Divine Etiquette
As It Pleases God

The Crème de la Crème People Skills for Believers

Copyright © 2025 by Dr. Y. Bur. All rights reserved.

Visit www.RoarPublishingGroup.com for more information. No part of this publication may be reproduced, stored in a retrieval system or transmitted in any way by any means, electronic, mechanical, photocopy, recording or otherwise without the prior permission of the author except as provided by USA copyright law.

Book design copyright © 2025 by R.O.A.R. International Group. All rights reserved.

R.O.A.R. Publishing Group
581 N. Park Ave. Ste. #725
Apopka, FL 32704
www.RoarPublishingGroup.com
DrY@DrYBur.com

Published in the United States of America
ISBN: 979-8-9990619-0-4
$22.88

Send *As It Pleases God* ®
Book Series **and** *Workbook* **Testimonies, Donations, Questions, or Orders to:**

Dr. Y. Bur
R.O.A.R. Publishing Group
581 N. Park Ave. Ste. #725
Apopka, FL 32704
ROAR-58-2316
762-758-2316
Dr.YBur@gmail.com

Visit Us At:

@AsItPleasesGodMovement
AsItPleasesGod

DrYBur.com
AsItPleasesGod.com

Please Donate

Please DONATE to this *Missionable Movement of God* as a GIVE-BACK to the Kingdom. Thanks for your support. Many Blessings.

AIPG Donation Link

Scan to Pay

Available Titles

ASITPLEASESGOD.COM

Table of Contents

Introduction 11
Chapter One 17
  Silent Acts of Unkindness 17
Chapter Two 23
  Reconciliation 23
    Being Vetted 25
    Each One Teach One 27
Chapter Three 31
  The Power of Greetings 31
    Respectful Leverage 37
    Spiritual Home Training 40
Chapter Four 43
  Dominating Peacemakers 43
    Combatting Fears 47
    The Power of Faith 52
    Entering A House 53
Chapter Five 59
  Pay Attention 59
    Living Without Boundaries 60
    Freedom In God 61
    Watch Out 64
    The Test 67

Chapter Six 69
Strongholds of Unkindness 69
Consuming Our Own Fruits 72
The Connection 77
Chapter Seven 81
Characteristics of the Holy Spirit 81
The Eye of Grace 90
The Problem 91
Owning the Room 93
Divine Power 98
Chapter Eight 103
The Overcoming...103
Seeds of Something Else...107
Law of Reciprocity 109
Chapter Nine 117
Divine Cleansing..117
Mental Cleansing..127
Bodily Cleansing 132
Soul Cleansing 136
Spiritual Cleansing...142
The Fasting Part...148
Chapter Ten...155
Spiritual Growth 155
Our Attitudes..156
Free Will 160
Spiritual Power Tool...162

Unanswered Prayers	165
The Power of Meditation	179
Chapter Eleven	**189**
The Power of Kindness	189
The Funny Feeling	192
Spiritual Needs	196
Spiritual Testing	199
Divine Illumination	207
Self-Fulfilling Prophecy	208
The Elimination Process	212
Chapter Twelve	**215**
Divine Etiquette	215
Spiritual Classroom	218
Selfless Commitment	228
Get Off The Sideline	232
Dealing With Anger	242
Dealing With Injustices	251
Dealing With Unforgiveness	254
Who Are We Pleasing?	256
Secrets of Discipline	262

Introduction

Impeccable people skills have somehow been exchanged with mockery, selectiveness, and rudeness that have gotten the Kingdom of God a bad reputation. Frankly, our Heavenly Father is not too happy about our negligent actions, thoughts, desires, beliefs, and language. It is disheartening for me to witness the decline of basic courtesy and respect, as well as the negative impact that mockery and rudeness have on the Kingdom of God.

Yet, amid the wave of instantaneous communication through social media, in workplaces, or even within families, we still justify and celebrate negativity, willful debauchery, selective prejudice, or behaving badly as if it were some sort of sport or pastime. Whether we do it for a click, for a show, to satiate our egos, to make us feel better about ourselves, or to get into someone's head, we do it so easily as if God is not watching or as if it does not matter to us. For this reason, it is my reasonable service to share profound information with those who are willing to learn, grow, and sow back into the Kingdom when called upon as the *Crème de la Crème of Kingdom Poshness*.

Introduction

To say the least, impeccable people skills and *Divine Etiquette* are not for the weak at heart. While they form the bedrock of compassionate interactions, *As It Pleases God*, our love, kindness, and understanding, along with our ability to forgive, will be tested and thoroughly tried in this area.

What is the purpose of being tested? First, we are the beacon of hope for God's precious sheep. Secondly, we do not truly understand what is hiding within the psyche until we are tested. Thirdly, it is for those who have a desire to become the *Crème de la Crème of Kingdom Poshness* on a level that puts the enemy to boot. Lastly, unkindness and rudeness create a disconnect from what is Divine, causing us to remain average in a bed of mediocrity. So, according to the Heavenly of Heavens, we will be tested and pruned to become the *Crème de la Crème*.

Of course, we have those proclaiming to want to become one of the upper echelons of the Kingdom, capturing the respect and admiration of our Heavenly Father and their peers in business, politics, or social circles. While at the core of this phenomenon, they envision themselves as leaders, visionaries, or pioneers, ready to inspire change for the Greater Good, *As It Pleases God*. Yet, and still, they continue to engage in free will low-level behaviors, undermining their credibility, integrity, and potential. Clearly, I am not calling anyone low-level here; I am only referring to charactorial beliefs, thoughts, actions, words, and fruits that are not Christlike.

What are considered low-level behaviors in the Eye of God? It is considered anything that violates or negates the Fruits of the Spirit or violates the conscience of mankind, especially when knowing right from wrong and continuing to engage in negativity anyway. Nonetheless, the biggest one on the Spiritual Table today is our social biases and open discrimination. Why is this such a big deal? We never know who God is using to BLESS us. Plus, Divine Blessings from

Introduction

the Heavenly of Heavens will come in all different shapes, sizes, colors, and intellects, allowing us the opportunity to accept or reject them.

Low-level behaviors can manifest in various ways, like gossiping about people when it has nothing whatsoever to do with us, undermining colleagues to get ahead, making dismissive comments, being impatient during difficult times, publicly belittling others, or indulging in petty rivalries to throw someone under the bus. Unfortunately, they reveal deeper inconsistencies within the psyche that are exposed in our everyday interactions with people.

With *Divine Etiquette: As It Pleases God*®, we promote respect and collaboration from the least to the greatest rather than conflict and division or thumbing our noses at people. We never know who God is using in the next phase of our lives, and most often, the answers to our requests will be presented in a package we would often reject, making self-reflection and discernment crucial.

For example, I sat with many individuals who openly voiced their petitions for what they needed from God. As I answered their questions, guiding them on what to do next, *As It Pleased God*, they rejected it because I did not appear as they envisioned. While sometimes openly proclaiming the Holy Spirit was speaking to them about me, they had no clue that I was Dr. Y. Bur, the WHY Doctor that could make their baby leap, for real, for real. As they proceeded to insult or disrespect me underhandedly with their *Silent Acts of Unkindness* as if I were a nobody, my kindness was undeniable and unrefutable because the Fruits of the Spirit do not lie.

According to the Heavenly of Heavens, their Spiritual Discerning Faculties should have kicked into high gear, clueing them in on something. And, if they received nothing whatsoever, it meant that their Spiritual Compass was keeled without them knowing it. How do I know? Spirit knows Spirit! Instead of accepting, gleaning, and documenting the

Introduction

information *As It Pleased God*, they interjected envy, pride, and negative competitiveness into the equation, voiding their Divine Help due to their lack of readiness, fear, anxiety, lack of humility, or societal pressures.

God was faithful enough to send them what they needed, but they were not faithful enough to receive. So, I have a few questions for you: 'When God sends the answer, are you able to recognize it?' Better yet, 'Are you ready to receive?' Then again, 'Will you reject it altogether?'

This book, *Divine Etiquette: As It Pleases God*®, will prepare you to receive all that God has for you, but you must do your part with the internal preparation. Now, if you think you already have it together, then it is fair to say that confusion and disillusionment have a negative grip on your psyche. How so? In all simplicity, we are Spiritual Beings having a human experience; thus, we are all a work-in-progress, so we must remain on a learning curve to become truly WISE, *As It Pleases God*.

The development of our emotional intelligence is important in enhancing our personal and professional relationships, fostering self-awareness and growth. All of which allows us to promote empathetic interactions, facilitating better communication and conflict resolution skills.

On the other hand, to get to *The Crème de la Crème People Skills for Believers*, the expansion of our Spiritual Intelligence with authentic values is even more crucial. By developing our Spiritual Awareness, *As It Pleases God*, it ensures that we do not miss the MARK or ANSWER. Can we really miss it? Absolutely! It happens all the time, but we tend to cover it up, whitewashing the effects. Unfortunately, this is why we often feel regret following our acts of disobedience. Even 1 Samuel 15:22 says, *"To obey is better than sacrifice."*

Introduction

Once we get an understanding of the Divine Blueprint for our lives, we are better able to recognize and align our values, morals, and standards, *As It Pleases God*, with a sense of meaning and balance from the inside out. As we cultivate both intelligences, we must refuse to remain imbalanced, confused, unfocused, and clueless about the reason for our being while fostering a more compassionate understanding of the world in which we live.

The foundation of *Divine Etiquette: As It Pleases God®* is built on trust, integrity, reconciliation, and respect for God, ourselves, and others in or out of the Kingdom. In this book, we accentuate *The Power of Greeting* others to ensure we are well-received and respectful in any situation, circumstance, or event.

Why is respectfulness so important for Believers? In a world that often feels divided, confused, and contentious, respectfulness stands out as a fundamental virtue for Believers across all walks of life. More importantly, we are the *Dominating Peacemakers* for our Heaven on Earth Experiences, but for some reason, we have forgotten who we are in the Eye of God. James 1:22 advises us on this: *"But be doers of the word, and not hearers only, deceiving yourselves."* Even I write with respect; therefore, I am granted an overflow of Divine Wisdom that supersedes human reasoning. Conversely, I must say that it is often the elements of disrespect that typically TRIGGER the overflow of Divine Revelation. Really? Yes, really!

The bottom line is that we must *Pay Attention* to ourselves, others, and life. In the same way that everyone has a story to tell, life has one as well. The moment we think respectfulness is not important, self-deception is at play, Mentally, Physically, Emotionally, and Spiritually, with a *Stronghold of Unkindness*. As a result, the Vicissitudes and Cycles of Life will thrust us into a Cycle of Déjà vu with or without our

Introduction

permission. Why? They are committed to doing their job, *As It Pleases God*, with unwavering consistency.

Throughout history, and according to the Ancient of Days, the only vessels continually refusing to do what they were called to do are mankind. Although we are endowed with the ability to reason, create, steward, care, and love. Yet, time and time again, we do the opposite. Instead of reasoning, we create problems. Instead of creating, we find pleasure in demolishing. Instead of stewarding, we get a thrill from enslaving. Instead of caring, we become insensitive. Instead of loving authentically, we engage in hating, using, and abusing, invoking all types of selfish desires, unnecessary conflict, and unjustified discord. Instead of meeting people where they are, we want them to come up to our level without leading by example.

In light of these serious concerns, if you are ready to go to the next level in your authentic people skills, *As It Pleases God*, then without further ado, let us go deeper as ONE in Christ Jesus.

Chapter One

Silent Acts of Unkindness

In the world in which we live today, the *Silent Acts of Unkindness* have penetrated the fabric of our being in a way that has publicly and privately astounded us as Believers and non-believers alike. Although the psyche of mankind has a story to tell, but according to the Ancient of Days, our REALITY speaks louder, exposing our workable, unworkable, underlying, and avoidable charactorial traits, truths, and quirks. Even though no one is perfect, we still must recognize and account for the behavioral factors extended openly, outwardly, behind the scenes, or underhandedly, especially for the next phase of our lives or when it is affecting our bottom lines.

Why are behavioral factors so important in the Eye of God, especially for Believers? The *Silent Acts of Unkindness* that go unnoticed, undealt with, or unrepentant weaken our Kingdomly Power and the Body of Christ altogether. At the same time, it also keeps us Mentally, Physically, Emotionally, and Spiritually Exhausted as they quietly permeate our

Silent Acts of Unkindness

interactions and relationships with the hidden seeds of unkindness.

According to the Heavenly of Heavens, the UNSAID can speak louder than what is being voiced, which leads to bullying and other negative forms of abuse, allowing this negative Spirit to manifest continually with or without our permission. As Believers, we tend to normalize unkind and negative behaviors or think it is harmless when they are actually abnormal according to Kingdom Standards and Principles.

How do *Silent Acts of Unkindness* manifest? In the Eye of God, it is a willful manifestation. How so? We choose the fruitful behaviors, thoughts, actions, and beliefs that we serve to ourselves and others. With all simplicity in answering the above question, there are many ways to create a free will atmosphere of discomfort and alienation; however, listed below are a few examples, but not limited to such:

- ☐ Social exclusion is a big one: Deliberately leaving someone out of conversations, activities, or the loop is one of the most prominent signs.
- ☐ Dismissive gestures and attitudes.
- ☐ Passive-aggressive remarks, subtle remarks, or sarcasm.
- ☐ Not acknowledging someone's existence.
- ☐ An insincere expression of underlying unkind feelings.
- ☐ Withholding information or intentional sabotage.
- ☐ Avoiding eye contact or turning away from someone when speaking.
- ☐ Not offering help or encouragement.
- ☐ The ultimate silent treatment.
- ☐ Negative gestures, like crossing arms or rolling eyes.
- ☐ Talking about someone in their presence in a semi-coded language.
- ☐ Failing to smile or reciprocate warmth.

Silent Acts of Unkindness

- ☐ Backhanded compliments.
- ☐ Speaking negatively about someone when they are not present.
- ☐ Replying with brief, minimal, or uninterested responses.
- ☐ Spreading unverified negative information.
- ☐ Not responding or helping when someone asks for assistance.
- ☐ Engaging in snide comments that are made under one's breath.

What is the purpose of knowing this information? The Power of Dominion is laid up for the just at heart; however, a compassionate environment is required. As a matter of fact, unkindness in itself has blinded most Believers into not being able to decipher between right and wrong, just and unjust, good and bad, and so on, based on the clique they are committed to.

Whereas, in the Kingdom of God, it is imperative to understand the kindness that God, our Heavenly Father, expects from us to feed His sheep. If not, we will lack Spiritual Discernment while confusing genuine helpfulness with someone having an agenda without having all the facts associated with our suspicions.

Why would suspicions happen to us when we genuinely operate with outright integrity and goodwill, all in the Spirit of Righteousness and Excellence? Unfortunately, when we knowingly or unknowingly interject jealousy, envy, pride, greed, coveting, or competitiveness into the equation, it can become a recipe for disaster.

What does this disastrous recipe mean in layman's terms? They cancel out our ability to properly discern genuineness and good intent while interjecting chaos, confusion, and division where there should not be. James 3:16 says this best:

Silent Acts of Unkindness

"For where envy and self-seeking exist, confusion and every evil thing are there." Picturesquely, this is when one person has a problem with another, and the other remains clueless until a third party voices it.

When one person nursing a grievance against another remains silent like a brooding lion or viper, while the second party remains entirely oblivious to the existence of any issue, it unveils an even bigger underlying issue. What type of issue is at hand? At the core, it will be fundamental COMMUNICATION. For the record, just because we can audibly speak does not mean it is effective, righteous, or accurate.

Without effective communication, all else will begin to fail, bringing the Tower of Babel to the forefront of our lives. Blasphemy, right? Wrong. Jesus said, *"Every kingdom divided against itself is brought to desolation, and every city or house divided against itself will not stand."* Matthew 12:25. So, on an individual basis, we are no different!

If we use our tongues to divide, insult, or abuse negatively, we will have issues. Conversely, if we fail to use our tongues, withholding viable information, we will still have problems. Although we do have free will in what to say, what not to say, and to whom, we are required as Believers to bring forth unity in the Body of Christ. Here is what 1 Corinthians 1:10 shares with us: *"Now I plead with you, brethren, by the name of our Lord Jesus Christ, that you all speak the same thing, and that there be no divisions among you, but that you be perfectly joined together in the same mind and in the same judgment."*

Misunderstandings and unexpressed feelings are often more common than we realize, eventually initiating emotions such as defensiveness, misunderstandings, anger, guilt, frustration, or shock. Valid or invalid reasons for the dissertation do not negate the need for constructive dialogue. Here is why: Matthew 18:15 says to us, *"Moreover, if your brother*

Silent Acts of Unkindness

sins against you, go and tell him his fault between you and him alone. If he hears you, you have gained your brother." And then, Proverbs 27:5 says, *"Open rebuke is better than love carefully concealed."*

Why must we tell people something, especially when they should know? We do not all think, behave, and react alike; plus, we are all different, with varying backgrounds and traumas. Thus, self-examination and a commitment to exemplify the Fruits of the Spirit unveil the ability to effectively communicate without excommunicating those who do not fit into our expectations. What makes this so important in the Eye of God? First, the Law of Reciprocity is real! The seed sown, positively or negatively, will bring forth its 'Like-Kind' in due season. Secondly, Galatians 5:15 says, *"If you bite and devour one another, beware lest you be consumed by one another!"*

In the Eye of God, most often, when living real life, we do not realize our *Silent Acts of Unkindness* unless they are pointed out or measured against the Fruits of the Spirit. Nor do we realize that God is UNPLEASED with our behaviors, thoughts, beliefs, conversations, mindsets, desires, and heart postures due to our conditioning and biases.

How would we not know when God is UNPLEASED with us? First, we will all appear right in our own eyes, making it easy to overlook the subtleties of our interactions, engagements, and encounters. Secondly, as we navigate our days filled with tasks, responsibilities, and noise, we are trained to emotionally or physically react or respond. Unfortunately, by falling into patterns of reacting and responding, we overlook the necessity of mentally understanding the reasons behind our whys. In addition, we also typically negate asking fact-finding questions to evaluate the full impact of our unintentional actions, thoughts, beliefs, habits, and desires. Thirdly, if we do not include God in the equation of all things, *As It Pleases Him*, we can lack Spiritual

Silent Acts of Unkindness

Discernment, developing Spiritual Blindness, Deafness, or Muteness, even if we appear to have it going on.

Where our *Silent Acts of Unkindness* may have inadvertently taken root, we must make a conscious attempt or put forth the effort to break this negative cycle using the Fruits of the Spirit (Love, Joy, Peace, Patience, Kindness, Goodness, Faithfulness, Gentleness, and Self-Control) to bring ourselves into Divine Oneness, *As It Pleases God*. Does this really make a difference? Absolutely! Having peace, Mentally, Physically, Emotionally, and Spiritually, makes a world of difference in the life of a true Believer. According to the Heavenly of Heavens, RECONCILIATION is of the utmost importance for a time such as this.

Now, before we move on, let me say this: REAL PEACE is not elusive; it is available to all when built upon the Foundation of Christ. Do we need God to have peace? No, we can have peace without Him when using peaceful principles. Still, they will have timestamps and limitations that God Almighty predetermines. In fostering Divine Awareness, *As It Pleases Him*, we CANNOT have REAL internal or lasting peace from the inside out without Him or the Fruits of the Spirit. Why not? It is prewired within our DNA to develop a *Spirit to Spirit* Relationship with Him when we are ready and to use the Fruits of the Spirit to behave Christlike.

Encapsulated in Colossians 1:20, here is what we must know to Spiritually Align accordingly: *"And by Him to reconcile all things to Himself, by Him, whether things on earth or things in heaven, having made peace through the blood of His cross."*

Chapter Two

Reconciliation

In the Reconciliation Process, the Blood of Christ still works, and it still speaks loudly, shaking the foundation in which we live today for the personalized remission of our known and unknown sins. On behalf of our Forefathers from the Ancient of Days, here is what I mean: According to Matthew 26:28, *"For this is My blood of the new covenant, which is shed for many for the remission of sins."* This passage not only reflects the nature of Christ's Sacrificial Offering on our behalf. But, it also underscores the ongoing IMPACT and COVERING of His Blood, enabling us to do our part in the equation of all things Spiritual for our Heaven on Earth Experiences.

What does doing our part have to do with anything as Believers? God is counting on us to restore friendly relations and bring harmony where there was once conflict through our ability to live by example. Even if people think we are too fake to be really authentic, hear me when I say this: The Fruits of the Spirit do not lie, and they work as they should when used properly, *As It Pleases God*.

Reconciliation

When engaging in Divine Relations, *Spirit to Spirit*, with our Heavenly Father and when operating in our Spiritual Gifts or Offerings, *As It Pleases Him*, we must bring forth reconciliation. Is this Biblical? I would have it no other way: *"Therefore, if you bring your gift to the altar, and there remember that your brother has something against you, leave your gift there before the altar, and go your way. First be reconciled to your brother, and then come and offer your gift."* Matthew 5:23-24.

What if we choose not to reconcile? We have the free will to do so or not. But know this: *"He who justifies the wicked, and he who condemns the just, both of them alike are an abomination to the Lord."* Proverbs 17:15. Although we do have grace to refine us, still, right is right, and wrong is wrong. And we must know the difference to ensure we do not turn on ourselves without knowing it.

When it comes to Kingdom Stature in the Eye of God, we must MASTER reconciling, apologizing, forgiving, and repenting. Why must we do all of this? We serve the Kingdom better and more effectively, *As It Pleases Him*. Plus, we will have fewer internal hiccups or fewer bouts with Spiritual Indigestion caused by unhealed wounds, unresolved trauma, or bossing God around.

It is a trend now on who has first dibs on God (Who is the most anointed or gifted), but if we are not humble or our character is not aligning with what He expects of us, it is all VAIN IDOLATRY, hidden in plain sight! If we cannot be down to earth, it is possible to be of no earthly good. Is this an underhanded or backhanded insult to the Body of Christ? Absolutely not!

The Cycle of Life will begin to create all types of warfare to correct us or take us out unless reconciliation occurs, *As It Pleases God*. We often refer to this as the pruning process; still, it can become excessively brutal if we are resistant, rebellious, or too religious, thumbing our noses at those who appear less

Reconciliation

than us. All of these things cause hidden rifts in the psyche of mankind, disrupting the natural order and creating discord between Heaven and Earth. As a result, our Heaven on Earth Experiences may cause us to feel overwhelmed and unusable in the Eye of God. Only to put on masks, pretending to be more than who we are to please ourselves or coax a hidden longing.

In the *Reconciliation Phase* of our lives, we all will go through vetting and being vetted. Nonetheless, in the Eye of God, we cannot put a human perspective on what is Divine. Why can we not vet from our own perspectives? We can if we like, based on free will. Unfortunately, when doing so outside of the Will of God, we will often get God's method of operation all wrong. How so? For example, I get people telling me who I am without knowing me, how I think, or my relationship with my Heavenly Father.

To add insult to injury, they proclaim the Holy Spirit told them this and that about me without asking me one question to reconcile their thoughts and projections. So my response is always, 'Really?' I do not try to correct, convince, or debate with them because the prejudgment prevented them from resolving their internal qualms. Here is what Isaiah 5:20 says, *"Woe to those who call evil good, and good evil; Who put darkness for light, and light for darkness; Who put bitter for sweet, and sweet for bitter!"* Above all, in the Eye of God, we are constantly *Being Vetted* on how we interpret our WOES, what we CALL people, places, and things, and where we PUT them, positively or negatively.

Being Vetted

In the *Reconciliation Process* of transparency and accountability, the woes associated with Being Vetted are real. Vetting is often seen as a necessary measure to ensure safety, integrity, and trustworthiness; it also comes along with all types of biased, founded, or unfounded judgments.

When *Being Vetted*, please understand that no one is flawless. And those appearing as such have definitely learned the psychology of beating the system in the pursuit of approval and acceptance. Even though *Being Vetted* can be invasive and overreaching, there are also Spiritual Woes associated with being judged under a microscope for the same things we are secretly or openly guilty of under a different label.

In a world that is supposed to promote fairness and equality, we are now becoming self-consumed with pegging someone's psychological status and credentials rather than heart postures and mindsets. Clearly, we have free will to choose what is best for us; we must also account for the woes associated from a Spiritual Perspective.

For me, to avoid anyone's woes from becoming mine, I let them think whatever they like with whomever, and I keep it moving in the Spirit of Excellence, doing what I am called to do. Here is the deal: In the *Reconciliation Process* with myself, I make a conscious attempt to use the Fruits of the Spirit and behave Christlike faithfully and self-correct when needed. So, if someone attempts to read my mail, Mentally, Physically, Emotionally, and Spiritually, without having a clue about the use of the Fruits of the Spirit whatsoever, or is clueless about behaving Christlike, rest assured, the VETTOR is being VETTED.

What does the VETTOR being VETTED mean in layman's terms? In all simplicity, I am gleaning the relevant information needed to feed God's sheep, *As It Pleases Him*, without breaking cover or flinching an inch. The goal of the Kingdom of God is to build a culture rooted in acceptance rather than scrutiny for those who are willing to do what it takes to get to the next level. So, if I have to become the guinea

Reconciliation

pig to bring forth Divine Information for a time such as this, then so be it!

In a place where information is readily available at the drop of a dime, it is often distorted with half-truths, flavorful lies, misleading interpretations, skewed doctrines, and worldly distractions. In a world needing Divine Healing, there is a rising concern about the negative impacts of unawareness and the misunderstandings about our Spiritual Lives from a Divine Perspective, especially when surrounding *Divine Etiquette*.

With intentional effort, commitment, and openness, I refuse to sit back and watch Believers destroy themselves for the lack of knowledge regarding the Divine Expectations from the Heavenly of Heavens that lead them further away from their Divine Purpose. As a Spiritual Vessel of the Most High God, I must do my part in providing strength, clarity, and direction while allowing God to do the rest, *As It Pleases Him*. While simultaneously inspiring others to do likewise with the '*Each One Teach One*' Mindset.

Each One Teach One

In Earthen Vessels, we are required to become teachers to the younger generation to ensure Spiritual Growth, Maturity, and Care in the Kingdom of God. In the Spirit of Love, we do not need to go to the Nations, use grand gestures, or grace large platforms unless we are on Divine Assignment. All we need to do is start with one person with the '*Each One Teach One*' Mindset, where love and patience can flourish, *As It Pleases God*.

Regardless of where we are in life or what we have going on, it is our responsibility and the essence of our mission to impart wisdom or what we have learned to the younger generation. A commitment to become teachers ensures they

Reconciliation

too, can thrive in their Spiritual Journeys and withstand the wiles of the enemy.

For example, Titus 2:3-4 says this to women: *"The older women likewise, that they be reverent in behavior, not slanderers, not given to much wine, teachers of good things—that they admonish the young women to love their husbands, to love their children."* For the men: Ephesians 6:4 says, *"And you, fathers, do not provoke your children to wrath, but bring them up in the training and admonition of the Lord."* Each conversation about faith, each shared testimony, and each moment of encouragement contribute to the Kingdom.

What if they do not listen to us? It is not our responsibility to make people listen to us. In cultivating this Teaching Spirit, As It Pleases God, the goal is to present the information in palatable seed form and allow them to see us applying it or setting an example. Frankly, this is why Proverbs 22:6 tells us to: *"Train up a child in the way he should go, and when he is old he will not depart from it."* Moreover, as a Divine Bonus, the more we selflessly share, the more we grow, becoming better, stronger, and wiser to continue this process on another level to equip the next generation.

Here is a list of ways to teach others with the '*Each One Teach One*' Mindset, but not limited to such:

- ☐ Personal Mentorship: Offer your time to mentor a young person, sharing experiences and insights to foster personal growth.

- ☐ Storytelling: Use personal and relatable stories to convey important lessons, making concepts more accessible and memorable.

Reconciliation

- [ ] Hands-On Learning: Engage them in hands-on activities related to Spiritual Growth, like community service or creative projects.

- [ ] Small Group Discussions: Create intimate groups where young people can discuss their thoughts and questions about faith in a safe environment.

- [ ] Encouraging Questions: Foster a culture that values curiosity by encouraging them to ask questions and express their thoughts without judgment.

- [ ] Lead by Example: Model the values and behaviors you wish to impart; let your life serve as a living illustration of Spiritual Principles, *As It Pleases God*.

- [ ] Creative Expression: Encourage art, music, or writing as forms of expressing Faith and Spirituality, helping to deepen their understanding, *As It Pleases God*.

- [ ] Workshops, Book Clubs, and Classes: Organize workshops or classes on relevant topics, inviting people to participate actively, *As It Pleases God*. In addition, with a focus on Spiritual Literature, it allows for shared reading experiences and discussions as well.

- [ ] Prayer Partners: Pair young individuals with each other and encourage them to pray for one another, building a supportive Spiritual community, *As It Pleases God*.

- [ ] Role-Playing Scenarios: Use role-playing to handle real-life situations and decision-making in a faith context, fostering critical thinking, *As It Pleases God*.

Reconciliation

- ☐ Lead Service Projects: Involve them in community service projects, showing the importance of faith in action, *As It Pleases God.*

- ☐ Using Technology: Leverage social media or online platforms for discussions and sharing resources, making learning more accessible, *As It Pleases God.*

- ☐ Goal Setting: Help them set Spiritual Goals and guide them on how to achieve these through actionable steps, *As It Pleases God.*

- ☐ Invite Participation: Encourage them to share their knowledge with others, empowering them to teach what they have learned, *As It Pleases God.*

- ☐ Celebrate Milestones: Acknowledge and celebrate their achievements in Spiritual Growth, reinforcing the value of their Spiritual Journey, *As It Pleases God.*

For the record, any sheep in the Kingdom of God in the milking stages of Spirituality is our child in Christ Jesus. Plus, according to the Ancient of Days, we must treat them accordingly. What if we do not have time? We make time for whatever we desire. Nevertheless, if we fail to do so, a statement found in Hebrews 5:12 would apply to us: *"In fact, though by this time you ought to be teachers, you need someone to teach you the elementary truths of God's word all over again. You need milk, not solid food!"* Simply put, if we are not reaching back to help another, it is time to step back into the Spiritual Classroom for Divine Updates.

Chapter Three

The Power of Greetings

The hidden secrets from the Ancient of Days are upon us, demanding our attention. We can proclaim New Age this and that, but in the Eye of God, there is nothing new under the sun.

Nonetheless, let us discuss *The Power of Greetings* to ensure that we gain access to the Divine Wisdom, Treasures, and Secrets of the Kingdom, *As It Pleases God*.

In Romans 16:16, Paul instructs, *"Greet one another with a holy kiss."* Of course, we cannot literally kiss someone, but the greeting in itself symbolically kisses the psyche of mankind without physically kissing. How do we make this make sense? It means fellowship and unity are important for our Heaven on Earth Experiences. More importantly, it breaks down barriers and fosters a sense of belonging, setting a conducive tone for interacting with others.

What if they are not one of us? Then, my question would be, 'Who are we?' and 'Who is us?' If one is of the Kingdom of God, one must take the higher road and greet those who are not like us as well, even if they offend us. Matthew 5:47 says,

The Power of Greetings

"And if you greet your brethren only, what do you do more than others? Do not even the tax collectors do so?"

For example, the moment we think we are too good to speak or greet others, there is an even bigger problem within the psyche, causing us to get a BIG Side-Eye from God. How so? As Servants of the Kingdom, we are greeters by nature. The moment we lose our ability to greet others, especially our ELDERS, the Spirit of Pride has robbed us of Divine Access and Wisdom from the Heavenly of Heavens.

What is the big deal about greetings, especially as Believers? Here is the deal: If God cannot trust us by simply greeting our family members, neighbors, foes, and most of all, His sheep, what makes us think He is going to trust us with the Treasures of the Kingdom? He is not! Even if we pretend to have Divine Access to impress others, there are still Spiritual Principles associated with gleaning from the Heavenly of Heavens.

From the Throne Room of the Most High God, the moment we think we are too good to speak, we become subjected to regular or learned knowledge instead of Supernatural Wisdom, Knowledge, and Understanding from the Heavenly of Heavens. Is this fair? Absolutely! Rudeness in the Kingdom comes with Spiritual Bars and Blockages, causing us to be placed on the sidelines for Spiritual Development or Revamping.

Why are we sidelined while wholeheartedly serving the Kingdom? In all simplicity, the expression of love, respect, and community is required, and we cannot pick and choose the disbursement of them. Actually, the disbursement is a free-will offering. The moment we block the free-will expression of the Fruits of the Spirit on our behalf or that of another, we can become seemingly cultic while appearing right in our own eyes.

In our daily interactions, whether good, bad, or indifferent, greetings serve as the socialistic glue that connects us to

The Power of Greetings

others and the Spiritual Glue that keeps us together. Here are the styles of greetings:

- **Verbal Greetings**: 'Good morning, afternoon, or evening.' In addition, we have 'Hello,' 'How are you?' 'Good to see you,' or 'Have a good day.'
- **Formal Greetings**: Using a person's name, such as Mr. or Mrs. [their name], and Ma'am or Sir.
- **Titled Greetings**: Use of titles such as President, Judge, Doctor, Brother, Sister, Elder, Bishop, Pastor, and Reverend where appropriate.
- **Non-verbal Greetings**: Smiles, nods, open arms, thumbs up, handshake, bow, high five, fist bump, air kiss, clap, facial expression, head tilt, body lean, and waves.
- **Written Greetings**: Cards, emails, and text messages with Dear ......, Hello......, Greetings ......, and so on.

Despite the method of greetings used, the essence of a greeting lies in its intention, respect, and connection. Here are the key characteristics of informal greetings:

- Use clear and respectful language.
- Maintaining a polite and attentive demeanor.
- Avoid slang or colloquialisms unless appropriate.
- A handshake or slight bow can often be appropriate. (Be mindful of cultural norms and preferences.)
- Using first names or nicknames (when appropriate).
- Expressing genuine warmth and care.
- Sharing a brief personal update or asking about their well-being.
- A friendly hug (when appropriate and welcomed) or a warm smile.

The Power of Greetings

☐ Make sure one's body language is open and receptive. (Avoid crossing arms or legs).

In the hustle and bustle of living real life, a simple greeting can often be overlooked, especially when we are distracted. *The Power of Greeting* extends the invitation to engage when welcome or a silent clue to disengage when unwelcome. Moreover, incorporating specific boundaries is equally important. How so? Listed below are a few examples, but not limited to such.

☐ **Cultural Sensitivity:** Be mindful of cultural differences in greetings. What is considered appropriate in one culture may be offensive in another. Learn about the customs of different cultures and adapt your greetings accordingly. For instance, while a handshake may be standard in some cultures, others may prefer a nod or a bow.

☐ **Personal Boundaries or Space:** Always respect personal space boundaries. Not everyone is comfortable with physical touch, such as hugging. Pay attention to non-verbal cues and adjust your greeting accordingly.

☐ **Authenticity:** The most important aspect of any greeting is authenticity. Be genuine in your expression of warmth and care. People can sense insincerity, so always strive to be true to yourself and your faith.

☐ **Adaptability:** Be prepared to adapt your greeting to the situation. A formal greeting may be appropriate in one setting, while an informal greeting may be more suitable in another. Use your best judgment and be

The Power of Greetings

flexible. For example, we can say 'Hey' to our friends, but we greet our parents with a 'Good Morning, Good Afternoon, Good Evening, or Good Night.'

- ☐ **Time Boundaries**: Everyone has different schedules, constraints, and commitments. A quick, friendly greeting can show acknowledgment without imposing on someone's time. Being mindful of this boundary can enhance respect and understanding.

In a world where opinions are readily shared and judgments are often broadcast without fail, the concept of *Divine Etiquette: As It Pleases God*® offers a refreshing perspective on how we interact with one another. Frankly, it is all about the energy and intention behind our words, gestures, and responses. The true essence of *Divine Etiquette* lies in maintaining a mindset that is unwaveringly positive, regardless of our external feedback or internal qualms.

When dealing with *Divine Etiquette: As It Pleases God*®, whether people like us or not, or whether we are received or not, the impact of our greetings is our Powerhouse. As a rule of thumb, we must keep this in a zone of positivity, which means no complaining, bickering, fussing, or fighting. We may have to make a conscious effort to avoid descending into negativity, but it is doable.

Will everyone respond to us? Absolutely not! We must become content with people rejecting our greetings, just accept the Spiritual Brownie Points from God, and move on to pave the way for healing conversations to uplift, empower, and cultivate positivity, *As It Pleases God*. Here are a few tips to always use:

- ☐ **Make eye contact**: Eye contact conveys sincerity, trust, and genuine engagement, fostering a sense of

The Power of Greetings

openness and honesty. Remember, a deceptive Spirit, on the other hand, will keep their eyes moving all over the place. It is vital to understand that avoiding eye contact creates feelings of mistrust or discomfort. The bottom line is that eye contact speaks volumes, positively or negatively.

- ☐ **Smile:** A smile is universally welcoming and can instantly put others at ease. As a matter of fact, it is considered to be the simplest form of communication for mankind, transcending language barriers, cultures, and distances. Always smile when greeting or meeting someone, starting a conversation, or connecting or reconnecting with people. When you smile, your brain releases neuropeptides that help combat stress, leading to a better mood. Endorphins are released as well, creating a sense of happiness. In all simplicity, smiling is a win-win for all involved.

- ☐ **Use the person's name:** Addressing someone by name shows that you recognize and value them. If you cannot remember their name, use ma'am or sir. Whether you are in a meeting, a classroom, or a social gathering, addressing people directly can make them feel more comfortable and included.

- ☐ **Be present:** Focus your attention on the person you are greeting, rather than being distracted by your phone or other tasks. In our fast-paced microwave world, where distractions are just a tap away, we can easily lose focus by sneaking glances at our phones, thinking about our to-do lists, or multitasking when we should be concentrating on the conversation at hand.

The Power of Greetings

- ☐ **Tailor your greeting to the situation:** Adjust your greeting based on the context, relationship, and cultural norms.

- ☐ **Be authentic:** A genuine greeting is more impactful than a forced or insincere one.

- ☐ **Listen actively:** Pay attention to the other person's response and adjust your approach accordingly.

Will this list help us with *The Power of Greetings*? Absolutely! At first impression, it helps people to determine if we are operating with proper home training or not. Plus, it ushers in the essence of *Respectful Leverage*, or it denies it therein, allowing us to know and understand the difference between respectfulness, *As It Pleases God*, and disrespectfulness that displeases Him.

Respectful Leverage

We are often taught not to judge a book by its cover, but God requires us to evaluate our fruits and those of another to ensure our discerning faculties are working properly, and *As It Pleases Him*. For this reason, our GREETINGS convey the first taste of anyone's fruit, even if we are pretending to be the best things since sliced bread, or we are credentialed up.

Supposedly, if an applicant arrives late, dresses inappropriately, or fails to greet the interviewer politely, they may be immediately dismissed or overlooked, regardless of their qualifications. In the Kingdom, the same applies as well, especially with *The Power of Greetings*. For example, if one is a Spiritual Elite ordained by the Heavenly of Heavens for real, for real, RESPECT is a must.

The Power of Greetings

What makes Spiritual Elites in the Eye of God so special? Frankly, it boils down to an OBEDIENT vessel over a disobedient one and their level of faith. When operating in the Divine Will of God according to our Predestined Blueprint, it comes with a Supernatural Spiritual Covering that we do not want to violate, offend, or contend with.

The profound reassurance of Divine Protection is unveiled in Psalm 91:11-12 as a powerful reminder that God watches over what and who belongs to Him wholeheartedly. Here is what it says: *"For He shall give His angels charge over you, to keep you in all your ways. In their hands they shall bear you up, lest you dash your foot against a stone."* Once again, disrespect on any level will get us sidelined due to the lack of discernment.

How do we know the difference between a Spiritual Elite and a non-elite? We may not know unless the Holy Spirit reveals it to us because they will not say a word or bring correction until after the fact. Moreover, they may even appear weak, unkempt, or fragile, but all are so Spiritually Powerful in the Eye of God. Even Hebrews 13:2 alerts us in this manner: *"Do not forget to entertain strangers, for by so doing some have unwittingly entertained angels."* So, it is always best to be kind and do good to all, even if they do not appear good to us, and keep it moving in the Spirit of Excellence.

Before going any further, please allow me to align this Divine Principle regarding good and bad fruit. *"For a good tree does not bear bad fruit, nor does a bad tree bear good fruit. For every tree is known by its own fruit. For men do not gather figs from thorns, nor do they gather grapes from a bramble bush. A good man out of the good treasure of his heart brings forth good; and an evil man out of the evil treasure of his heart brings forth evil. For out of the abundance of the heart his mouth speaks."*

In addition, when dealing with *Respectful Leverage*, it appalls me to witness proclaimed Shepherds decline to greet the sheep God is allowing them to steward on His behalf. While

The Power of Greetings

at the same time, operating as if they are doing the congregation a favor by presenting them with idolistic measures. Come on, we have to do better than this!

What is required of us as Believers and Shepherds who are leading flocks? Although everyone's path is different; thus, we must take it to God, *Spirit to Spirit,* for the Divine Blueprint or Instructions while documenting as an element of *Respectful Leverage,* leading all things back to the Kingdom of God. While doing so, here are a few Divine Expectations, but not limited to such:

- ☐ **Expectation One**: *"That you may walk worthy of the Lord, fully pleasing Him, being fruitful in every good work and increasing in the knowledge of God."* Colossians 1:10.

- ☐ **Expectation Two**: *"That you may approve the things that are excellent, that you may be sincere and without offense till the day of Christ."* Philippians 1:10.

- ☐ **Expectation Three**: *"And let our people also learn to maintain good works, to meet urgent needs, that they may not be unfruitful."* Titus 3:14.

- ☐ **Expectation Four**: *"But also for this very reason, giving all diligence, add to your faith virtue, to virtue knowledge, to knowledge self-control, to self-control perseverance, to perseverance godliness, to godliness brotherly kindness, and to brotherly kindness love. For if these things are yours and abound, you will be neither barren nor unfruitful in the knowledge of our Lord Jesus Christ."* 2 Peter 1:5-8.

The Power of Greetings

Why are these expectations needed in the Kingdom of God? In the same way that we do home training to develop a framework for interacting with the world around us, we cannot stop there.

Spiritual Home Training

Foundational training not only helps us navigate social situations, which include social etiquette, manners, respect for others, and the ability to communicate effectively. We also have Spiritual Home Training in the Kingdom of God with the use of Spiritual Fruits and Christlike Charactorial Traits, making us approachable with a sense of comfort and trust.

For example, when possessing Spiritual Home Training, *As It Pleases God*, even if people attempt to block people from connecting to us, our Heavenly Father will find another way to get us what we need or get people what they need. According to the Heavenly of Heavens, the ONLY person who can stop Him from operating as such is the one with the Spiritual Training to get the job done with a mission-accomplished mindset.

What about those who do not possess *Spiritual Home Training*? According to the Heavenly of Heavens, they should be in a Spiritual Classroom developing themselves *As It Pleases God* with a work-in-progress mentality. For this reason, we are given the Fruits of the Spirit in Galatians 5:22-23 for Kingdomly Training and Counteracting. Here is what it says: *"But the fruit of the Spirit is love, joy, peace, longsuffering (patience), kindness, goodness, faithfulness, gentleness, self-control. Against such there is no law."*

Listen to me and listen well: Individuals lacking proper Spiritual Training or home training will often display rudeness, disobedience, rebellion, dullness, jealousy, envy,

The Power of Greetings

disregard for others, lack of humility, unresolved trauma, or a lack of basic social skills. All of which will usher us into a pruning process, *As It Pleases God*. Is this Biblical? Absolutely. Plus, I would have it no other way: Here is what Matthew 7:16-20 says, *"You will know them by their fruits. Do men gather grapes from thornbushes or figs from thistles? Even so, every good tree bears good fruit, but a bad tree bears bad fruit. A good tree cannot bear bad fruit, nor can a bad tree bear good fruit. Every tree that does not bear good fruit is cut down and thrown into the fire. Therefore by their fruits you will know them."* Most often, we do not think about *Spiritual Home Training* as much due to the lack of understanding from a Divine Perspective. Nevertheless, here is how *Spiritual Home Training* can help us, but not limited to such:

- ☐ **Inner Peace**: It fosters a deeper sense of inner peace and tranquility, enabling us to manage stress more effectively.

- ☐ **Emotional Resilience**: Regular practice helps build emotional resilience, allowing us to navigate life's challenges with greater ease.

- ☐ **Helps us Connect to Self**: It encourages self-discovery, self-awareness, self-mirroring, and understanding, leading to a stronger connection to our true selves.

- ☐ **Strengthened Relations**: By cultivating compassion and empathy, we improve our interactions and relationships with others.

- ☐ **Improved Focus**: Spiritual Focus can enhance concentration, proactiveness, and attentiveness, benefiting productivity in our personal values and

The Power of Greetings

beliefs. All of which are guiding us to live more authentically.

- ☐ **Enhances Well-being**: It supports Mental, Physical, Emotional, and Spiritual Well-Being, creating a more balanced lifestyle. It also helps us to detox, relax, and reduce stress levels.

- ☐ **Increased Gratitude**: This encourages thankfulness and contentment, which can shift our perspective towards positivity.

- ☐ **Purpose and Direction**: It can aid in finding purpose, passion, and direction in life, giving us something meaningful to strive for.

- ☐ **Conflict Resolution**: Providing tools for conflict resolution, both within ourselves and in our interactions with others, helps us make better decisions. With increased self-awareness and clarity, we can make more informed and aligned decisions.

- ☐ **Enhanced Creativity**: A connected Spiritual State of being can open up pathways for creativity and innovative thinking.

Incorporating these practices into our daily lives can lead to profound transformation and fulfillment, making us *Dominant Peacemakers* by default.

Chapter Four

Dominating Peacemakers

In today's world, filled with conflict, chaos, confusion, and division, most of us are pondering on what to do and how we got to this state. Still, when reflecting on our values and teachings of our beliefs, the role of a peacemaker is more crucial than ever, especially in a time such as this. Above all, our Heavenly Father is not looking for grandiose gestures of peace. He is sweeping the earth, looking for the peace found in our everyday actions, thoughts, beliefs, words, desires, and charactorial traits. As the Divine Sweep is in full effect at this very moment, the goal of this chapter is to unearth the Power of Peacemaking, *As It Pleases God*.

As Believers, the Ambassadors of Harmony, we are considered the *Dominating Peacemakers*, not hell-raisers or hellions on wheels. According to the Heavenly of Heavens, we are designed to seek to resolve conflicts and promote understanding in situations of discord. If this is not happening, we have work to do to become more proactive than reactive, striving to find solutions rather than escalating tensions. For this reason, Luke 10:5 gives us specific

Dominating Peacemakers

instructions: *"But whatever house you enter, first say, 'Peace to this house.'"*

What does peace have to do with anything? Better yet, would people think we are a little weird? Peace is not weird; it is the lack of peace that makes us weird.

For instance, the word 'Shalom' is often translated simply as 'peace,' but its meaning is far more profound and multifaceted than most would think. Although rooted in Hebrew culture and Biblical Tradition, Shalom encapsulates a sense of completeness, wholeness, and well-being that transcends the absence of conflict. It incorporates harmony, Mentally, Physically, Emotionally, and Spiritually, to bring forth Spiritual Balance, *As It Pleases God* amid chaos, confusion, malice, or Spiritual Warfare.

According to Numbers 6:24-26, it conveys a prime example of what is needed to coax the psyche of mankind: *"The Lord bless you and keep you; the Lord make His face shine upon you and be gracious to you; the Lord lift up His countenance upon you and give you peace."* The Word of God is a source of strength and unity that propels us to pursue peace.

Dominating Peacemaking or becoming an Agent of Unity requires courage to contend against the tide of negativity and contention with respect and understanding, *As It Pleases God*. Now, with a mindset anchored in love, here are a few ways to make peace, but not limited to such:

- ☐ Practice Forgiveness: Release grudges and forgive those who have wronged you, just as we are forgiven.

- ☐ Practice Repentance: Turning away from anything or anyone leading you away from the Kingdom of God.

Dominating Peacemakers

- ☐ Engage in Active Listening: Take the time to truly listen to others, showing empathy and understanding in conversations.

- ☐ Promote Understanding: Encourage open dialogue among people with differing opinions to foster a Spirit of Respect and Cooperation.

- ☐ Show Kindness: Perform random acts of kindness to uplift others and create a positive environment or situation.

- ☐ Volunteer Your Time and Serve: Share your time, skills, and talent with those in need, helping to build community and support in and out of the Kingdom.

- ☐ Pray for Peace: Make prayer an integral part of your life, asking for guidance and strength to be a peacemaker in all situations.

- ☐ Share Your Faith: Share your beliefs and values gently and respectfully, promoting a dialogue about peace and understanding.

- ☐ Advocate for Justice and Righteousness: Stand up against injustices in your community, seeking fair treatment and dignity for all people.

- ☐ Cultivate Inner Peace: Engage in practices like meditation, silence, and reflection to maintain your own peace, allowing it to flow into your interactions with others.

Dominating Peacemakers

- ☐ Create Inclusive Spaces: Work to build environments where everyone feels welcome and valued, regardless of background, belief, nationality, or color.

- ☐ Resolve Conflicts Early: Proactively address conflicts before they escalate, approaching disagreements with a calm and peaceful demeanor.

- ☐ Encourage Collaboration: It is often said, *'Teamwork makes the dream work.'* It is always wise to foster teamwork and collaboration in your community to create solutions together as ONE, rather than becoming divided over issues.

- ☐ Promote Environmental Stewardship: Advocate for the care of the earth, emphasizing responsibility and love for creation as part of being a good steward in Earthen Vessels.

- ☐ Lead by Example: Be a living example of peace in your home and community, reflecting your beliefs through your actions, thoughts, beliefs, words, and desires.

- ☐ Teach Peace: Educate others, especially children, about the importance of peace, patience, tolerance, sharing, and understanding.

- ☐ Stay Humble: Approach conversations with humility, recognizing that we can all learn from one another. Humility is a prerequisite for Divine Wisdom.

- ☐ Use Gracious Words: Speak with respect and kindness to others, even in disagreement. Choose words that uplift rather than tear down.

Dominating Peacemakers

- ☐ Seek Common Ground: When faced with differing views, identify shared values or goals and build on them to foster unity.

- ☐ Support Peace Initiatives: Get involved in or support organizations that work towards peace and conflict resolution.

- ☐ Live a Life of Gratitude: Cultivate a thankful heart, recognizing the good in your life and in others, which helps to promote a peaceful mindset.

Although nothing is foolproof, having a point of direction on what to do, how to do it, and why you are doing so will help save time and energy while combating the relevant fears that come along with living life.

Combatting Fears

Above all, the Heavenly Peace of Jesus is desired by all, used only by a few due to the underlying FEARS of yesterday, today, and our tomorrows. Most often, we talk a good game as if we are big, bad, and bold, but a Spiritual Yoke will bring the strongest person to their knees if not handled correctly, or *As It Pleases God*. So let me say this: Yes, fear is real, and it also affects and infects us, Mentally, Physically, Emotionally, and Spiritually. Really? Yes, really! Unfortunately, in the Eye of God, the most fearful individuals are the most proud and judgmental, lacking humility and self-control.

Why would the elements of fear Spiritually Yoke Believers? We have unawaringly come into agreement with our fears without counteracting them, *As It Pleases God*. All we need to do is check our self-talk, words, beliefs, and thoughts; they

Dominating Peacemakers

tell us everything we need to know about our Spiritual State of Being and worldly state. On the other hand, if we make a conscious choice to lie to ourselves, then who are we really fooling? Unfortunately, we fool ourselves; while, at the same time, playing ourselves short when we should be standing tall in and out of the Kingdom of God. Here are the most common underlying fears we deal with or deny, but not limited to such:

- ☐ Fear of the unknown.
- ☐ Fear of change.
- ☐ Fear of rejection.
- ☐ Fear of failure.
- ☐ Fear of embarrassment.
- ☐ Fear of exposure.
- ☐ Fear of losing faith.
- ☐ Fear of lack of readiness.
- ☐ Fear of losing loved ones.
- ☐ Fear of a broken heart.
- ☐ Fear of eternal damnation.
- ☐ Fear of judgment from others.
- ☐ Fear of not being good enough.
- ☐ Fear of abandonment.
- ☐ Fear of not fulfilling a Divine Purpose.
- ☐ Fear of being ostracized.
- ☐ Fear of life's hardships.
- ☐ Fear of conflicting religious teachings.
- ☐ Fear of inadequate understanding of Scripture.
- ☐ Fear of being misled by false teachings.
- ☐ Fear of the end times or Revelation.

In our lives, fear often manifests in various forms and for many reasons. These fears can lead to feelings of anxiety and uncertainty that might seem overwhelming at times. Yet, they can also be opportunities for growth and a deeper

Dominating Peacemakers

understanding of faith if we allow them to teach us, *As It Pleases God*. Real or imagined fears affect us in various ways that Science has yet to truly understand. However, what we do know is that we can cancel and redirect our fears to prevent negative outcomes, such as but not limited to:

- ☐ Lack of faith
- ☐ Wavering doubt or disbelief.
- ☐ Negative environment.
- ☐ Unresolved trauma.
- ☐ Loss of desire or purpose.
- ☐ Complacency.
- ☐ Toxic relationships.
- ☐ Lack of education.
- ☐ Addictions.
- ☐ Procrastination.
- ☐ Materialism.
- ☐ Coveting and competitiveness.
- ☐ Envy, jealousy, pride, and greed.
- ☐ Isolation.
- ☐ Unmet basic needs.

Fear is a natural human response, acting as a protective mechanism, alerting us to potential dangers or threats. Actually, fear is not necessarily a negative emotion as long as we handle it correctly, *As It Pleases God*. In fact, a balanced amount of fear can be beneficial for us, provided that we comprehend it. On the other hand, unregulated or unchecked fears will lead to anxiety and a decline in health due to the over-release of cortisol and adrenaline.

The physiological responses elicited by fear can knowingly or unknowingly lead to significant chemical imbalances in our bodies, affecting our Mental, Physical, Emotional, and Spiritual Health. In *Combatting Fears*, let us break this down for a moment. When faced with a perceived threat, the body enters a state known as the 'fight or flight' response, initiated by the autonomic nervous system. No one is exempt from this happening; still, we must get an understanding of what is happening to counteract it properly.

This complex 'fight or flight' physiological reaction begins in the brain, particularly in the amygdala, which processes fear and triggers the hypothalamus to activate a stress response. For the sake of mankind, this results in the release of hormones, primarily adrenaline (epinephrine) and cortisol, into the bloodstream. If this happens too often, it will begin to work against us negatively, affecting our *Divine Etiquette* until it becomes counteracted positively, *As It Pleases God*. Please allow me to explain:

- ☐ **Adrenaline Surge**: Adrenaline prepares the body for immediate action. It increases heart rate, elevates blood pressure, and boosts energy supplies. While this is beneficial in short bursts, chronic exposure to fear can lead to persistently high levels of adrenaline, resulting in increased anxiety and other cardiovascular issues.

- ☐ **Cortisol Release**: As a longer-term stress hormone, cortisol helps manage how the body uses carbohydrates, fats, and proteins. It also plays a crucial role in regulating blood sugar levels, inflammation, and immune responses. Elevated cortisol due to continuous fear can lead to various problems, including weight gain, digestive issues, and weakened immune function.

For these two reasons and to preserve our lives, it is imperative to face our fears, even if trauma is involved. Why must we deal with fear and trauma as Believers? When fear and trauma are trapped in the psyche of mankind, we become susceptible to being yoked by the enemy or turning against ourselves. Above all, it cannot be whitewashed...it only lays dormant within the psyche, waiting for the opportune moment to express itself. Unfortunately, this is one of the reasons that we 'Click' when we are hurt, offended, or betrayed, zapping our peaceful state of being.

As we navigate through life, facing our fears head-on, these feelings can lead us to question our decisions, our capabilities, and sometimes even our beliefs. We should only rely on fear as a temporary measure until we address the root causes of our insecurities and vulnerabilities through Spiritual Growth, inner peace, physical activity, balanced nutrition, mindset strengthening, and sometimes through professional help. Once we achieve this goal, we can become Spiritually Fearless, possessing an unshakable confidence that transcends human understanding.

If we wallow in our fears and embrace our ability to remain afraid of things we cannot control, then it becomes an unhealthy fear and not a survival mechanism. If we allow fear to become our shadow, we will become susceptible to becoming overbearing, pompous, and controlling. Then again, we can also become weak, easily influenced, or bullied.

According to the Heavenly of Heavens, ungoverned fear crushes our self-reliance, enthusiasm, and initiative, promoting procrastination and leading to weak character. In addition, fear defeats our ability to love efficiently and effectively, *As It Pleases God*. Without love, our fears will eventually lead to known or unknown misery, heartaches, betrayal, and sadness. However, we must not lose hope, as fear and a lack of courage are simply states of mind that can be overcome by reshaping our character and embracing our unique traits. All of which can be transformed by the faithful use of the Fruits of the Spirit and behaving Christlike.

The Power of Faith

Our faith is our power! Moreover, our Divine Power is hidden within our faith. Is there a difference? Absolutely. One is self-developed through our words, thoughts, beliefs, desires, and decisions, positively or negatively. In contrast, Divine Power is Divinely or Heavenly Transferred, *As It Pleases God*, and maintained in the Spirit of Righteousness with Spiritual Principles at the forefront.

Without basic faith, life becomes a little more complicated to understand, which causes us to fear and judge life through our own eyes, with our perception of God nowhere in our equational efforts. When it comes down to the root of our fears, our perception must meet up with the truth of our reality. If not, our perceptions can become warped while placing them on others without asking fact-finding questions first.

Why is asking questions so important? Simply put, we do not all think alike, nor do we operate on the same level of faith or use Divine Wisdom over common knowledge. For example, with me, it is only wise to ask me why I do what I do. Someone else's perception of an ungoverned query can get me totally wrong, even while appearing right in their own eyes. What is the big deal here? I operate on a Divine Level, *As It Pleases God*. And, for someone operating on their own terms to please themselves, satiate their ego, find fault, or satisfy their curiosities, they will get me all wrong, including a psychiatrist, prophet, or priest who is not Spiritually Aligned, *As It Pleases God*.

Why must they be Spiritually Aligned, *As It Pleases God*? The Divine Secrets, Wisdom, and Treasures of the Kingdom are not for everyone. God will place a Spiritual Guard protecting what is Divine and what truly belongs to Him, that is also in Purpose on purpose. In my opinion, this analogy is similar to the Garden of Eden being Divinely Guarded from

Dominating Peacemakers

mankind. The moment we attempt to supersede what is Divine or override the Will of God with anything or anyone, we will lose peace in that particular area. So, BEWARE. If we take the proper channels, *As It Pleases God*, our peace will remain, even amid chaos.

In John 14:27 lies our instructions from Jesus: *"Peace I leave with you, My peace I give to you; not as the world gives do I give to you. Let not your heart be troubled, neither let it be afraid."* As a Word to the Wise: When dealing with *The Power of Faith*, we have a Spiritual Right to place a Spiritual Demand on our Divine Peace, casting down all turmoil and fear while replacing them with Divine Order and Courage.

What if we choose not to overcome our fears? Unfortunately, unnecessary or useless fear will place a vice grip on the psyche that can become contagious, zapping our peacefulness from within, in our homes, and in the homes of others.

To fully embrace our role as *Dominating Peacemakers*, we must transform conflict into compassion, patience, and empathy, especially when visiting others.

Entering A House

According to the Heavenly of Heavens, we must bring peace to our homes and the houses of others, not chaos, debauchery, or confusion. If peacefulness is not the intent, then we should not enter another man's house with ill will. Why? We will bring that same energy back to our domain, plus whatever negative energy they possess. Is this real? It is as real as the oxygen we are breathing!

What if we are not accepted into someone's home? Unbeknown to most, everyone has the right to accept or reject us, and there is nothing we can do to change this Spiritual Birthright. On the other hand, if we are rejected,

Dominating Peacemakers

then here is what Jesus said to do according to Matthew 10:14: *"And whoever will not receive you nor hear your words, when you depart from that house or city, shake off the dust from your feet."* Is it that simple? Yes, we cannot violate the free will of anyone. If they are not our children, then people need to make their own choices, and we need to kindly keep it moving in the Spirit of Excellence, being about our Father's Business, doing what we were called to do.

What if we are compelled to keep trying to win someone to the Kingdom of God? The Kingdom is not by force, nor do we need to hit people over the head with the Bible. Here is what we must know:

- ☐ When we are called to complete a Divine Mission, we do what we are called to do and step back and allow God to do His part. We are not to play His role; let God be God, period.

- ☐ We must keep this Scripture in mind at all times to exercise Spiritual Discernment: *"Do not give what is holy to the dogs; nor cast your pearls before swine, lest they trample them under their feet, and turn and tear you in pieces."* Matthew 7:6.

- ☐ Rejection comes with the territory. And if we cannot handle rejection, it is time to step back into the Spiritual Classroom. Then again, rejection is sometimes our protection. 1 Corinthians 15:33 says, *"Do not be deceived: 'Evil company corrupts good habits.'"*

- ☐ We are required to live by example, using the Fruits of the Spirit and behaving Christlike at all times, even if people do not like us.

Dominating Peacemakers

No one is exempt from Spiritual Opposition, nor are we obliged to settle for this state. We have Spiritual Authority to overcome whatever with whomever, but we must know it to apply it, *As It Pleases God.* Unfortunately, this is how the enemy shakes us down, causing us to turn on ourselves first and then others. Sadly, this tactic has not changed since the Garden of Eden Experience. Nonetheless, our lack of understanding of Spiritual Duality has caused us to become confused about Kingdom Authority, Dominion, and Expectations.

Throughout history, from the Ancient of Days until now, one of the most deceptive strategies employed by our adversaries has been the art of division. For example:

- ☐ A Divided Mind, Body, Soul, or Spirit.
- ☐ Divided Thoughts, Words, and Actions.
- ☐ Divided Obedience and Reverence.
- ☐ Divided Goals, Seeds, and Multiplying Factors.
- ☐ Divided Strength and Fellowship.
- ☐ Divided Healing and Power.
- ☐ Divided Light and Illumination.
- ☐ Divided Language and Truth.
- ☐ Divided Communication and Peace.
- ☐ Divided Skills, Talents, and Purpose.
- ☐ Divided Love, Oneness, and Joy.
- ☐ Divided Homes and Relationships.
- ☐ Divided Workplaces and Governments.
- ☐ Divided Churches and Denominations.
- ☐ Divided Beliefs and Righteousness.
- ☐ Divided Loyalty and Service.
- ☐ Divided Character and Fruits.
- ☐ Divided Faith and Hope.
- ☐ Divided Connections and Unity.
- ☐ Divided Understanding and Execution.
- ☐ Divided Jealousy, Envy, Pride, Greed, and Coveting.

Dominating Peacemakers

Spiritual Duality refers to the existence of opposing forces that influence our lives positively and negatively. As a matter of fact, it encompasses the internal and eternal battle between good and evil, right and wrong, light and darkness, positive and negative, and just and unjust. All of which shape our thoughts, beliefs, desires, actions, words, character, and interactions with ourselves and others.

How do we make this make sense? For example, the enemy first sows seeds of discord, triggering insecurities, traumas, and fears that prompt self-doubt, anger, hatred, resentment, or unforgiveness, causing us to react negatively or disobediently. As a result of the negativity without a positive counteraction, *As It Pleases God*, it will begin to spoil our good fruit from within, spreading outwardly and inciting conflict, chaos, and confusion. While at the same time, we appear right and justified in our own eyes, thinking the problem lies within everyone else besides us—the trigger point or point of origin.

Rather than standing firm in our Spiritual Dominion, *As it Pleases God*, we may fearfully or selfishly yield our Divine Power to adversarial forces, further perpetuating division from within ourselves, as well as inside and outside of the Kingdom. To counteract these dubious, underhanded tactics, we must cultivate a deeper understanding of Spiritual Duality and the reversal process while embracing our Kingdom Identity and Stance for our Heaven on Earth Experiences (Our Reason for Being).

Regardless of where we are in life or what we have going on, we need to seek peace in every facet of life, even when life is lifing with the Cycles and Vicissitudes at full force. One thing is for sure: According to the Heavenly of Heavens, life is designed for us, so it is our responsibility to *Pay Attention* and maximize it, *As It Pleases Him*. If not, we will get what we get. Plus, the enemy's age-old strategy of dividing and conquering

Dominating Peacemakers

from the Garden of Eden will remain in full effect until we step up to the plate, doing what we are called to do!

What are we called to do as Believers? Everyone's Divine Calling is different, with varying Spiritual Blueprints and intricately designed paths guiding, protecting, and training us for our Heaven on Earth Experiences and the Greater Good of mankind. Yet, in Earthen Vessel, everyone is PREWIRED to step up to the plate to use the Fruits of the Spirit, *As It Pleases God*, and develop a *Spirit to Spirit* Connection with Him. If not, we will face some form of division or shame from the inside out based on our personalized kryptonite, overlooked triggers, or hidden traumas.

What happened to our free will choice, opting out of division and shame, especially in our own homes? The free will of mankind is not lost in this matter because, as living beings, we are grafted into Spiritual Duality by default. For example, we have a free will choice between unity or division, self-respect or shame, positivity or negativity, good or bad, right or wrong, and so on. In the intricate tapestry of existence, regardless of whether the use is in the home or not, no one is exempt from Spiritual Duality, and we all possess the power to change its course, positively or negatively.

In shaping our choices and the paths we take when entering or exiting our homes or those of another, we still have free-willed freedom to use the Guiding Principles of the Fruits of the Spirit, where there are zero laws against their use. Then again, we can also opt out of their use, subjecting ourselves to Spiritual Laws, Principles, and Protocols.

What is the big deal here, especially when we are not under the law? Ultimately, not being under the law does not exempt us from Spiritual Laws, Principles, and Protocols or the Laws of the Land. It only removes the sting or stench of death, replacing it with grace (the refinement or empowerment process). Secondly, the deal is that if we do not make the correct choices in life, our homes are impacted, including the

Dominating Peacemakers

ones belonging to others, extending outwardly to our neighborhoods and communities.

Plus, we do not want to spread bad or negative energy, period. Just know this: Energy, whether positive or negative, is contagious and contributes to a chain reaction. For example, a home filled with chaos, contention, anger, resentment, unforgiveness, or confusion will often feel heavy and unwelcoming, making it difficult for peace and joy to thrive. Even Proverbs 4:23 tells us: *"Keep your heart with all diligence, for out of it spring the issues of life."*

The Divine Cornerstone of *Divine Etiquette* is to become the *Dominating Peacemaker* and a beacon of hope, turning our environments into a place of harmony, love, patience, and understanding, fostering positivity and inclusivity regardless of our struggles, traumas, weaknesses, and triumphs. In the Eye of God, to get to this point goes far beyond mere social or expected niceties. We must *Pay Attention* to our people skills and character traits, *As It Pleases God*, without becoming distracted by spreading gossip, slandering the innocent, harboring resentment, engaging in debauchery, neglecting our responsibilities, or anything eroding our foundation of peace or undermining our good-willed focus.

In essence, the heart of being a *Dominating Peacemaker* encompasses the pursuit of authenticity and a commitment to Lead by Example, *As It Pleases God*, with unifying inspiration, catalyzing to Heal the Land. Although this Spiritual Journey is both challenging and rewarding, but gaining Spiritual Access to the Divine Wisdom, Treasures, Protection, and Secrets of the Kingdom is well worth the pursuit.

In doing our due diligence, *As It Pleases God*, let me say this: When entering another man's house, do not and I mean do not, enter their domain with the attempt to curse them. Always *Enter A House* with the intent to BLESS; if not, then keep your distance to ensure you do not curse your own hand.

Chapter Five

Pay Attention

Amid living our best lives, we must also *Pay Attention* to our commitment to our Divine Interconnectedness and those who are Kingdomly USABLE. What is the purpose of Kingdom Usability over Kingdom Anointing? According to the Heavenly of Heavens, we cannot become truly Kingdomly Anointed until we can become Kingdomly Usable.

Nevertheless, we can become self-anointed and self-appointed with zero Spiritual Fruits, *As It Pleases God*. Or, we can have a track record of leaving rotten fruits all over the place with all types of lies, debauchery, and confusion. Here is what Romans 16:17-18 leaves for us to Spiritually Glean: *"Now I urge you, brethren, note those who cause divisions and offenses, contrary to the doctrine which you learned, and avoid them. For those who are such do not serve our Lord Jesus Christ, but their own belly, and by smooth words and flattering speech deceive the hearts of the simple."*

Serving the Kingdom of God with a grudge, anger, revenge, or any negative attributes will cause the unresolved overflow of negativity to leak out on others. Unfortunately, it most

Pay Attention

often leaks on the innocent while appearing right in our own eyes, enhancing Kingdom Polarity (A Divided Kingdom). For this reason, Philippians 1:27 advises us in this fashion: *"Only let your conduct be worthy of the gospel of Christ, so that whether I come and see you or am absent, I may hear of your affairs, that you stand fast in one spirit, with one mind striving together for the faith of the gospel."*

Living Without Boundaries

What if we prefer to allow life to just happen? We have free will to choose our paths in life, even if it is fancy-free or reckless. Yet, one thing is for sure: We cannot complain about the side effects of living our lives without boundaries. Sometimes, this is our training ground for learning, understanding, and growing. Then again, it can also create a bed of negativity and sacrifice or a cycle of déjà vu, especially if God is nowhere in the equation.

When *Living Without Boundaries*, I do not wish ill will upon anyone; actually, I want the best for every living being, regardless of whether they are good, bad, or indifferent. Still, as a Divine Vessel of the Most High God, I must emphasize the importance of self-control and discipline due to the inherent vulnerabilities of the human psyche, even if we are clueless about what is taking place.

What makes boundary awareness so important for Believers? According to Proverbs 25:28, *"Whoever has no rule over his own spirit is like a city broken down, without walls."* By allowing anything or anyone into the Mind, Body, Soul, or Spirit, we will pick up the negative debris called Spiritual Yokes, mind germs, and soul ties. If we do not know or understand how to reverse-engineer negativity, *As It Pleases God*, the negative grip will become tighter, especially when we are clueless, disobedient, or pompous.

Pay Attention

In the Eye of God, to grow Mentally, Physically, Emotionally, Spiritually, and Financially, we must exhibit self-control and discipline. So, we must make a choice:

- ☐ Embrace Freedom in God, our Heavenly Father. *"Now the Lord is the Spirit; and where the Spirit of the Lord is, there is liberty."* 2 Corinthians 3:17.

- ☐ Embrace worldly freedom, catering to ourselves and others. If this is our choice, know this: *"For he who sows to his flesh will of the flesh reap corruption, but he who sows to the Spirit will of the Spirit reap everlasting life."* Galatians 6:8.

In this book, *Divine Etiquette: As It Pleases God*, it is urging us to choose wisely and follow the path that leads to life through love, faith, and obedience. Clearly, we do not need to be perfect. We only need to be a WILLING Vessel ready to please our Heavenly Father by any means necessary, especially with the simple stuff, such as being kind, respectful, and merciful.

Freedom In God

Can we really experience Freedom in God, our Heavenly Father? Absolutely. Freedom is a concept that resonates deeply within the Mind, Body, Soul, and Spirit, establishing our heart postures. *Freedom In God* is often associated with the absence of constraints, unlimited potential, the free will to choose, the power to live authentically, or the ability to live and have our being, *As It Pleases Him*. So, you see, there is a lot to consider when opting for *Freedom In God*.

Once we understand the nature of God Almighty and develop an intimate *Spirit to Spirit* Relationship with Him in

Pay Attention

outright obedience, as a Loving Father, He will grant us things that money cannot buy. What can money not buy? There are many things, varying from person to person, trauma to trauma, situation to situation, and so on. From a broad perspective, here is a list, but not limited to such:

- ☐ Money cannot buy us SALVATION.
- ☐ Money cannot buy us DIVINE PURPOSE.
- ☐ Money cannot buy us RIGHTEOUSNESS.
- ☐ Money cannot buy us LOVE.
- ☐ Money cannot buy us JOY.
- ☐ Money cannot buy us PEACE.
- ☐ Money cannot buy us PATIENCE.
- ☐ Money cannot buy us KINDNESS.
- ☐ Money cannot buy us GOODNESS.
- ☐ Money cannot buy us FAITHFULNESS.
- ☐ Money cannot buy us GENTLENESS.
- ☐ Money cannot buy us SELF-CONTROL.
- ☐ Money cannot buy us DIVINE WISDOM.
- ☐ Money cannot buy us KEYS TO THE KINGDOM OF GOD ALMIGHTY.

Why can money not buy these things? They are FREE if we do what it takes to receive them, *As It Pleases God*. Really? Yes, really. They are Free-Will Gifts from our Heavenly Father.

Although Ecclesiastes 10:19 says, "*A feast is made for laughter, and wine makes merry; but money answers everything.*" And, yes, we need money to finance our lifestyles and facilitate the Kingdom of God. Then again, it can also play a critical role in addressing our external needs, wants, desires, dreams, and concerns, facilitating temporal happiness.

Nevertheless, when it comes to the Spirit Man in Earthen Vessel, we need BALANCE between what money can and cannot buy. When choosing between material gain over

Pay Attention

Spiritual Growth, it can indeed become a tricky situation, but the choice must be made. If not, we will eventually come to a crossroads, Mentally, Physically, Emotionally, or Spiritually, with varying conflicts, causing us to chase after fleeting pleasures that ultimately leave us feeling empty, lost, confused, traumatized, and insecure.

Spiritual Nourishment, *As It Pleases God*, on the other hand, can provide the best of both worlds once we get in Purpose on purpose, according to our Predestined Blueprinted Mission. How do we get in Purpose on purpose, *As It Pleases God*? Clearly, everyone's Divine Mission is different, but we can begin with:

- ☐ Come into an AGREEMENT with God, *Spirit to Spirit*.
- ☐ Become ONE with the Holy Spirit for guidance.
- ☐ COVER ourselves with the Blood of Jesus as Spiritual Atonement.
- ☐ PRAY, REPENT, and FORGIVE.
- ☐ READ the Word of God.
- ☐ GIVE THANKS in all things.
- ☐ USE the Fruits of the Spirit.
- ☐ BECOME a work-in-progress, *As It Pleases God*.
- ☐ BEHAVE Christlike and self-correct immediately.
- ☐ DOCUMENT our conversations with God.

Can this work for anyone? Absolutely. We all must begin somewhere, so it may as well be here and now.

Once we are set free, *As It Pleases God*, Galatians 5:1 has a word for us: *"Stand fast therefore in the liberty by which Christ has made us free, and do not be entangled again with a yoke of bondage."* The call to 'stand fast' is a reminder that maintaining our Divine Liberty in Christ Jesus requires willing intentionality and attentiveness.

Pay Attention

Above all, we must avoid being manipulated. *Freedom In God* grants us the ability to self-correct at the drop of a dime and say 'yes' or 'no' when necessary. Doing so will help us avoid a lot of negative influences. In addition, Matthew 5:37 says, *"But let your 'Yes' be 'Yes,' and your 'No,' 'No.' For whatever is more than these is from the evil one."* So, when operating in this state, please 'Watch Out!'

Watch Out

When operating in freedom, *As It Pleases God*, why must we *Watch Out* and remain attentive? Our known and unknown enemies will shoot their shots, and if our discerning faculties are warped or lack peacefulness, we will 'get got' by the enemy's wiles. For this reason alone, this is why a lot of witches and warlocks are in the church, stealing the dreams of weaker vessels. Really? Yes, really!

What if we do not believe witches and warlocks exist? We have free will to believe whatever we like...but anyone who willfully violates the free will of another, manipulates people out of selfishness, or engages in the works of the flesh with rebellion could be operating in the Spirit of Divination. Clearly, we do not have to believe in them, but if we BEHAVE like them, then where are the boundaries set? Or better yet, have we crossed the line without realizing it? Here is what Galatians 3:1 states: *"O foolish Galatians! Who has bewitched you?"*

Those who know know, and those who do not know will 'get got' when they least expect it, especially when straying away from the Truth and the Word of God. Then again, Ephesians 6:12 says, *"For we do not wrestle against flesh and blood, but against principalities, against powers, against the rulers of the darkness of this age, against spiritual hosts of wickedness in the heavenly places."*

Pay Attention

If we think we are exempt from the factors of wrestling, then think again. Ephesians 6:10-11 tells us what to do: *"Finally, my brethren, be strong in the Lord and in the power of His might. Put on the whole armor of God, that you may be able to stand against the wiles of the devil."*

As a Word to the Wise: Do not play around with Spiritual Things you do not understand to override the Will of God. Here is what 1 Samuel 15:23 states: *"For rebellion is as the sin of witchcraft, And stubbornness is as iniquity and idolatry. Because you have rejected the word of the Lord, He also has rejected you from being king."* Does this not apply to King Solomon only? The Divine Judgment was directed toward King Solomon, but the Spiritual Principle regarding disobedience, idolatry, and stubbornness will remain until the end of time.

For the record, we do not get a free pass for Spiritual Negligence. Yes, we do have grace and mercy to save us from death and destruction, but it does not override Seedtime and Harvest or the Law of Reciprocity. Besides, where I am from, we have this saying, *'What is good for the goose is good for the gander.'* And if we think that God is going to endorse our selfish debauchery of unrighteousness, we are sadly mistaken, especially when it comes to His precious or innocent sheep.

Now, if we think we are big, bad, and bold enough to contend with God Almighty, then carry on! Do people really contend with Him? Of course. Actually, I have met a few witches and warlocks who were really bold. They were so confident in their method of operation that they openly stated that they wanted to get to know me to steal my destiny. Although I did not flinch an inch or show my hand too quickly, I wanted to see how far they would take it before I shut them all the way down.

How is it possible to shut someone down? First, you must become Divinely Accurate. Secondly, if you do not know who you are in the Kingdom of God or you operate in willful debauchery or disobedience, then you may become 'Stuck like Chuck.'

Now, being that I operate in a Divine Realm, *As It Pleases God* and *Spirit to Spirit*, I can see, hear, and speak what most cannot. What does this mean in layman's terms? I shut them or their vile intents down by canceling, rebuking, or disagreeing with their projections while not mumbling one single word audibly. I do this based on James 4:7, *"Therefore submit to God. Resist the devil and he will flee from you."*

In addition, I will also operate with a pleasant smile while exhibiting the Fruits of the Spirit and behaving Christlike simultaneously in the Spirit of Righteousness. Above all, I apply the appropriate Scriptures to the situation, circumstance, or event, quoting them back to God as a Spiritual Seal on His Divine Promises for me and my house.

According to the Heavenly of Heavens, there is no need to be rude, mean, hateful, condescending, or engage in name-calling. Lovingkindness with Divine Authority will get the job done without behaving irrationally or immorally.

Why must we remain in a State of Righteousness or Positivity? First, Spiritual Duality is real—We cannot fight negativity with negativity. In the Eye of God, we must contend with the righteous opposites. Secondly, negative behaviors zap our Divine Power. Unfortunately, this is why the enemy tries to get into our heads to ruffle our feathers or push our buttons to get us off our squares. Thus, when contending on any level, we must remain calm.

I must admit, getting to this Spiritual Level by keeping my composure takes a lot of work, correction, and training, especially when my known and unknown enemies attempt to make me look like boo-boo the fool, throw me under the bus, out me publicly, or bring shame to my name. Nevertheless, if you begin with the Fruits of the Spirit and behave Christlike, it will develop your Spiritual Senses, Peacefulness, and Accuracy.

Pay Attention

However, when you are in Purpose on purpose, operating in the Fruits of the Spirit, and behaving Christlike, they can only take what you give them or what you come into agreement with. For me, I was not surrendering anything to them, nor did I agree with their negative antics. Instead, I interjected a Divine Counteraction. And then, I gleaned the story to feed God's sheep, letting them know that dream killers or stealers are on the prowl and are boastfully within the pews and pulpits.

The Test

How do we know the difference between the righteous and the unrighteous? The difference is revealed through the works of their flesh and their fruits. Unfortunately, this is where most Believers get confused and miss their Spiritual Cues. How so? Here is how Isaiah 5:20 puts it: *"Woe to those who call evil good, and good evil; who put darkness for light, and light for darkness; who put bitter for sweet, and sweet for bitter!"* In all simplicity, they do not know the difference between positive and negative fruits, behaviors, thoughts, words, and beliefs.

Conversely, we also have those who go on feelings, and our feelings are not always accurate based on our perceptions, mindsets, biases, or traumas. For this reason, we are required to TEST the Spirit. According to 1 John 4:1, it says: *"Beloved, do not believe every spirit, but test the spirits, whether they are of God; because many false prophets have gone out into the world."*

And then 1 Thessalonians 5:21 tells us what to choose: *"Test all things; hold fast what is good."* If, for some reason, we do not know what is good or what the compositional factors of good character traits are, then it is time to get in the know. Even if it takes us to get in God's Face, *Spirit to Spirit*, seeking answers, then do it! If one needs to use James 1:5 as Divine Leverage, then do it! It says, *"If any of you lacks wisdom, let him ask of God,*

Pay Attention

who gives to all liberally and without reproach, and it will be given to him." It costs us nothing to ask questions and seek answers, but it could cost us everything for not doing so.

In *Divine Etiquette: As It Pleases God®*, we are required to know good character traits to become better, stronger, and wiser, *As It Pleases Him*, and to be about our Father's Business. In addition, we are also required to know the bad ones that are not conducive to our well-being or Spiritual Journey.

In *The Testing Phase*, here is how Galatians 5:19-21 clearly outlines negative behaviors that are contrary to a faith-based life and warns of their consequences. *"Now the works of the flesh are evident, which are: adultery, fornication, uncleanness, lewdness, idolatry, sorcery, hatred, contentions, jealousies, outbursts of wrath, selfish ambitions, dissensions, heresies, envy, murders, drunkenness, revelries, and the like; of which I tell you beforehand, just as I also told you in time past, that those who practice such things will not inherit the kingdom of God."*

In the Eye of God, any of these negative attributes can be reversed into a positive or a win-win, but we must make the effort to put in the work, *As It Pleases Him*. Without Him added into the equation, we may lay down one negative thing, only to pick up another one, putting us in a worse condition than before.

Can we really become worse by getting rid of negative attributes and yokes? Absolutely. Here is what Matthew 12:43-45 says about this condition: *"When an unclean spirit goes out of a man, he goes through dry places, seeking rest, and finds none. Then he says, 'I will return to my house from which I came.' And when he comes, he finds it empty, swept, and put in order. Then he goes and takes with him seven other spirits more wicked than himself, and they enter and dwell there; and the last state of that man is worse than the first. So shall it also be with this wicked generation."* What do we do in this case? We must break the *Strongholds of Unkindness*.

Chapter Six

Strongholds of Unkindness

To break the *Strongholds Of Unkindness*, we must know what and with whom to engage or disengage. Although PLEASING God or doing things God's Way is the best, we must still recognize when we are pleasing ourselves or people-pleasing due to our secret or open insecurities and traumas. By placing God on the back burner, the effectiveness of our fruitfulness or communicative skills is negatively impacted, even if we think we are the best thing since sliced bread.

Who am I to judge, right? No judgment intended. Nevertheless, Matthew 6:33 says, *"But seek first the kingdom of God and His righteousness, and all these things shall be added to you."* And then we have Proverbs 3:5-6 saying, *"Trust in the Lord with all your heart, and lean not on your own understanding; in all your ways acknowledge Him, and He shall direct your paths."*

In addition to the use of the Fruits of the Spirit and behaving Christlike, here are a few items that can crumble negative strongholds of our past, present, and future, but not limited to such:

Strongholds of Unkindness

- ☐ We need to exhibit empathy and understanding of situations and circumstances from other people's perspectives, especially when we do not have all the facts.
- ☐ Create an environment where people feel safe expressing their feelings and experiences.
- ☐ Stay aware of how others might perceive your body language, tone, and words.
- ☐ Acknowledge and celebrate the achievements of others.
- ☐ Foster a sense of community, teamwork, and support.
- ☐ When you witness unkind behaviors being normalized, speak up positively.
- ☐ Diffuse negative feelings with positive thoughts, relevant Scriptures, and positive affirmations.
- ☐ Lead by example with positivity and kindness.
- ☐ Become grateful in all things, pinpointing the win-win.
- ☐ Distance yourself from individuals or situations that perpetuate unkindness with no remorse or correction.
- ☐ Reverse negative thoughts, beliefs, and desires into positive ones.
- ☐ Let go of grudges, unforgiveness, and resentment.
- ☐ Find constructive ways to address issues.
- ☐ Exhibit patience in all things.
- ☐ Become positively proactive.
- ☐ Acknowledge and repent of all negative behaviors, thoughts, beliefs, words, and desires.

When dealing with *Strongholds Of Unkindness*, this list can enhance our ability to bring forth reconciliation in or out of the Body of Christ and from within the depths of our souls.

What does reconciliation have to do with the *Silent Acts of Unkindness*? Without the reconciliation properties flowing through our veins, *As It Pleases God*, we become susceptible to

Strongholds of Unkindness

the eminent wiles of the enemy, causing us to play ourselves short while thinking we are standing tall. What does all of this mean for Believers? Picturesquely, this is when we feel as if we are on fire for God while lighting a match to the unhealed or ungoverned psyche with zero understanding of what is going on. As a result, we feel a sense of burnout but usually cannot tell anyone about it, which causes us to become a melting pot of negative thoughts, emotions, and desires.

Regrettably, the melting pot effect usually happens when we play in God's face while having to lick our wounds continually behind closed doors. Often, this is due to the lack of Spiritual Healing from the Heavenly of Heavens. In addition, it can also happen when we are operating in outright disobedience or when being misaligned with God's Divine Will with a time-sensitive Missionable Purpose.

As we deepen our relationship with God, we have three options associated with His Divine Plan that lead to positive or negative outcomes:

- ☐ Option One: God's Way, *As It Pleases Him*.
- ☐ Option Two: Our own way to please ourselves.
- ☐ Option Three: To please others.

What is the purpose of knowing the three? It helps us to recognize whether we are *Pleasing God*, ourselves, or others on a moment-by-moment basis.

How do we make these options make sense for Believers? For example, when operating in Purpose on purpose, *As It Pleases God*, if someone attempts to block us or the Divine Will of God, the opposite of their intent will happen, and He provides another way of escape. For instance, if we repeat Psalm 119:105, "*Your word is a lamp to my feet and a light to my path,*" while simultaneously using the Fruits of the Spirit and behaving Christlike, He will fine-tune our Spiritual Compass to ensure we are on time, every time, not missing a beat. But know this: *"Therefore, whether you eat or drink, or whatever you do, do all to the glory of God."* 1 Corinthians 10:31.

On the other hand, when operating out of purpose, the wiles of the enemy can cause our minds to jump the track, placing us on an emotional rollercoaster while contemplating more plots and schemes against one another. By far, when operating in such a manner, it closes our eyes to the Divine Glory, Presence, and Manifestation of the Holy Trinity.

For example, a security guard will focus on external thieves while missing the thieves in his circle in plain sight, with whom he lollygags daily. Whereas, the same applies to the Believers in or out of the Kingdom; for this reason, we are required to examine the Fruits of the Spirit as outlined in Galatians 5:22-23. Indeed, they play a vital role in shaping our character, thoughts, and actions, *As It Pleases God*.

Consuming Our Own Fruits

The benchmark of Spiritual Health, Ultimate Wellness, Good Success, and Kingdom Growth, *As It Pleases God*, are all hidden within the Fruits of the Spirit. In light of *Divine Etiquette*, they provide a clear guideline or roadmap for living a life reflective of our faith, integrity, and loyalty from a Divine Perspective, superseding human reasonings.

Now, if for some reason, we are experiencing Spiritual Depravity, Yokes, or Bondage, we are required as Kingdom Citizens to examine our Spiritual Fruits to ensure they are not mangled, rotten, or unripe. In addition, we must also ensure that we are NOT consuming our own fruits through our selfish ambitions, debauchery, or competitiveness.

What if we begin to consume our own fruits through selfishness or pompousness? Many things can happen depending upon our relationship with our Heavenly Father,

Strongholds of Unkindness

our level of understanding, our level of traumas, our cultural backgrounds, or our level of obedience. Here are a few things that can happen, but are not limited to such:

- ☐ We will begin to turn on ourselves from the inside out without realizing we are doing so. But the evidence will leave a paper trail in our thoughts, words, actions, reactions, and beliefs.

- ☐ We may become self-centered and overly focused on our own Spiritual Journey, neglecting the needs of others.

- ☐ We may find ourselves isolated from friends, family, and community, refusing to serve or support others.

- ☐ We may become stagnated in our Spiritual Growth. Then again, we may experience a Spiritual Plateau, recycling what we already know without receiving new and refreshed Heavenly Downloads.

- ☐ We may begin to lack accountability or downplay our Spiritual Commitments without realizing it.

- ☐ We may experience a decline in internal joy or avoid sharing our experiences with others.

- ☐ We may experience an increased desire or hunger for ungodly temptations, making us extremely vulnerable to negative influences, habits, and vices. All of which brings the lust of the eye, the lust of the flesh, and the pride of life to the forefront with stigmatic shame attached.

Strongholds of Unkindness

- ☐ We may experience a severe bout with guilt, shame, and fear of being overlooked or missing out.
- ☐ We may encounter all types of debauched glitches, misunderstandings, confusion, and chaos coming out of nowhere.
- ☐ We may willfully refuse to share our Spiritual Gifts to prevent others from getting ahead or outdoing us.
- ☐ We may experience all types of unregulated bitterness, hatefulness, resentment, anger, and unforgiveness, oppressing and traumatizing others.
- ☐ We may experience a lapse in gratefulness while beginning to fuss and complain about everything and not being satisfied with anything or anyone. In my opinion, this is the 'Nothing is ever good enough' mentality.
- ☐ We may experience decreased fulfillment with all kinds of negative reports while second-guessing and doubting ourselves, others, and most of all, God.
- ☐ We may begin to lack inspiration or a desire to continue in the Will of God while secretly giving up without voicing it.
- ☐ We may lose sight of our Divine Purpose while plugging and playing or doing anything, hoping something will stick.
- ☐ We may lose our ability to love unconditionally. In this phase, we may find ourselves looking for love in all the wrong places, expecting others to do what we are not willing to do for ourselves.

Strongholds of Unkindness

- We may begin to feel vulnerable, therefore hiding our struggles to avoid becoming a victim of potential preying vultures or wolves in sheep's clothing.

- We may begin to experience an identity crisis, not knowing whether we are coming or going. As a result, we will anchor our identity in a role, title, degree, or status instead of being our authentic selves.

- We may experience feelings of unworthiness while masking them with materialism, causing us to become consumed with power, money, and sex for a temporary boost.

- We may begin to engage in the blaming game while faithfully feeding ourselves lies. When we begin to believe our own lies, we must shift from the blaming game to owning our truth to develop a work-in-progress mindset and heart posture.

- We may miss out on viable Blessings and Miracles designed to take us from where we are into our NEXT. Due to the lack of investment into the Seedtime and Harvest Principle based on the Law of Reciprocity, we can indeed sideline ourselves.

Our Spiritual Fruits are designed to build us up Mentally, Physically, Emotionally, Spiritually, and Financially in order to give back to the Kingdom of God when called upon.

Suppose we are on the take more than we give or become a miser. In this case, we cannot be fruitful and multiply as Divinely Commissioned, according to Genesis 1:28. Here is what it says, *"Then God blessed them, and God said to them, 'Be fruitful*

Strongholds of Unkindness

and multiply; fill the earth and subdue it; have dominion over the fish of the sea, over the birds of the air, and over every living thing that moves on the earth.'"

Why is a miser frowned upon in the Kingdom of God? When we willfully withhold goodness, we limit ourselves in Kingdom Usage, *As It Pleases Him*. For the record, I know a few very BLESSED and very wealthy misers, but when it comes to Divine Wisdom, Peace, Understanding, and Illumination, they are void of them while coveting what their money cannot buy. All of which lead to varying struggles, addictions, abusiveness, or bad habits. Here is what Proverbs 23:6-7 warns about this type of heart posture: *"Do not eat the bread of a miser, nor desire his delicacies; for as he thinks in his heart, so is he. 'Eat and drink!' he says to you, but his heart is not with you."*

What is the big deal as long as they have money? First, in the Eye of God, we are *'Blessed to Be A Blessing.'* He uses people like us in Earthen Vessels to become the conduits of Blessings. Secondly, being a miser is not just about money; it also involves our time, wisdom, talents, love, support, and kindness. If God cannot trust us to help, mentor, or inspire others, we erect Spiritual Blockages within the human psyche by default. Please allow me to share 2 Corinthians 9:6 and its take on this matter: *"But this I say: He who sows sparingly will also reap sparingly, and he who sows bountifully will also reap bountifully."*

The bottom line is that we must become good stewards of what we have while proactively tilling and nurturing whatever, whenever, however, wherever, whyever, and with whomever, *As It Pleases God*. In all simplicity, we are responsible for the resources we have at our disposal, even if they are not fully developed or they are in the milking stages.

Procreation and stewardship of the earth and mankind serve as the foundational command for humanity to thrive and grow in numbers, skills, talents, servanthood, purpose, and dominion. For the record, it is not just about popping out

Strongholds of Unkindness

babies, nor does it exempt it. Being fruitful and multiplying is a concept of being proactive, producing, and sharing our resources, knowledge, and love in ways that inspire others and promote growth, respect, and connection for others or the NEXT in line.

If we do not begin with the basic things of subduing, *As It Pleases God*, we cannot make it to the Divine Status that we all have access to but lack the Spiritual Astuteness, *As It Pleases God*, to tap into, *Spirit to Spirit*.

The Connection

A genuine connection to God, *Spirit to Spirit*, contains Divine Healing and Wisdom characterized by love, trust, understanding, and open communication.

Why must we operate *As It Pleases God* when dealing with the *Silent Acts of Unkindness*? Regardless of how HOLY or unholy we think we are, here is the deal:

- ☐ We can become a stepping stone.
- ☐ We can become a cornerstone.
- ☐ We can become a wall.
- ☐ We can become a roadblock.
- ☐ We can become a bridge.
- ☐ We can become a gap.
- ☐ We are diamonds in the rough.

They all work both positively and negatively, even if we are clueless about them. More importantly, we must know and understand the difference to effectively heal, reconcile, repent, forgive, and harmoniously move on in the Spirit of Excellence. If not, the Divine Plan or Predestined Blueprint will be withheld to prevent us from making a mess in a bed of unrest and confusion. But, yes, there is a but in this...the longing for Divine Purpose will remain within the depths of our soul, eventually driving us to our knees in due season.

Why would we become driven to our knees? Our Divine Purpose or Predestined Blueprint must include God, our Heavenly Father, the Creator of it all. Without Him, we are subjected to plugging and playing, hoping to hit the mark while missing it royally.

How do I know if someone will miss the mark or not? We are Spiritual Beings having a human experience; therefore, to get to anything Divine, we must include God, *As It Pleases Him*. Please allow me to Spiritually Align: First, here is what Matthew 6:33 tells us: *"Seek first the kingdom of God and His righteousness, and all these things will be added to you."* Secondly, here is what Colossians 3:23-24 says, *"And whatever you do, do it heartily, as to the Lord and not to men, knowing that from the Lord you will receive the reward of the inheritance; for you serve the Lord Christ."*

Then again, we still have free will to settle for being average. But for a time such as this, we may as well take possession of what rightly belongs to us by Spiritually Activating one of my favorites, Proverbs 3:5-6. *"Trust in the Lord with all your heart, and lean not on your own understanding; in all your ways acknowledge Him, and He shall direct your paths."*

What if we do not recognize the Hand of God or the help that He sends? All this means is that our Spiritual Discerning Faculties are off. Often enough, and with all due respect, what we proclaim as being the Holy Spirit may not be. In or out of our *Silent Acts of Unkindness* or Kindness, the Holy Spirit does not miss or make mistakes; we do! The Holy Spirit does not become emotional or think negatively; we do! The Holy Spirit does not lack obedience; we do! For this reason, Psalm 37:4 tells us this: *"Delight yourself also in the Lord, and He shall give you the desires of your heart."*

Strongholds of Unkindness

Above all, the Blood of Jesus can and will cover us in all things if we allow it to do so, even if we are a work-in-progress. Now, here is what is required of us: *"And do not be conformed to this world, but be transformed by the renewing of your mind, that you may prove what is that good and acceptable and perfect will of God."* Romans 12:2.

How do we know if we are being transformed? We will begin to see or experience things differently, or *As It Pleases God*. Here is a list of things that can happen, but are not limited to such:

- ☐ We may begin experiencing awe in the natural world, like a breathtaking sunset or a serene landscape, which can feel like a touch from the Heavenly of Heavens.

- ☐ We may begin witnessing or participating in selfless acts of kindness, love, and compassion.

- ☐ We may begin experiencing inner peace amid chaos and confusion.

- ☐ We may begin feeling God's presence and guidance when worshipping, praying, or meditating.

- ☐ We may begin experiencing answered prayers and thoughts unexpectedly.

- ☐ We may begin receiving support during difficult times for exactly what we need.

- ☐ We may begin experiencing unexplained comfort from within, like Divine Intervention on another level.

- ☐ We may begin noticing perfect timing, feeling like a guiding hand.

Strongholds of Unkindness

- ☐ We may begin experiencing deep *Spirit to Spirit* Connection with God and others.

- ☐ We may begin experiencing a sudden burst of Divine Clarity or Divine Wisdom guiding us.

- ☐ We may begin experiencing miraculous events that defy human explanation or reasoning.

- ☐ We may begin experiencing personal transformation Mentally, Physically, Emotionally, Spiritually, or Financially for the Greater Good or Divine Purpose.

- ☐ We may begin experiencing Divine Inspiration, Creativity, or Insight from seemingly out of nowhere.

- ☐ We may begin finding meaningful passages that Divinely Align with what we are experiencing, thinking, saying, or doing.

- ☐ We may begin experiencing Supernatural Peace while making significant choices.

- ☐ We may begin experiencing healing Mentally, Physically, Emotionally, and Spiritually.

- ☐ We may begin experiencing unexpected opportunities that align with our Divine Path or Blueprinted Purpose.

When engaging in *The Connection* with a *Spirit to Spirit* approach with our Heavenly Father, *As it Pleases Him*, it will always come with Spiritual Benefits, especially when mastering *The Characteristics of the Holy Spirit*.

Chapter Seven

Characteristics of the Holy Spirit

When it comes to the Characteristics of the Holy Spirit, for some odd reason, we trip over ourselves thinking one thing about Him that is totally opposite of Him from a Divine Perspective. Often enough, this occurs due to us attempting to bring Him to our level when we are supposed to COME to Him or INVITE Him in.

For example, Matthew 11:28 places a Spiritual Seal on this Divine Invitation, *"Come to Me, all you who labor and are heavy laden, and I will give you rest."* True enough, in a world full of chaos and uncertainties, in our labors, ladens (Heavy Loads or Burdens), and unrest, this is usually when most of us seek the Lord. Still, John 7:37 shares: *"On the last day, that great day of the feast, Jesus stood and cried out, saying, 'If anyone thirsts, let him come to Me and drink.'"*

Does John 7:37 not say Jesus instead of the Holy Spirit? Yes, it does. Nonetheless, in the Eye of God, they are ONE, but Jesus will always be THE MEDIATOR (The Go-Between) for us, especially in partaking of the Gift of Salvation. Here is what is being referred to: *"And the Spirit and the bride say, 'Come!'*

Characteristics of the Holy Spirit

And let him who hears say, 'Come!' And let him who thirsts come. Whoever desires, let him take the water of life freely." Revelation 22:17.

I hear people walking around saying the Holy Spirit said this, and the Holy Spirit said that, but they lack the understanding of His Divine Character and the reason for His Divine Existence. Once we truly come to an understanding of what is Divinely Expected of us, with outright simplicity, we will self-correct or self-adjust accordingly to align with the *Divine Etiquette* of the Kingdom.

While not having a clue about the *Characteristics of the Holy Spirit*, we tend to do our own thing or the wrong thing, allowing the chips to fall where they may. Then again, we have those frolicking around as self-proclaimed conduits of the Holy Spirit. Still, they are as mean as junkyard dogs, casting people (God's first love and innocent sheep) into the PIT with zero love for human life, zero mercy, and zero grace, as if He (the Holy Spirit) is telling them to play a demigod for a view, click, or bait.

Whether we seek rest, nourishment, companionship, or redemption, the Holy Spirit is here to guide us back to the Kingdom and to lead others, *As It Pleases God.* The Holy Spirit, often described as the Breath of God and the Comforter, stands ready, willing, and able to guide, nourishing the Mind, Body, Soul, and Spirit of all mankind. In addition, He also has a unique way of providing illumination, insight, understanding, inspiration, and challenges that lead toward Spiritual Growth, Maturity, and getting us to the Divine Status.

As we walk through trials and triumphs associated with the Cycles and Vicissitudes of Life, the Holy Spirit accompanies us, whispering words of encouragement and love, guiding us back to the Path of Righteousness. On the other hand, if we are getting negative, abusive,

Characteristics of the Holy Spirit

condescending, or backhanded chatter or self-talk, leading to unrighteous acts, rest assured, it is not the Holy Spirit.

Even if we do not know anything about the Holy Spirit, it is still best not to grieve Him. Why should we not grieve the Holy Spirit? We do not want Him to perceive us as an enemy. Can this really happen? Absolutely. The consequences of rebellion, pompousness, and disobedience are no joke, as they are greatly frowned upon in or out of the Kingdom of God. Here is what can happen to us: *"But they rebelled and grieved His Holy Spirit; So He turned Himself against them as an enemy, And He fought against them."* Isaiah 63:10.

In a time of profound change and uncertainty, we are seeking more. More of what we do know and more of what we do not. But, for a time such as this, in the embodiment of love, wisdom, and truth, the Heavenly of Heavens wants us to understand the Character Traits of the Holy Spirit. These attributes are foundational and serve as a guide to develop our charactorial traits, *As It Pleases God* to ensure that what we need will avail itself at the right time.

On this Spiritual Journey of *Divine Etiquette: As It Pleases God*® with an ongoing reflective mirror, here are a few directives on the Holy Spirit, but not limited to such:

- ☐ He is a Comforter: The Holy Spirit provides comfort and support during difficult times. Even if we are clueless, abandoned, or traumatized, healing and hope are at our beck and call. Here is what John 14:16-17 shares with us: *"And I will ask the Father, and he will give you another Helper, to be with you forever, even the Spirit of truth, whom the world cannot receive, because it neither sees him nor knows him. You know him, for he dwells with you and will be in you."*

Characteristics of the Holy Spirit

- ☐ The Holy Spirit is a Will Call Counselor: He offers guidance, support, direction, and wisdom to help us as Believers make wise and thoughtful decisions based on fact and not fiction. Even Acts 2:38-39 says: *"Peter replied, 'Repent and be baptized, every one of you, in the name of Jesus Christ for the forgiveness of your sins. And you will receive the gift of the Holy Spirit. The promise is for you and your children and for all who are far off—for all whom the Lord our God will call.'"*

- ☐ He is a Helper: The Holy Spirit assists us with Spiritual Growth, Understanding, and Know-how in our daily lives to shape and guide our actions, thoughts, beliefs, desires, mindsets, bottom lines, and Divine Instructions set forth prior to our human existence. *"But the Helper, the Holy Spirit, whom the Father will send in My name, He will teach you all things, and bring to your remembrance all things that I said to you."* John 14:26.

- ☐ The Holy Spirit is a Teacher: He educates and reveals truths about God and His Word while illuminating our understanding of Divine Information, Treasures, Wisdom, and Mysteries to deepen our *Spirit to Spirit* Relationship with the Kingdom Building process. *"So Christ himself gave the apostles, the prophets, the evangelists, the pastors and teachers, to equip his people for works of service, so that the body of Christ may be built up."* Ephesians 4:11-12.

- ☐ He is an Intercessor: The Holy Spirit will make intercession on our behalf according to God's Divine Will and Blueprinted Mission. When life is lifing, we may not know what to pray for. So, it is wise to give it to the Holy Spirit at this point to ensure we are not sending out wrong, manipulative, or debauched

Characteristics of the Holy Spirit

prayers. *"Likewise the Spirit also helps in our weaknesses. For we do not know what we should pray for as we ought, but the Spirit Himself makes intercession for us with groanings which cannot be uttered."* Romans 8:26.

- ☐ The Holy Spirit is a Convictionist: He convicts our conscience of sin, ill will, unrighteousness, and judgment, prompting us to reflect deeply, change, or repent. *"Now He who searches the hearts knows what the mind of the Spirit is, because He makes intercession for the saints according to the will of God."* Romans 8:27.

- ☐ He is an Empowerer: The Holy Spirit gives us strength and courage to live a faithful life while actively working within us. With clarity and understanding, He also helps us grasp the meanings and applications of God's Word as we read Scripture, meditate, engage in prayer, and witness the Gospel of Jesus Christ. *"But God has revealed them to us through His Spirit. For the Spirit searches all things, yes, the deep things of God. For what man knows the things of a man except the spirit of the man which is in him? Even so no one knows the things of God except the Spirit of God. Now we have received, not the spirit of the world, but the Spirit who is from God, that we might know the things that have been freely given to us by God."* 1 Corinthians 2:10-12.

- ☐ The Holy Spirit is a Giver of Spiritual Gifts: He distributes SPECIFIC GIFTS among believers for the Greater Good of all mankind and the Glory of God. *"We have different gifts, according to the grace given to each of us. If your gift is prophesying, then prophesy in accordance with your faith; if it is serving, then serve; if it is teaching, then teach; if it is to encourage, then give encouragement; if it is giving, then*

Characteristics of the Holy Spirit

give generously; if it is to lead, do it diligently; if it is to show mercy, do it cheerfully." Romans 12:6-8.

- ☐ He is a Guide: The Holy Spirit directs us as Believers in our lives and paths according to God's Divine Purpose and the areas of our Divine Giftings. 1 Corinthians 14:12 says, "So it is with you. Since you are eager for gifts of the Spirit, try to excel in those that build up the church."

- ☐ The Holy Spirit is a Spiritual Seal: He confirms the believer's salvation and marks them as belonging to God as Promised. "In Him you also trusted, after you heard the word of truth, the gospel of your salvation; in whom also, having believed, you were sealed with the Holy Spirit of promise, who is the guarantee of our inheritance until the redemption of the purchased possession, to the praise of His glory." Ephesians 1:13-14.

- ☐ He is a Source of Unity: The Holy Spirit promotes unity among Believers to ensure we operate in the Spirit of Oneness in or out of the Kingdom of God. "Now I plead with you, brethren, by the name of our Lord Jesus Christ, that you all speak the same thing, and that there be no divisions among you, but that you be perfectly joined together in the same mind and in the same judgment." 1 Corinthians 1:10.

- ☐ The Holy Spirit is a Sanctifier of Divine Guarantee: He works to purify and help Believers grow in authentic Holiness, As It Pleases God. "Now He who establishes us with you in Christ and has anointed us is God, who also has sealed us and given us the Spirit in our hearts as a guarantee." 2 Corinthians 1:21-22.

Characteristics of the Holy Spirit

- [ ] He is an Enabler of Witnessing and Worshiping: The Holy Spirit assists Believers in worshiping God sincerely and passionately through Christ Jesus. Moreover, He helps us live out our faith boldly, without shame, to convey the GOOD NEWS effectively. *"But you shall receive power when the Holy Spirit has come upon you; and you shall be witnesses to Me in Jerusalem, and in all Judea and Samaria, and to the end of the earth."* Acts 1:8.

- [ ] The Holy Spirit is a Helper in Abiding Weaknesses: He aids Believers in overcoming their weaknesses and struggles by engaging in righteous acts with a work-in-progress mentality. *"Now he who keeps His commandments abides in Him, and He in him. And by this we know that He abides in us, by the Spirit whom He has given us."* 1 John 3:24.

- [ ] He is a Spirit of Truth: the Holy Spirit leads and guides into all truth. *"But when the Helper comes, whom I shall send to you from the Father, the Spirit of truth who proceeds from the Father, He will testify of Me."* John 15:26.

- [ ] The Holy Spirit helps us with our Compassion: He helps a hardened heart become tenderhearted. *"Finally, all of you be of one mind, having compassion for one another; love as brothers, be tenderhearted, be courteous."* 1 Peter 3:8.

- [ ] He is a Promoter of Love: The Holy Spirit helps us foster love among our Brethren, ourselves, and most of all, for the Holy Trinity in totality (The Father, Son, and Holy Spirit). *"But above all these things put on love, which is the bond of perfection."* Colossians 3:14.

Characteristics of the Holy Spirit

☐ The Holy Spirit oversees the initiation of Single-Minded Joy: He helps us to become like-minded to bring about joy and peace amidst trials and challenges. In addition, if we are dealing with scatterbrain syndrome or scattered thoughts, the Holy Spirit is the Divine Antidote for this fog or scattered condition. *"Fulfill my joy by being like-minded, having the same love, being of one accord, of one mind."* Philippians 2:2.

☐ He is an Agent of New Birth: The Holy Spirit initiates regeneration in Believers being born again in Spirit and Truth, leading them to the Free Gift of Salvation based on John 3:3. It says, *"Jesus answered and said to him, 'Most assuredly, I say to you, unless one is born again, he cannot see the kingdom of God.'"* And then, 1 Peter 1:23, *"Having been born again, not of corruptible seed but incorruptible, through the word of God which lives and abides forever."*

How does the Holy Spirit play a part in the decision to be born again? Titus 3:5 says it best: *"Not by works of righteousness which we have done, but according to His mercy He saved us, through the washing of regeneration and renewing of the Holy Spirit."* With this built-in re-gening system, we can indeed cover ourselves with the Blood of Jesus while allowing the Holy Spirit to go to work on our behalf in the transformative process of Spiritual Awakening.

☐ The Holy Spirit is a Presence of God: He represents and re-presents God's presence in the lives of Believers and the Church. Know this: *"Nevertheless the solid foundation of God stands, having this seal: 'The Lord knows those who are His' and, 'Let everyone who names the name of Christ depart from iniquity.'"* 2 Timothy 2:19.

Characteristics of the Holy Spirit

Despite God's unwavering faithfulness to us, if we turn away from Him, the Holy Spirit, or reject the Blood of Jesus as our Spiritual Atonement to do our own thing, He views this as a breach in our covenant relationship.

How is a breach formed as Believers? Anything that contradicts the Will of God can form a breach due to acts of disobedience, lukewarmness, stiff-necked behaviors, or when having a debauched heart and mind posture. For example, suppose we choose to follow our selfish desires, engage in our untamed lust, inflict harm on the innocent, or engage in rebellion rather than adhering to His commands. In this case, He will put our *Divine Etiquette* on lockdown, leading us straight into Mental, Physical, Emotional, and Spiritual turmoil. In all simplicity, we will turn on ourselves!

Now, if repentance, obedience, or uprightness does not occur, *As It Pleases God*, we will remain in this state until we return to our FIRST LOVE. *"But this I have against you, that you have forsaken your first love. Remember then from where you have fallen. Repent and do the deeds you did at first. If not, I will come to you and remove your lampstand from its place—unless you repent."* Revelation 2:4-5.

Can our Lampstands be removed? Absolutely. Our Lampstands (the essence of our purpose, roles, beliefs, identity, and unique contributions with Divine Guidance, Hope, Clarity, Provisions, and Direction) are removed all the time. It is just hidden or whitewashed most of the time.

Even my lampstand was removed for some time due to my willful acts of disobedience to do my own thing. It is for this reason that I write and speak passionately about obedience, humility, and our Blueprinted Purpose. By embracing change and reshaping the narrative, *Spirit to Spirit*, I know what I am speaking about and have the experience of becoming the Teacher and Messenger to feed God's sheep, *As It Pleases Him*.

Characteristics of the Holy Spirit

Amid all this, in *The Eye of Grace*, the goal of *Divine Etiquette* is to return to our FIRST LOVE.

The Eye of Grace

What if we are under grace? Grace has nothing to do with our return to our FIRST LOVE. Whether we return or not, grace is still available to all mankind.

Grace is a GIFT of Refinement, and our return is an ACTION of Restoration. Please do not confuse the two because accountability and repentance are a must to restore the foundation of our faith, our Divine Light, and a loving relationship with the Holy Trinity.

What is the *Eye of Grace* all about? It is about gaining a Divine View of Grace from God Almighty based on our situations, circumstances, or conditions. In my opinion, it is like having grace on a sliding scale. Blasphemy, right? Wrong. Romans 5:20-21 says, *"Moreover the law entered that the offense might abound. But where sin abounded, grace abounded much more, so that as sin reigned in death, even so grace might reign through righteousness to eternal life through Jesus Christ our Lord."* If grace reigns from righteousness to Eternal Life, there is a Spiritual or Sliding Scale involved.

Although we are all saved by grace, according to John 1:16, *"And of His fullness we have all received, and grace for grace."* Now, if we do not use it *As It Pleases God* or approach Him, *Spirit to Spirit*, then we invoke a limit on it, especially in our times of need. Simply put, we settle for ordinary grace instead of Supernatural or Divine Grace. Here is what Hebrews 4:16 tells us about what to do: *"Let us therefore come boldly to the throne of grace, that we may obtain mercy and find grace to help in time of need."*

Does Supernatural or Divine Grace have a Throne? Yes. It is designed to REFORM us, *As It Pleases God* through Salvation

Characteristics of the Holy Spirit

(The shedding of Blood through Christ Jesus). If we opt out of the reforming process or ignore it altogether while continuing in our folly, rest assured, DISGRACE is on the horizon. Blasphemy again, right? Absolutely not! Spiritual Duality applies to grace as well, and the moment we think it does not, we will 'get got' by the enemy's wiles. James 4:6 has a perfect example of Spiritual Duality when dealing with grace: "*But He gives more grace. Therefore He says: 'God resists the proud, but gives grace to the humble.'* "

God is paying attention to our charactorial developmental process, even if we think we can beat the system through grace. Listen, He is not condemning us for our humanness, but it is our reasonable service to make a willful attempt to become better, stronger, and wiser, *As It Pleases Him*, instead of seeking to please ourselves. What is the big deal? In the areas that we receive grace should become a place of our Testimonies; if not, there is a problem or a glitch in our system of conveyance.

The Problem

What type of problem would Believers have with their Testimonial Grace? We must be willing to give back to the Divine System that has graced us. If we are hiding or negating our giving back, then therein lies some type of Spiritual Negligence. Here is the deal: Testimonial Grace embodies the AWARENESS that grace is not only a gift received but also one that should be reciprocated through acts of gratitude, service, and love within the Divine Context gracing us.

It is not enough to simply accept these free will gifts from our Heavenly Father and then sit on our hands, doing, saying, or becoming nothing. We, as Believers, are called to TESTIFY regarding our faith through our actions, thoughts, words, beliefs, and contributions. Whether it is through sharing our

Characteristics of the Holy Spirit

time, talent, purpose, knowledge, or treasures, they are deemed as a natural response to the grace received. If it is not occurring, we may have a problem going from the milk to the meat stages in our Divine Walk with God.

Here is what Hebrews 5:12-14 shares with us: *"For though by this time you ought to be teachers, you need someone to teach you again the first principles of the oracles of God; and you have come to need milk and not solid food. For everyone who partakes only of milk is unskilled in the word of righteousness, for he is a babe. But solid food belongs to those who are of full age, that is, those who by reason of use have their senses exercised to discern both good and evil."* Who is considered the Oracle? The one who is gleaning the grace, mastering Spiritual Duality, or enduring the refinement process for Spiritual Maturity, Nourishment, and Growth in the faith.

Unbeknown to most, we are all Oracles of our Predestined Blueprinted Purpose, but we must master knowing the difference between right and wrong, good and evil, just and unjust, positive and negative, and so on.

What if we opt to accept the grace bestowed upon us and do nothing else? We have free will to do or not to do; however, feelings of loneliness or emptiness will occur if we do nothing. In addition, we will also begin to experience the strain of unfulfillment, lagging faith, confusion from within, and disconnecting from others without understanding why. When it is all said and done, we are called to become an ACTIVE participant in our graceful endeavors or put our Faith in Action, *As It Pleases God*.

Keep in mind that no one is exempt from the cycle of GIVING and RECEIVING. Still, we should keep this cycle working in our favor to ensure our growth and enrichment do not become stunted, preventing us from becoming our Highest and Greatest Self.

All in all, in the *Eye of Grace*, when one comes to me talking about grace, I expect to see some type of refinement taking

Characteristics of the Holy Spirit

place. If not, there is some sort of Spiritual Abuse or Oversight occurring without them realizing it. To be clear, I am not here to judge anyone; I am here to bring Divine Revelation regarding this matter and help to gain a few Divine Notches on our belts with the mindset of *Owning the Room*.

When dealing with a Divine Mindset, *As It Pleases God*, issues like conflict, division, disobedience, and negativity can easily cloud our interactions, intentions, perceptions, and sense of good judgment, causing us to become *The Problem* instead of THE SOLUTION.

According to the Heavenly of Heavens, by becoming the Answer or Solution to *The Problem* with *Divine Etiquette* in hand, we can better navigate challenges or issues, regardless of who is right or wrong. Behaving in a self-aware manner that reflects compassion, love, kindness, mercy, and respect for others with a HIGHER PURPOSE allows us to transform all things into opportunities. Really? Yes, really! Spiritually Speaking, using Kingdomly Core Principles, *As It Pleases God*, provides hidden opportunities for growth, understanding, refinement, and harmony within a Spiritual Framework, especially when *Owning The Room* with the Holy Trinity at the forefront.

Owning the Room

Most often, when we speak of '*Owning The Room*,' our minds drift to images of charming, charismatic individuals effortlessly captivating everyone around them. We picture confident leaders, entertainers, or social butterflies who naturally draw attention and admiration. However, in a deeper and more profound sense, *Owning The Room* can take on an altogether different meaning, especially within the context of Faith and Spirituality.

Characteristics of the Holy Spirit

In the Kingdom, we *Own The Room* with the Divine Presence of the Holy Spirit, not through our looks or allure, but through extraordinary LOVE, MERCY, and GRACE. With this type of shift in our perspectives, we take the focus from mere charisma to the TRANSFORMATIVE POWER of Spiritual Connection. According to the Heavenly of Heavens, it is an atmosphere of reverence, love, and empowerment through the use of the Fruits of the Spirit that changes the trajectory of any space or person we encounter.

Picturesquely, imagine walking into a room and feeling an immediate sense of warmth and welcome. Unbeknown to most, the palpable presence of the Holy Spirit creates an inviting atmosphere of Divine Authenticity, Safety, and Trust. Actually, the Holy Spirit empowers us to engage with others in a meaningful, genuine, and polite way, offering us wisdom and guidance on demand, becoming a conduit of Greatness with Divine Influence.

What if we do not have Divine Influence? The goal is to possess normal influence first. Then, focus on building our character traits using the Fruits of the Spirit and behaving Christlike. Using this method will help us to lift others, just as Christ Jesus supports us because the Covering of the Blood still works.

What if we are alone in this process as Believers? We are never alone in our endeavors unless we choose to be. With the Holy Spirit, we can face difficult situations with courage and resilience, knowing that we are, quite literally, filled with Divine Strength. Still, in order to use it effectively, *As It Pleases God*, we must know it without wavering, which thrusts us into our Divine Dominion.

What is Divine Dominion? For example, in *Owning the Room*, we must believe that it is ours from the onset. If not, we digress instead of progressing, multiplying, and replenishing, *As It Pleases God*. But first, in Earthen Vessel, here are a few things to do, but not limited to such:

Characteristics of the Holy Spirit

- ☐ We must open the Mind, Body, Soul, and Spirit to our Heavenly Father, *Spirit to Spirit*.
- ☐ We must come into Agreement with the Holy Spirit.
- ☐ We must cover ourselves with the Blood of Jesus as Spiritual Atonement.
- ☐ We must forgive and repent of anything unholy, owning our truth.
- ☐ We must set the Atmosphere of Worship.
- ☐ We must properly govern our thoughts and words, revamping them from negative to positive.
- ☐ We must be willing to become a work-in-progress for the Kingdom of God.
- ☐ We must give thanks in all things.
- ☐ We must look for and locate the win-win.
- ☐ We must document, document, document!

In addition, we can also ask ourselves, 'How can I contribute positively to this situation?' And then document the answer instead of merely pointing out flaws, expressing dissatisfaction, or outright complaining.

When people see us truly walking by faith and not by sight, it will encourage them to do likewise, transforming the world around us and, most of all, within us, *As It Pleases God*. Here are a few things to do when engaging in *Owning the Room*, but not limited to such:

- ☐ Practice Humility: Approach the situation with a humble mind and heart posture, recognizing that your Divine Purpose is to serve others.

Characteristics of the Holy Spirit

- ☐ Speak with Confidence: Use a clear and steady voice when you speak, which conveys authority and self-assurance.

- ☐ Make Eye Contact: Engage with your audience by maintaining eye contact, creating a connection, and showing sincerity.

- ☐ Dress Appropriately: Wear attire that reflects respect for the setting and the people present. Please do not overdo or underdo it; modesty works well.

- ☐ Use Positive Body Language: Stand tall, smile, and use gestures that invite engagement and warmth.

- ☐ Listen Actively: Show genuine interest in what others are saying, validating their thoughts and feelings.

- ☐ Be Prepared: Have a clear understanding of the topic or event and solve problems, ensuring you can contribute thoughtfully, strategically, and helpfully.

- ☐ Share Personal Stories: Relate personal experiences that highlight your points and help build rapport with your audience.

- ☐ Encourage Participation: Invite others to share their thoughts, creating an inclusive atmosphere.

- ☐ Stay Calm Under Pressure: Maintain composure, even in challenging situations, to set a positive tone.

- ☐ Use Humor Wisely: Lighten the mood with humor that is appropriate and relatable, bringing joy to the moment.

Characteristics of the Holy Spirit

- ☐ Be Authentic and Show Respect: Embrace your true self, allowing your personality and values to shine through your actions. At the same time, acknowledge, respect, and honor the beliefs and values of those around you.

- ☐ Pray or Meditate: Take a moment for reflection and connection with God before entering the room, aligning your intentions.

- ☐ Stay Focused and Express Gratitude: Keep the conversation on point, gently steering it back if it strays off topic. Thank others for their contributions and involvement, fostering goodwill.

- ☐ Be Solution-Oriented: Approach challenges with a mindset geared towards finding constructive solutions.

- ☐ Lead with Kindness and Positive Tone: Treat everyone with respect and compassion, reflecting God's love. Start the interaction with an upbeat attitude, inspiring others to follow suit.

- ☐ Seek Guidance: Continuously pray for wisdom and discernment in your actions, thoughts, and words, ensuring they align with God's Divine Will.

In *Divine Etiquette: As It Pleases God*®, by *Owning The Room* with the Presence of the Holy Spirit and covering ourselves with the Blood of Jesus, it contains POWER. Yes, that is, Supernatural *Divine Power*, to be exact.

Characteristics of the Holy Spirit

With the Spiritual Mindset of service, compassion, understanding, and community when *Owning the Room*, our humility will naturally come forth. What can humility do for us as Believers, especially when we are already *Owning The Room*? First, when making a conscious effort to avoid the negative pitfalls humbly, we can operate with integrity for the Greater Good without overreacting or underreacting. Secondly, when used correctly, *As It Pleases God*, operating in such a manner allows us to move away from being part of the problem to become the solution as beacons of Divine Light. Lastly, we can prevent envy, jealousy, pride, coveting, greed, confusion, or competitiveness from zapping our *Divine Power*. Does it really make a difference? Absolutely! Let us talk about it in the next section.

Divine Power

Regardless of what we believe about *Divine Power*, righteous charactorial pleasantries are required of us. In all simplicity, we cannot walk around behaving like hellions on wheels and expect the Divine Heavens to crack open for us. On the other hand, if it does open, it will be for corrective measures or a wake-up call and a prompt for accountability. Now, if for some reason it does occur, all we need to do is repent, forgive, and reassess our actions, thoughts, beliefs, words, desires, or intentions from selfishness to selflessness, *As It Pleases God*.

Is repenting, forgiving, and reassessing that easy? Sometimes 'yes,' and sometimes 'no,' but they are doable. *Divine Etiquette* wants us to know that our choices really matter. When we choose to engage thoughtfully, willfully, and respectfully, *As It Pleases God*, we align ourselves with the Greater Good that could usher us into a Higher or Divine Purpose, depending on our readiness.

Characteristics of the Holy Spirit

As we walk through life, there is no need to walk on eggshells when we become ONE with the Holy Trinity. According to the Heavenly of Heavens, by acknowledging our shortcomings and weaknesses to become better, stronger, and wiser, we will find our hidden strength and clarity IN HIM. This Trinitarian Approach frees us from the fear of judgment and ridicule, allowing our thoughts, beliefs, desires, and emotions to be articulated genuinely through a *Spirit to Spirit* Connection with our Heavenly Father.

How does this Divine Connection thing work for Believers? The Holy Trinity (The Father, Son, and Holy Spirit) represents a profound relationship that exemplifies unity, love, and guidance for all mankind. This Divine Relationship is not about losing our identity; rather, it is about gaining the knowledge of who we are from the inside out as Spiritual Beings having a human experience. Above all, it is all by choice, not by force!

With the dispensation of grace, *As It Pleases God*, we do not need to force anything on anyone—it is about Free Will. Everything works better in the Eye of God, especially when we want it, whatever it is or is not, for ourselves.

God's unmerited favor is for those who make a willful choice to embrace it. What must we embrace? The Pathway to Salvation. It is a path that redefines our relationships, encourages inclusivity, and emphasizes transformation through faith in *The Overcoming* Process, regardless of where we are in life or what we have going on.

Furthermore, on this Spiritual Journey of *Divine Etiquette*, when dealing with *Divine Power* in the Eye of God, we must become willing to empower others Mentally, Physically, Emotionally, Spiritually, and Financially. The Spiritual Duty to empower, uplift, and build others is what bridges the gap between us and what is Divine, making us sharp, astute, and wise in harnessing our own potential, *As It Pleases God*.

Characteristics of the Holy Spirit

What if we decline Spiritual Duty? We have free will to decline. Once again, this is not by force, but rest assured, it comes with a state of mediocrity and commonality with little to no poshness, causing us to fall into the category of lukewarmness, dullness, idleness, or stiff-neckedness. Now, if this is what you desire, then have at it! Unfortunately, this is not why I have taken the time to document this information.

My Spiritual Duty, according to the Heavenly of Heavens, is to provide you with an opportunity to break the yoke of the negative mindset of mediocrity and bondage first. Secondly, to give you the opportunity to activate the Law of Reciprocity to help someone else while you, yourself, become better, stronger, and wiser, *As It Pleases God*. And finally, to help you master the Fruits of the Spirit and behave Christlike according to Kingdom Standards.

In a world increasingly defined by division, confusion, and discord with a cancel culture, zapping our *Divine Power*, we need Spiritual Help from the Heavenly of Heavens. If we do not step up our game to get the Divine Help we need, we will self-destruct, get sidetracked, or become railroaded while appearing right in our own eyes.

Our interconnectedness and our responsibility to uplift one another are on the Table of God for reevaluation. But why use the term 'reevaluation' rather than simply 'evaluation'? Evaluation suggests a one-time assessment, a moment to check off the boxes and move on. In contrast, reevaluation implies an ongoing, dynamic process of reflection, assessment, pruning, training, and reconsideration that takes courage, tenacity, and humility.

Here is the deal before moving on to *The Overcoming* in the next chapter: As we stand at this crossroads, if we were not designed to learn, grow, sow, transform, and develop, *As It Pleases God*, I would not be writing this book. In this Divine Call, if we were on point with our Spiritual Principles,

Characteristics of the Holy Spirit

Protocols, and Laws, or if we were self-correcting as we should, I would not have been called to the forefront for such a time as this. In re-evaluating our *Spirit to Spirit* Relations with our Heavenly Father, with the correct heart and mind posture, we must begin to ask ourselves the hard questions about our rooting systems and seeds, aligning them with the *Characteristics of the Holy Spirit*.

Why can we not be our authentic selves when it comes to the Holy Spirit? We can be who we are, for real, for real. It is He who knows the truth about us in more ways than one, even amid our lies, half-truths, or masks.

According to the Heavenly of Heavens, we must always remember that there is MORE to us lying dormant from within that we do not have Divine Access to as of yet. Regardless of whether we think we have it going on or we are the best thing since sliced bread, there is always MORE. In all simplicity, if we think our human self (the fleshly being) is authentic or the best version of ourselves, then we are sadly mistaken. If you do not believe this, let someone intentionally step on your big toe, and then gauge your response thereafter.

Once again, we are Spiritual Beings having a human experience, and if we have not tapped into our Spirit Man, *As It Pleases God*, it is fair to say that we have more work to do. What does this mean for us as Believers? We do not have Divine Access to our Predestined Blueprinted Purpose as of yet. Nevertheless, we may have an inclination or glimpse of it with a mountaintop view. Still, we cannot possess the Blueprinted Promise until certain Spiritual Criterias are met, *As It Pleases God*. Until then, we will remain in the desert, wandering around Mentally, Physically, Emotionally, and Spiritually with Divine Barriers or Blockages.

When dealing with Divine Power, *As It Pleases God*, the Holy Spirit is our point of contact for empowerment, guidance, and transformation. Therefore, to access deeper parts of ourselves or the inner man with Spiritual Growth working in our favor,

Characteristics of the Holy Spirit

it is only wise to become Spirit-Led instead of self-led in the Eye of God. What makes this so important for WISE Believers? First, it allows the Holy Spirit to work out the hidden kinks in our character as the Blood of Jesus covers us in the process of becoming, *As It Pleases God*. Secondly, it helps to sharpen our Spiritual Compass or Discerning Faculties, especially when dealing with Divine Power.

Is normal power and Divine Power one and the same? Absolutely not! Normal power can be derived from anywhere and from different perspectives or sources. In contrast, Divine Power can only come from the Creator of it with a Supernatural Catalyst. What does this mean in layman's terms? We cannot beat the Heavenly System surrounding what is Divine. If we attempt to violate Spiritual Protocols, we will begin to turn on ourselves by default due to Spiritual Violations and the lack of Spiritual Readiness. Unfortunately, this is the reason for most of us opting for normal power rooted in the lust of the eyes, the lust of the flesh, and the pride of life to please ourselves instead of Divine Power, *As It Pleases God*.

A demigod mindset or heart posture cannot contend with a Kingdomly Commissioned Mindset and Heart Posture from the Heavenly of Heavens. Why not? Idolatry contaminates us, preventing our *Divine Power* from coming forth as it should. Here is what Exodus 20:3-5 shares with us: *"You shall have no other gods before Me. You shall not make for yourself a carved image—any likeness of anything that is in heaven above, or that is in the earth beneath, or that is in the water under the earth; you shall not bow down to them nor serve them."*

The transformative power of the Holy Spirit is here to help us take our normal to Divine with *The Overcoming* Process. Yet, we must become a work-in-progress, being Spiritually Trained, Pruned, and Tested, *As It Pleases God*. *"Therefore, my beloved, flee from idolatry."* 1 Corinthians 10:14.

Chapter Eight

The Overcoming

As we navigate life's complexities, *The Overcoming* incorporated in our *Divine Etiquette* is within our reach, exempting not a soul. In the Eye of God, our shared experiences contain Healing Powers to restore us and inspire others in ways confounding human reasoning. In the Kingdom of God, although we are all different, when our legacy is rooted in love and understanding, *As It Pleases God*, we can take Divine Dominion over what rightly belongs to us. So, let us talk about this Divine Phenomenon in this chapter.

With our shared experiences, we cannot leave God, our Heavenly Father, out of the equation because we truly overcome through the Power of our Testimonies. Really? Yes, really! Revelation 12:11 states: "*And they overcame him by the blood of the Lamb and by the word of their testimony, and they did not love their lives to the death.*" In the same way that we say, 'Closed mouths do not get fed.' It applies to the Kingdom as well, saying, 'A closed mouth who refuses to use their Testimony as a Spiritual Weapon, *As It Pleases God*, will remain traumatized and yoked within the psyche by their past, present, and future.'

Unbeknown to most, the Divine Healing Power we need is often hidden in our personal or private Testimonies, whether good, bad, or indifferent. Stemming from personal challenges, triumphs, or everyday struggles, no one, and I mean no one, is exempt from what contains the growth elements of the next level for us. The Cycle and Vicissitudes of Life will continue with or without our permission, thrusting us into a cycle of déjà vu until we get it. Nevertheless, they will all serve as powerful connections that bind us together as ONE in the Eye of God.

In addition to the vibrant tapestry of the human experience pre-coded in our DNA, we already possess what we need to succeed. Suppose we allow the Divine Presence of the Holy Spirit to permeate our interactions, reactions, and environments. In this case, we will become a force to be reckoned with in and out of the Kingdom of God with Transformative Power and Authority.

Each thread or chapter of our lives represents a unique story with its fruits, positively or negatively. Fortunately, it is our responsibility to reverse engineer the negative experiences into positive win-wins. Here is what Isaiah 11:5 shares with us: "*Righteousness shall be the belt of His loins, and faithfulness the belt of His waist.*" With the presence of the Holy Trinity, this is doable for strength, lineage, and preparedness, As It Pleases God. All of these are designed to feed His precious sheep and keep them uplifted when straying out of the Divine Fold.

Why would sheep stray off, especially when being Believers? It is in our nature to wander off when we become weak, distracted, or bored. Just like a sheep may wander away in search of greener pastures, we may find ourselves drifting off, feeding our hidden pangs of hunger.

The Overcoming

At the core of our being, we are pre-wired to seek comfort, security, and satisfaction. As a result, when operating out of purpose, operating in outright disobedience, or lacking a *Spirit to Spirit* Relationship with our Heavenly Father, we will often find ourselves chasing after fleeting desires. We will tend to pursue the ones that promise Mental, Physical, Emotional, Spiritual, or Financial Fulfillment, which produces distractions in the Eye of God.

Enticing alternatives divert and stagnate the Mind, Body, Soul, and Spirit from our intended path or Predestined Blueprinted Purpose. In my opinion, pleasing ourselves in such a manner leads to a cycle of straying and returning back to God when things do not work out as we envisioned.

The truth is that the faith, doubt, or confusion struggle happens to every Believer, even if we do not talk about it, admit it, or pretend it does not happen. Many Believers wrestle with the fear that admitting doubtfulness or uncertainty might undermine their faith, so they opt for lies and pretense, concocting an insta-perfect persona. Whereas, in accordance with *Divine Etiquette: As It Pleases God*® with a work-in-progress or do-it-yourself mindset, we must understand that acknowledging our struggles is a vital part of our Spiritual Journey.

In reflecting on my own experiences, I have had my share of this back-and-forth motion in my Milking Stages of Spirituality when I lacked understanding, *As It Pleased God*. I wavered between confidence and uncertainty, wondering if my struggles were a sign of weakness as my name was dragged through the dirt. To add insult to injury, I was thrown under the bus, left for dead several times, and called everything but a Child of God. And yet, still, I rise with *The Overcoming* Mindset with the Divine Wisdom and Strength to know the difference and to properly feed God's precious sheep, *As It Pleases Him*!

The Overcoming

According to the Heavenly of Heavens, the wondering (the questioning phase of our lives) or wandering process (the desert experience) does not define us. It is the testing methods, learning processes, getting back on track, understanding our triggers, and knowing what to do when this happens that define us in the Eye of God.

What if we do not get back on track, understand our triggers, or refuse to do anything to self-correct? We will feel lost, confused, or dismayed while using negative habits, thoughts, beliefs, desires, or words to satiate the longings from within the psyche temporarily.

In essence, refusing to confront our vulnerabilities, *As It Pleases God*, gives way to the lust of the eyes, the lust of the flesh, and the pride of life. As a result, we become consumed with the desire for power, money, sex, fame, and status to make us feel better about ourselves, with idolatry tagging along with golden calves. Unfortunately, this is how it gets started, and this is how we become consumed without realizing what is happening until we are in too deep.

In *The Overcoming* Process, just as sheep need their Shepherd for protection, guidance, and direction, we too require the steady Hand of God to lead us through the complexities of life to safe pastures and secured folds. As life is full of choices, we also need the Holy Spirit to guide us on our Spiritual Journey to avoid unnecessary detours, hiccups, or *Seeds of Something Else*. Plus, we need the Blood of Jesus to cover us as Spiritual Atonement, the reconciliation between God and humanity, restoring our internal and external harmony for *The Overcoming* Process, freeing us from guilt and shame.

What if we still feel a sense of guilt and shame? Lingering guilt and shame can be indicative of something deeper. Also, it is an indication of an ongoing seed or root attempting to place a Spiritual Yoke to keep us bound, weighing us down, and preventing us from living freely, authentically, and fully,

The Overcoming

As It Pleases God. Once negativity is planted and has taken root in our psyche, it will silently influence our behaviors, thoughts, beliefs, desires, and choices. So, let us go deeper.

Seeds of Something Else

In our Spiritual Endeavors, we must be mindful of the *Seeds of Something Else* that might take root in our hearts and minds, stemming from childhood experiences, societal pressures, unresolved traumas, thwarted expectations, or personal failures.

Once again, please do not become alarmed about hidden pangs of hunger; we all have them. Even if we deny or hide them in a metaphorical 'something else' filing cabinet, blurring the lines from within. When it is all said and done, they will have a desire to be fed at some point due to underlying seeds of whatever.

How do we overcome the 'something else' seeds? They must be uprooted and placed under the Blood of Jesus. Anything or anyone who negatively challenges, impedes our growth, and attempts to sway our understanding away from God Almighty, the Kingdom, or Divine Blueprint must be uprooted, period. They are like weeds that often bring us into the negative mindset of 'What else?'

Unfortunately, it is those negative thoughts, doubts, fears, or deceptive influences that find a way to disrupt our relationship with God. In addition, if they are not recognized and addressed, *As It Pleases Him*, they will lead us astray, affecting our well-being and manifesting as anxiety, guilt, temptation, shame, anger, lust, habits, or confusion, to name a few.

Just as a gardener must uproot weeds to cultivate a healthy garden, we too, must do likewise with a Garden of Eden reminder. What is the reminder? To Spiritually Till our own

The Overcoming

ground without allowing the enemy to play mind games or have an opportunity to play on words. Regardless of what season we are in, we must identify and remove harmful seeds or weeds associated with societal pressures, personal insecurities, self-induced yokes, unresolved traumas, or even Spiritual Attacks.

According to the Heavenly of Heavens, this is a continual process that requires vigilance, faith, diligence, self-reflection, self-awareness, and action. Still, we must know what we must overcome first. Here is a list of examples, but not limited to such:

- ☐ Mediocrity.
- ☐ Failure.
- ☐ Lack.
- ☐ Negativity.
- ☐ Stagnation.
- ☐ Ignorance.
- ☐ Disobedience.
- ☐ Shame.
- ☐ Poverty.
- ☐ Mental Anguish.
- ☐ Hurt.
- ☐ Betrayal.
- ☐ Waywardness.

- ☐ Anger.
- ☐ Unforgiveness.
- ☐ Envy or Jealousy.
- ☐ Loneliness.
- ☐ Abuse.
- ☐ Backwardness.
- ☐ Failure.
- ☐ Fear.
- ☐ Doubt.
- ☐ Pride.
- ☐ Other:_____
- ☐ Other:_____
- ☐ Other:_____

According to the Ancient of Days, if we proactively operate with the Fruits of the Spirit continually and behave Christlike, we can save ourselves a lot of precious time. Doing so will cause all things to work together for our good, even if it does not feel good at the time. All we need to do is learn, understand, grow, document, and sow back into the Kingdom

The Overcoming

when called upon. Does this really work? Absolutely! The *Law of Reciprocity* does not miss a beat, positively or negatively. So, it is only wise to keep the needle swinging toward the positive.

Why the positive? First, in a world often clouded by negativity, we must provide a counteraction that works with an optimistic outlook, even in difficult circumstances, lowering our anxiety, stress, depression, and reactiveness. Secondly, we cannot expect God to back up our negative mess or willful debauchery. I am not saying that He will not step in to save us, but we must approach all things with positive proactiveness with the correct heart and mind posture that PLEASES Him. Thirdly, with creativity and open-mindedness, positivity allows us to see possibilities, opportunities, or hidden treasures instead of the obstacles.

Law of Reciprocity

The Law of Reciprocity is an act or framework of sharing, often summarized by the phrase, 'You will reap what you sow.' By far, this Spiritual Law highlights the inherent give-and-take in our relationships and exchanges. Now, regardless of whether we believe it or not, or whether we experience delays, it has a mind of its own, keeping a tally of our positive or negative actions and reinforcements. Is this Biblical? I would have it no other way: Galatians 6:7 states: *"Do not be deceived: God is not mocked; for whatever a man sows, that he will also reap."*

In or out of season, this Spiritual Law, ranges beyond simple exchange or trading. Actually, it is a part of the giving and receiving module used in the Kingdom to bring alignment to what we know as Seedtime and Harvest. 2 Corinthians 9:6 says, *"But this I say: He who sows sparingly will also reap sparingly, and he who sows bountifully will also reap bountifully."* All of which

The Overcoming

embody a Spiritual and Moral Component of interplay that aligns our DNA with the DNG (Divine Nature of God).

When we openly discuss our vulnerabilities, lessons, and victories, *As It Pleases God*, leading all things back to His Kingdom, we will find the strength to carry on regardless of what we are going through or with whom.

How do we carry on as Believers, especially when things are going really south? Regardless of what direction we are headed, if God is at the forefront, He will never mislead us. All we need to do is listen, learn, grow, and prepare while documenting, leaving no stone unturned. Galatians 6:9 tells us: *"And let us not grow weary while doing good, for in due season we shall reap if we do not lose heart."*

Here is the Spiritual Seal to explain this better than any words I can string together. Luke 6:38 states: *"Give, and it will be given to you: good measure, pressed down, shaken together, and running over will be put into your bosom. For with the same measure that you use, it will be measured back to you."* So, if you desire positivity, give it. And the same applies to the negative as well, even if we think money can buy our way out of anything or buy anyone. Remember this Spiritual Law is way smarter than us on our best day.

When positively activating the *Law of Reciprocity* with the Spirit of Righteousness in our areas of need, God must bring forth what we need or bring us peace amid what we are enduring. In the Eye of God, it is not fair to beg or ask for something we are not willing to share that is within our power to do so. Simply put, we cannot be on the take more than we give. James 3:18 even states: *"Now the fruit of righteousness is sown in peace by those who make peace."* For example, when using the Fruit of Righteousness, *As It Pleases God*, here is what you must do to place a Spiritual Seal:

☐ If you need LOVE, give it.

The Overcoming

- ☐ If you need PEACE, give it.
- ☐ If you need JOY, give it.
- ☐ If you need PATIENCE, give it.
- ☐ If you need KINDNESS, give it.
- ☐ If you need GOODNESS, give it.
- ☐ If you need FAITHFULNESS, give it.
- ☐ If you need GENTLENESS, give it.
- ☐ If you need SELF-CONTROL, give it.
- ☐ If you need FORGIVENESS, give it.
- ☐ If you need MERCY, give it.
- ☐ If you need FREEDOM, give it.
- ☐ If you need COMPASSION, give it.
- ☐ If you need UNDERSTANDING, give it.
- ☐ If you need EMPATHY, give it.
- ☐ If you need a SECOND CHANCE, give it.

According to *Divine Etiquette*, whatever you need, freely give it without expecting a return from anyone aside from God Himself. How do we make this make sense, especially for Believers? In light of the Ancient of Days, the key to Divine Mastery is only to expect a return from God, our Heavenly Father, because He knows best. When we allow Him to orchestrate our Blessings or fill our longings, He does not make mistakes when doing so. Plus, it helps us with our heart and mind postures to ensure we are doing, saying, and becoming for the right reasons.

Conversely, if one does not know how to place God at the forefront above all things, one will continually look to fix whatever needs fixing through human vessels outside of the Will of God. Unfortunately, this is how we get control freaks who desire to be in charge of or know everything, including violating the privacy of others or outright making bad choices based on their perception.

The Overcoming

Then again, we may become focused on fixing others, making them what we desire, without taking the time to fix ourselves. As a result, this will include making a lot of selfish mistakes that could have been avoided. It is also the cause of many of our regrets derived from disobedience, arrogance, and self-centeredness. Clearly, no one is exempt from this phase of life; still, we must know what to do and why we are doing so to ensure we can participate in *The Overcoming* phase without being yoked, soul-tied, mocked, or overwhelmed.

On behalf of the Heavenly of Heavens, we were created to share and bond with people, not fix them. Fixing people is God's job, and the moment we exclude Him, our interactions can become toxic, abusive, and manipulative. Plus, the moment we think this is not happening to us, all we need to do is check our thoughts, words, actions, and responses. They will tell us everything we need to know about ourselves if we listen more to ourselves and speak less negative chatter.

What is the big deal here about fixing ourselves, and why should we stop trying to fix others? The *Law of Reciprocity* applies to our words, thoughts, desires, and actions. What we release into the atmosphere, we invite those same qualities back into our lives, positively or negatively, looking for the weakest vessels. Sadly, most often, the weakest will be found in our children.

Matthew 7:2 says, *"For with what judgment you judge, you will be judged; and with the measure you use, it will be measured back to you."* The moment we begin to focus on criticizing or attempting to change others, we inadvertently attract similar negative energy into our spaces.

In addition, we must avoid violating the free will of another unless we are raising or training our children, *As It Pleases God*, and according to Proverbs 22:6, *"Train up a child in the way he should go, And when he is old he will not depart from it."* Proverbs 29:15 states: *"The rod and rebuke give wisdom, But a child left to himself*

The Overcoming

brings shame to his mother." In addition to this Scripture, we have Ephesians 6:4 saying, *"And you, fathers, do not provoke your children to wrath, but bring them up in the training and admonition of the Lord."* Once done, *As It Pleases Him,* here is the Spiritual Seal from Isaiah 54:13, *"All your children shall be taught by the Lord, And great shall be the peace of your children."*

In the Divine Eye of God, it is imperative to embrace personal growth over fixing others while sharing our Testimony positively. By channeling our positive energy toward self-improvement with a work-in-progress mindset, we will gain better results over the long run. Our efforts to flourish without the pressure of our judgments, unwelcomed advice, resentment, and defensiveness are plausible for ourselves and others when applying Spiritual Principles, *As It Pleases God.*

As the world buzzes with expectations and demands, the goal is to become a powerful problem solver through the power of agreement and helping others. We are not a fixer, mending what we perceive as broken among the brethren. Nor are we fixating on others' flaws to make ourselves feel better or to neglect our own struggles or issues.

In the *Law of Reciprocity,* self-reflection, self-awareness, personal development, and healing are powerful tools that enable us to become the best version of ourselves by addressing our issues first, from the inside out. Once accomplished, *As It Pleases God,* in *The Overcoming Process,* we will become more compassionate, merciful, patient, and understanding towards others. More importantly, letting go of the urge to change others or when we can meet people where they are can indeed lead to wealthier, more authentic relationships of respect with trustworthy boundaries.

How do we set trustworthy boundaries as Believers? We must always add the Holy Trinity (Our Creator, our Salvation, and our Counselor) into the equation to invoke

The Overcoming

Divine Discernment. Why must we do this when setting real boundaries as Believers? According to the Heavenly of Heavens, Spiritual Blindness, Deafness, and Muteness are our biggest challenges in the Eye of God, preventing us from recognizing them as we should.

Clearly, boundaries are not meant to alienate, isolate, or put us in a box. Spiritually Speaking, they are used to protect us from people, places, and things that are unhealthy and unwise for our well-being or our Predestined Blueprinted Purpose.

In *The Overcoming* Process, it is WISE to withdraw from human influences and distractions to Divinely Connect to our Heavenly Father, *Spirit to Spirit*, to operate or move with discernment, confidence, and grace, *As It Pleases Him*. Listed below are a few tips on setting boundaries to LIVE BY EXAMPLE, but not limited to such:

- ☐ Add the Holy Trinity into the equation.
- ☐ Pray for Divine Wisdom and Guidance.
- ☐ Determine and become clear on established boundaries.
- ☐ Align boundaries with the Word of God.
- ☐ Cover the boundaries with the Blood of Jesus.
- ☐ Become ONE with the Holy Spirit for guidance.
- ☐ Use the Fruits of the Spirit and behave Christlike.
- ☐ Communicate boundaries effectively and positively.
- ☐ Practice active listening and proactivity.
- ☐ Balance boundaries with strength and kindness.
- ☐ Become accountable and supportive amid boundaries.
- ☐ Know the 'when'...when to say 'yes' or 'no' gracefully.
- ☐ Address breaches calmly and assertively.

The Overcoming

When activating the *Law of Reciprocity* with boundaries, we can truly protect the Mind, Body, Soul, and Spirit from unwanted, ungodly, and idolistic intruders, allowing our discernment faculties to kick into high gear. When we are able to discern, learn, and document what we have seen with lovingkindness, *As It Pleases God*, the *Divine Cleansing* Process will become a piece of cake, opening up the Floodgates of Divine Wisdom.

What if the *Law of Reciprocity* does not work on our behalf? First, this Spiritual Law does not lie. Now, it is very good at taking its time to respond, especially regarding our actions, reactions, human interactions, and relationships. According to *Divine Etiquette: As It Pleases God*®, when confronting our uncomfortable reality, we must be careful about allowing our negative thoughts, mental chatter, and feelings to make it into reality because the *Law of Reciprocity* will take it from there. For this reason, it is only wise to reverse unconscious negatives into conscious positives to change the trajectory of our seedful exchanges, shifting the narrative to *As It Pleases God*.

Secondly, when the *Law of Reciprocity* appears not to work on our behalf, it means that it is working AGAINST us due to some form of Spiritual Blindness, Deafness, or Muteness. To harness the *Law of Reciprocity* positively, *As It Pleases God*, it is crucial to turn inwardly and assess our known and unknown contributions, creating an opportunity for growth, taking responsibility, and embracing self-discovery for the Greater Good of mankind.

Why would the *Law of Reciprocity* work against Believers? When we are Kingdomly Unusable, we are off-balanced, we have misaligned expectations, we are too pompous, we are operating in willful disobedience, we have planted in the wrong ground, we are bound with unforgiveness, or there is underlying selfishness involved, the *Law of Reciprocity* will

The Overcoming

make its best attempt to help us self-correct. But rest assured, the *Law of Reciprocity* works, even when we feel otherwise, full of disappointment, frustration, revenge, or confusion.

According to the Heavenly of Heavens, the *Law of Reciprocity* is a GIFT to mankind, and we only need to learn how to use it to our advantage, *As It Pleases God*. Instead of opting for the disadvantages of cursing our own hands with rotten fruits all over the place to please ourselves, we should always opt for the proven, trusted, and chosen way by using the Fruits of the Spirit and the character traits of Christ Jesus.

Even if we are tempted to follow the path of least resistance, we can reverse it to a path of righteousness, catalyzing positive change. Regardless of whether we believe in the Fruits of the Spirit (Love, Joy, Peace, Patience, Kindness, Goodness, Faithfulness, Gentleness, and Self-Control), the fruits we choose today will nurture and define our Spiritual Gardens of tomorrow.

What if we do not have a Spiritual Garden? Unbeknown to most, we all have a Spiritual Garden containing the Tree of Life, symbolizing growth, vitality, and nurturing, and the Tree of Death, representing stagnation, decay, and the need for pruning that is hidden within every human being, regardless of whether we understand it or not.

In the realm of human experience based on the Breath of Life given to each of us, we are required to Spiritually Till our own ground based on the Divine Agreement set forth before taking our first breath. However, we may not be conscious of this at the present moment. All this means is that no one can fulfill this Divine Agreement or Mission for us but the one in charge of the Spiritual Garden in the Earthen Vessel from within. If we neglect it, the *Law of Reciprocity* will reflect likewise to AWAKEN us from our slumber.

In the *Divine Cleansing* Process, we must ensure we are on the up and up, *As It Pleases God*. So, let us break this process down in the next chapter for our Spiritual Garden's sake.

Chapter Nine

Divine Cleansing

In our quest to create a Heavenly existence on Earth, we often prioritize material possessions and financial gain over our well-being. While these things may be necessary for our survival, they do not necessarily bring us lasting joy, peace, contentment, or fulfillment within the human psyche. Instead, let us shift our focus toward discovering our true selves and what truly matters, *As It Pleases God* or from His Divine Perspective. By doing so, we can cultivate a more meaningful and fulfilling life that aligns with our deepest desires and values, according to our Predestined Blueprint.

To appreciate the real you, you must understand that God has given you everything you need. He has given you a SOUL to live, a MIND to think, a BODY to function, a SPIRIT to worship Him, FAITH to know Him, the HOLY SPIRIT to guide and teach you, His WORD to live by, and the BLOOD of Jesus to cover you. If you have a hard time understanding what I just said, let me break it down for you. You are a living SOUL with a SPIRIT dwelling within a BODY, which happens to be Blessed with a MIND to think, EMOTIONS to

Divine Cleansing

feel, and SENSES to discern. All of these are Protected and Covered by the Blood of Jesus, restoring your Divine Rights to living a fulfilled life according to your Predestined Blueprint. Now, with this being said, you must understand the difference between all four aspects of you: The Mind, Body, Soul, and Spirit.

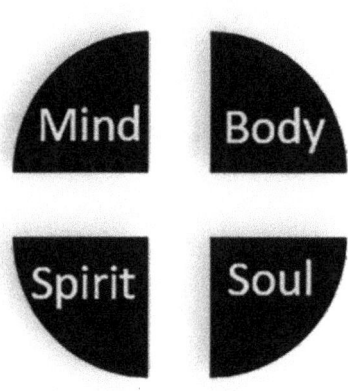

In *Divine Etiquette: As It Pleases God*®, let us go deeper to ensure you understand how I got it, how I can do what I do, and how you can do likewise, regardless of your weaknesses, idiosyncrasies, background, culture, or whatever. Once you comprehend the inner workings of the Mind, Body, Soul, and Spirit in this manner, the Holy Spirit will do the rest in your *Spirit to Spirit* Connection.

    Why do we need the Holy Spirit in the inner workings process? Everyone is different; therefore, your Cornerstone of Greatness will not be the same as mine. What does this mean in layman's terms? Your Blueprint is different from mine. Your Soul Print is unlike mine. Your Mind Print is unique as well. More importantly, your Spirit Print or *Spirit to Spirit* Relationship with the Holy Trinity is EXCLUSIVE; therefore, no one can do this for you, but you!

Divine Cleansing

It is imperative that you Spiritually Till your OWN ground to develop a Direct Connection to the Holy Trinity, getting to know the Divine Experience for yourself. What is the purpose of knowing this? Once you experience the Divine Presence of God, the inner workings of the Holy Spirit, and how the Blood of Jesus covers you...you would not want to experience anything less. Plus, you will become more than willing to let go of anything or anyone attempting to block you from operating, thinking, and becoming, *As It Pleases God*.

When it comes to *Divine Cleansing*, we must incorporate cleansing of the Mind, Body, Soul, and Spirit. In the same way that we bathe to cleanse the dirt and debris off our bodies to maintain proper hygiene, we need to do likewise with others. Even 1 John 1:7 says, *"But if we walk in the light as He is in the light, we have fellowship with one another, and the blood of Jesus Christ His Son cleanses us from all sin."*

In a world that often prioritizes physical appearance and tangible results, we frequently overlook the significance of the *Divine Cleansing* Process, *As It Pleases God*. The elements of physical care, mental clarity, emotional nurturing, and a Spiritual Connection are important in the Eye of God. This Divine Connection transcends the earthly realm in which we live, guiding us to a deeper understanding of our reason for being and the Divine Purpose that facilitates our Heaven on Earth Experiences.

Is this Divine Connection stuff real? Absolutely! We are here for a reason, and if we do not know or have forgotten the reason, it is fair to say that some form of unrest is occurring within the psyche, prompting us to self-correct or to awaken from our slumber.

Divine Etiquette: As It Pleases God® wants us to know that nurturing or *Divinely Cleansing* our Spiritual Selves can take many forms, including prayer, worship, writing, reading the Bible, or simply spending time in nature.

Divine Cleansing

When we prioritize our Spiritual Growth and Development, *As It Pleases God*, we open ourselves to Divine Wisdom and Guidance from the Heavenly of Heavens. More importantly, it also comes with a Divine Filtering Process that helps us to Spiritually Discern correctly through our senses, conscience, mindfulness, and Spiritual Eyes, Ears, or Mouth, creating a well-calibrated INTERNAL COMPASS.

How do we perfect our Internal Compass as Believers? By getting into God's Face, *Spirit to Spirit*, asking relevant fact-finding questions, and documenting the answers. By understanding what is important to us, we are better able to personally direct our Spiritual Queries to the Heavenly of Heavens.

How can we change the trajectory of our questions from negative to positive or irrelevant to relevant, *As It Pleases God*? We must get into a still, small place with pen and paper, invoking the presence of the Holy Trinity. Here are a few sample questions, but not limited to such:

- ☐ What do I need to learn?
- ☐ What is the lesson?
- ☐ Where did I go wrong?
- ☐ How did I get off track?
- ☐ Can You show me the purpose of this ordeal?
- ☐ What did I miss?
- ☐ How can I help others with this experience?
- ☐ What is the WISDOM I need to extract?
- ☐ What is the plan?
- ☐ Can You show me the way?
- ☐ Lord, can You take the wheel?
- ☐ Lord, can You show me how to steer this situation?
- ☐ Father, can You show me the win-win?

Divine Cleansing

What is the purpose of querying in such a manner? It develops our Spiritual Vision, Hearing, and Speaking in our communicable efforts with the Holy Trinity. The moment we negate our Spiritual Relations, *As It Pleases God*, we will begin to interject rationalities based on our thoughts, beliefs, traumas, and biases on a sliding scale.

What is the sliding scale? In the Eye of God, it is a sliding scale of worldliness. Our hidden or open biases are often portrayed as a form of godliness with spoiled rotten fruits and atrocious character traits bound by negativity. Regardless of whether we are querying ourselves or not, we have two options from a Spiritual Perspective:

- ☐ Awaken our AWARENESS.
- ☐ Ignore our RELEVANCE.

What is the big deal, whether or not we query ourselves? It will determine our developmental process and our ability to become proactively diligent or valuable for the Kingdom's Use.

The Kingdom of Heaven is predicated on workability, not contentability. What about Philippians 4:11 that says: "*Not that I speak in regard to need, for I have learned in whatever state I am, to be content.*" We must also read the second passage that says: "*I know how to be abased, and I know how to abound. Everywhere and in all things, I have learned both to be full and to be hungry, both to abound and to suffer need. I can do all things through Christ who strengthens me.*" Philippians 4:12-13.

According to the Heavenly of Heavens, if we do not understand something or someone and their relevance, we should get an understanding first. If not, do not play around with it or bring about a negative judgment without getting the facts first.

Divine Cleansing

Why should we not judge, especially when operating with free will? It contains a seed, and we may not like the fruit it produces. So, if we are unsure of the seed, do not sow it, in or out of season! We must query it first.

What is the purpose of querying people, places, things, or events? By concluding without having the facts or asking fact-finding questions, we leave ourselves open to speculations, half-truths, or untruths based on our biases, perceptions, traumas, or misunderstandings. Unfortunately, this happens to me all the time, even to Believers who claim to be Holy Ghost-Filled and Fire Baptized. As a result, I have to shake my head at the type of stuff people come up with while not asking me one question at all, especially when I think differently, strategically, systematically, proactively, and Kingdomly. Here are a few pointers on how to avoid defaulting on *Spiritual Commitments*, but not limited to such:

- ☐ Respect and Reverence our Heavenly Father as our Divine Creator.
- ☐ Use the Blood of Jesus as a Spiritual Sacrifice on behalf of the Kingdom of Heaven.
- ☐ Use the Holy Spirit in unison with our Spirit through Spiritual Baptism or Awakening.
- ☐ Use the Fruits of the Spirit consistently (Love, Joy, Peace, Patience, Kindness, Goodness, Faithfulness, Gentleness, and Self-Control).
- ☐ Operate with Christlike Character with a positive mindset.
- ☐ Develop a *Spirit to Spirit* Connection.
- ☐ Document information and answers that are given while obeying Divine Instructions.
- ☐ Use the Word of God as our Spiritual Armor and Alignment Apparatus.
- ☐ Become Merciful, Repenting, Forgiving, Thankful, and Humble.

Divine Cleansing

- ☐ Look for the GOOD in all things.
- ☐ We must operate in our Spiritual Gifts according to our Predestined Blueprint.
- ☐ We must give back to the building of the Kingdom of God, preparing others through our Testimony, passing the MANTLE when the time is right, or teaching the NEXT in line without hoarding or becoming selfish.

Does God not speak to everyone? Of course, He does. It is a matter of whether we can hear the Voice of God correctly, clearly understand Him, or whether we obey Him or not. For the record, I do not discount anyone's experience with God. Still, most often, we hear our prewired or conditioned echoes of the conscience or our natural instincts speaking, while we misinterpret it as being God, our Heavenly Father.

Then again, we must never forget that the lust of the eyes, the lust of the flesh, and the pride of life can speak as well; so, it behooves us to develop a *Spirit to Spirit* Connection, *As It Pleases God*. The bottom line is that in all things, we must look into ourselves through the Spiritual Examination Process by proactively DOING while interjecting the Holy Trinity as our Spiritual Reckoning Force. What does our DOING consist of?

- ☐ Our DOINGS for the Kingdom of Heaven.
- ☐ Our DOINGS with God's sheep.

In all simplicity, God is accounting for what we do, what we do not do, and how we self-correct. To take this a step further, when someone engages in deception with me, they often continue as if God has not already revealed them or the situation. As I hold my tongue, exhibiting a massive amount of self-control, and out of respect, I often leave clues that I know about whatever or whomever. Then again, I may ask a relevant question, providing a way of escape or an opportunity for them to self-correct. But, for some odd reason, most would often miss their cued clue, only to continue in their folly with a stiff neck, unchecked ego, hidden biases, or ungoverned agendas.

As I shake my head in dismay, I have to remind myself that I am on assignment to gather the information to present to the Kingdom in real-time. So, I do not relent; while at the same time, operating in outright humility, I allow them to play their games as if they have the upper hand as I glean Divine Wisdom, *As It Pleases God*, doing what I am designed to do.

As we are a work-in-progress, *As It Pleases God*, in the *Divine Cleansing* Process, we must be willing to do a few things, but not limited to such:

- ☐ We must be willing to feed the hungry without worrying about how much it costs.
- ☐ If someone is thirsty, give them something to drink.
- ☐ We must be willing to shelter, visit, or help people experiencing homelessness wisely.
- ☐ We must be willing to provide clothing for others or give away what we do not need to the less fortunate.
- ☐ We must be willing to visit, be kind, or help the sick, sharing our Spiritual Gifts.
- ☐ We must be willing to visit, help, or comfort those who are imprisoned, Mentally, Physically, Emotionally, or Spiritually.
- ☐ We must be willing to positively encourage or mentor others in the midst of what we are going through.

Are we buying brownie points with God by engaging in these works? Absolutely! Yet, I do hear some people saying we cannot buy God, but in my opinion, it depends on how we

Divine Cleansing

attempt to buy Him! If it is with money to avoid purpose, self-correction, wallow in folly, or engage in debaucherous efforts, then they are correct! We cannot pimp or prostitute God.

However, on the other hand, when it comes down to feeding His sheep with clean hands and a pure heart, while fulfilling our Missionable Purpose or aligning with our Divine Blueprint, we can buy God all day long. We can especially buy Him with the use of the Fruits of the Spirit because there is no Spiritual Law against their usage, according to Galatians 5:22-23.

Plus, using the Fruits of the Spirit is indeed a vital part of the *Divine Cleansing* Process. In the same way that we use some type of fruit to cleanse our meats, the same applies to taming the flesh of mankind. Whether we have perfected the Fruit of the Spirit in ONENESS or use the Fruits of the Spirit one-by-one with a work-in-progress mindset, they work nonetheless.

Painstakingly, those who disagree with fruitful brownie points are more than likely the ones who do not use Spiritual Fruits that PLEASE God. For me, I operate *As It Pleases Him*, and I do not make a secret about it! I know WHAT I am doing and the reasons why, and I faithfully use the Fruits of the Spirit to do it. So, it is my reasonable service to help others do likewise.

When it is all said and done, I did not get to this place in my Spiritual Anointing by luck; it was by SKILL! Spiritual Skills, Principles, and Tools, to be exact. Listen to me, and listen well, 'Do you think God will abandon us when we are Spiritually Aligning with the Kingdom of Heaven with a willful work-in-progress mindset?' The answer is 'No.' He is going to do everything in His Divine Power to Spiritually Train and Protect us in Kingdom Protocol, Principles, and Laws.

Brownie points or not, we must remember that the enemy does not attack what already belongs to him! Therefore, we need all the Spiritual Ammunition we can get, putting on the

Divine Cleansing

Whole Armor of God while being in the Spiritual Know. So, if this is a way to pay it forward to obtain the Favor of God, then so be it!

Besides, paying it forward helps fill or bridge the gap with our imperfections. How is this humanly possible? In perfecting Spiritual Duality, *As It Pleases God*, a counteraction or counterplay must be made. Here are a few examples of how the Law of Reciprocity or Seedtime and Harvest can work in our favor, but not limited to such:

- ☐ If we become sad about something or someone, it is wise to give a seed of happiness to another.
- ☐ If we need love, it is wise to give a seed of love to another.
- ☐ If we lack understanding, it is wise to give a seed of understanding to another without judgment.
- ☐ If we need wisdom, become the Wise One for another.
- ☐ If we need help, it is wise to give a seed of help to another.

According to the Heavenly of Heavens, when we ignore the gaps or our 'Give Back,' we tend to run into a bit of trouble, resistance, or contention in the Kingdom.

Regardless of where we are in life or what we are going through, we cannot tear down or lead people to the slaughter, period. In the *Divine Cleansing* Process, it does not matter what they have done or how they have treated us; Spiritual Integrity is a must when becoming Spiritually Committed to God, the Kingdom, or Righteousness.

The moment we open our mouth, using it as a gateway of unrighteousness, we close the door on many of our Blessings from the Kingdom by default. Yes, we have grace and mercy, but they do not provide a safety net to keep us wallowing in messiness or debauchery. Besides, Divine Grace and Mercy

Divine Cleansing

are designed to get us out of messiness and debauchery, not as a covering for it.

As we embark on this Spiritual Journey, this sought-after multi-dimensional experience is in the palm of our hands, and we only need to learn how to use it with *Divine Etiquette: As It Pleases God®*. So, let us talk about this a little more within the individual sectors of the Mind, Body, Soul, and Spiritual Dimension of *Divine Cleansing*.

Mental Cleansing

Mental clarity is of the utmost importance for Believers and non-believers alike. In the same way that we take a shower to refresh our bodies, we must also find ways to cleanse our minds of unwanted negative clutter, lies, hidden upsets, past grievances, whitewashed insecurities, and prolonged fears. All of this unnecessary stuff will become like dust piling up in an empty room with cobwebs, increasing our anxiety, stress, and edginess with a sense of unease and paranoia. In addition, it may also cause difficulty concentrating, including feelings of being overwhelmed, feelings of hopelessness, and a sense of dissatisfaction while pretending all is well.

In *Divine Etiquette: As It Pleases God®*, we must pride ourselves in stimulating our mental rejuvenation process to ensure that our minds are ready, willing, and able to work for us and not against us. More importantly, to clean anything *As It Pleases God*, we must also develop an understanding of it.

The Mind is the instrument used to OUTPUT what is stored in the Soul, producing your thoughts on a conscious or unconscious level. Although the Mind is essential in your day-to-day activities, it is a vital aspect of your brain that cannot be seen or touched. Without the Mind, you would only be able to INPUT information into the Soul, but not receive the OUTPUT.

Through the Mind, you receive the ability to think, learn, understand, compare, comprehend, research, analyze, choose, create, observe, plan, reflect, remember, imagine, and reason. When exercising your Mental Abilities, your manifested thoughts will contribute to your intellectual power, enabling you to experience the knowledge of your likes and dislikes. In addition, it helps with the expression of love or hate, happiness or sadness, desire or disgust, patience or anger, generosity or selfishness, as well as virtue or envy.

Let us not overlook the fact that fantasy, romance, visualization, and role-playing occur in the Mind, often referred to as your IMAGINATION or Mind's Eye. More importantly, this is a process in which your Mind creates positive or negative images of your desires, goals, failures, fears, proclivities, and achievements.

Here is the deal with our Spiritual Cognitive DNA, connecting us between our worldly existence and the Spiritual Realm. Your Mind is to your Soul as your finger is to your hand; they are connected but have different functions working together, creating the whole unit. Unbeknown to most, when used in unison with the other symbolic fingers of our WILL and EMOTIONS, it is referred to as the Human Psyche from a Spiritual Perspective.

What does all of this mean for Believers? When dealing with Kingdom Rationale, the Mind, Will, Emotions, Desires, and Senses are the connected divisions or departments of our Soul that we cannot neglect. From a Kingdom Perspective, they are considered the Spiritual Fingers of our entire Hand or Branches to the Tree of our Soul, often referred to as the Tree of Life or Death, Biblically.

If we take this a step further, whatever stems from us is a SEED, bearing much Fruit, positively or negatively, in due

Divine Cleansing

season. Therefore, we must target the department of the Seed to cleanse or heal the soul.

Picturesquely, if you broke your finger, would you put a cast on your whole hand? No, your physician would stabilize your finger, but the pain would be felt throughout your whole hand and possibly throughout your Body. Better yet, if you remove every finger from your hand, you would still have a hand, but it would not function properly. So, if your Mind, Will, Emotions, Desires, and Senses are in turmoil, the side effects will begin to permeate throughout your life, creating dysfunction within the depths of your Soul.

According to the Heavenly of Heavens, to maximize your Spiritual DNA, it is imperative to manage the time you spend with your Mind, exercising control over your thoughts, emotions, and behaviors. Why must we invest in ourselves in such a manner? The only person who can destroy you is YOU!

In all simplicity, your Mind is like a bank account; what you put in it is what you can take out. No more or no less. In so many words, whatever you deposit into your Mind, or what you think about for twenty-one to thirty days, will positively or negatively accrue interest that is deposited into your Soul. Can the Mind make such deposits? It happens all the time and sometimes too often.

It is often said that a Mind that is too idle makes the heart grow weary. However, we must also determine if the Mind is trained or untrained because we cannot stop the Mind from doing its job. Still, we must become proactive in doing our job as well. What is our job? It is called Mental Management and *Mental Cleansing*.

Idleness is one of the biggest time wasters known to man. Yes, it is good to rest, but resting too much will take a toll on your emotional well-being, causing you to overthink and over-rationalize issues. For example, an idle mind complains, whines, rationalizes, or makes excuses for not doing anything.

Divine Cleansing

As you very well know, it is through the Mind that Satan builds his playground, and if he can get you to sit around long enough doing nothing, he will have a heyday with your Mind. With this being said, *As It Pleases God*, you have two choices:

- ☐ Get a systematic way of managing your Mind.
- ☐ Sit around and allow your Mind to manage you.

In the *Mental Cleansing* Process, if you ever feel depressed about a situation, circumstance, or condition, just rev up your Mind by getting busy doing something positive, productive, and fruitful, benefiting you, your environment, or the Kingdom. How do we make this make sense in the real world? The brain releases one of the most significant chemicals prewired in our DNA during acts of kindness called Endorphins. It is often referred to as 'feel-good' hormones, but the endorphins function as natural painkillers and mood enhancers naturally.

We can also benefit from the bonding hormone called Oxytocin. This hormone is released during moments of connection, whether through acts of kindness, hugging, giving, or nurturing relationships. Oxytocin promotes feelings of trust and bonding, making us feel more connected to others.

In addition, acts of kindness can also elevate serotonin levels, a crucial neurotransmitter that regulates mood, appetite, and sleep to combat feelings of depression and anxiety.

Last, but not least, Dopamine, a neurotransmitter associated with the brain's reward system for performing good deeds, can trigger the release, creating a sense of pleasure and gratification.

This 4-in-1 Powerhouse Building Quaternity: Endorphins, Oxytocin, Serotonin, and Dopamine create a sense of well-being by getting our minds right and doing good deeds. We

Divine Cleansing

often look for external rewards, but in the Eye of God, the internal intangible rewards are already preset to release to us what really matters, with a chemical boost that can make our baby leap. It is so powerful that those witnessing an act of kindness can trigger a chain reaction, prompting bystanders to enact their own good deeds. This Divine Phenomenon is often referred to as the 'bystander effect,' where kindness spreads in a ripple effect, changing or enhancing the overall atmosphere.

What if we opt out of doing good or being kind? The opposite happens. We release Cortisol, a stress hormone that may affect our well-being, causing our minds to seemingly jump the track or wallow in a cycle of negativity, self-doubt, and worry, sometimes without realizing it. Although it is an essential hormone, it tends to hijack our emotional regulation system. Simply put, we need our counterbalancing hormones (Endorphins, Oxytocin, Serotonin, and Dopamine) to kick into high gear to prevent anxiety, depression, loneliness, and a host of other health issues.

All in all, we do not want Cortisol to hang around in our bodies too long. So, what do we do? Get busy using the Fruits of the Spirit (Love, Joy, Peace, Patience, Kindness, Goodness, Faithfulness, Gentleness, and Self-Control) to counterbalance it.

The use of the Fruits of the Spirit is the most POWERFUL counterbalancing system for the DNA of all mankind. It is so free and simple to the point that most of us, including the proclaimed Holy Ghost-Filled and Fire-Baptized, overlook using it. While simultaneously searching for the difficult and expensive ways that will always lead us back to the foolproofed, simple *Divine Etiquette!*

Always remember, when dealing with the Mind on any level, it is the small goals that eventually add up to the achievement of bigger goals. Besides, life is too short to throw away precious time being idle-minded. Now, before we move

Divine Cleansing

on to *Bodily Cleansing*, let me ask you this question: 'How are you really spending your time with your Mind?' 'Do you know?' Or, better yet, 'Do you care?'

Bodily Cleansing

When we think about *Bodily Cleansing*, our minds often jump to thoughts of personal hygiene, such as bathing, brushing our teeth, and keeping ourselves looking and smelling good. However, true *Bodily Cleansing* extends far beyond these daily routines. It encompasses a detoxification that includes:

- ☐ Nourishing our bodies with nutritious foods for fuel.
- ☐ Staying adequately hydrated.
- ☐ Engaging in regular exercise promotes circulation.
- ☐ Prioritizing rest to rejuvenate, enabling the body to recover from the wear and tear of everyday life.

In totality, these practices contribute to a healthy, balanced lifestyle that enhances the body's natural cleansing processes, but there is more to *Bodily Cleansing*.

In a world that often emphasizes physical health through juice cleanses and detox diets, there is another form of detoxification that often goes unmentioned: The cleansing of the Mind, Body, Soul, and Spirit through practices such as meditation, prayer, forgiveness, repentance, and thankfulness.

From a Spiritual Perspective in the *Divine Etiquette* Process, when people live predominantly from a physical perspective, they tend to refer to the body as 'flesh.' This terminology not only reflects a grounded existence in the tangible world of material desires, earthly pursuits, and immediate gratification. It also indicates a detachment from the Spiritual

Divine Cleansing

Essence that truly defines us as living a Spirit-led life, calling our bodies Temples that embody respect, care, and reverence.

Contrary to what most would think, the Body is NOT the real you! It is your means of coming into contact with the material or physical world. It is also the visible entity housing the invisible, intangible assets of your Mind, Soul, and Spirit in Earthen Vessels.

Take notice that you have two of every body part except for the commonly misused ones. For example, we have:

- ☐ One BODY that is prone to promiscuity, abuse, dullness, neglect, and laziness.

- ☐ One MIND is often plagued with negative thinking, debased mental chatter, and destructive thoughts.

- ☐ One NOSE that finds it more appealing to know everyone's business or have first dibs on gossip, slander, or the secrets of another.

- ☐ One MOUTH is inclined to gossip and belittle others or say things that we should keep to ourselves.

- ☐ One TONGUE that is apt to cut wounds into the heart of the innocent, especially when we are hurt or cannot have our way.

- ☐ One HEART that can potentially become quickly hardened and evil when we are hurt, betrayed, traumatized, or abused.

- ☐ One STOMACH which tends to consume too much or abuse food, alcohol, etc., when lacking the appropriate self-control or emotional regulation.

Divine Cleansing

- ☐ One HEAD that is likely to become vain or arrogant when we think we are better than others.

- ☐ One SEXUAL ORGAN that is often misused before and during marriage, while also having a direct connection to the lust of the eyes, the lust of the flesh, and the pride of life.

Knowing what you know now, my question is, 'What if you had two minds, two bodies, two noses, two mouths, two tongues, two hearts, two stomachs, two heads, or two sex organs?' In my opinion, this would be devastating to humanity. I must admit that God had a Divine Plan for His creation, and it is apparent you are genuinely a MASTERPIECE.

Accepting yourself for who you are does not mean you are not to take care of yourself. Your Body is a Temple, so you have to take care of it. Choose the type of hairstyle, makeup, or clothing that reflects your style and uniqueness.

As we navigate through life's complexities, natural beauty is not just on the outside; it also comes from within. Therefore, change the things you can, accept the things you cannot change, and love everything about you without complaining.

In the framework of *Divine Etiquette*, God has given you one Body, lasting you a lifetime. And, 'NO,' He did not make a mistake when He created you. So, whether you like it or not, you must take care of it and strive to honor your Body as the Divine Temple housing your Spirit Man. Why is this so important for a Believer? It possesses an unseen but all so powerful Spiritual Compass, guiding you toward a richer and more fulfilling Spiritual Journey, *As It Pleases God.*

For the most part, what God has Blessed you with, believe it or not, people are paying money to have! Your unique

Divine Cleansing

attributes, talents, skills, body type, and characteristics are not only valuable but also sought after by many. The next time you doubt your worth or feel inadequate, remember this: You possess treasures within you that others would pay dearly to have. And what you take for granted every day may be the answered prayer for someone else.

Nonetheless, once the *Bodily Cleansing* occurs, *As It Pleases God*, keep in mind that your Blessings and unique Gifts, Talents, or Creativity are not just for you; they are meant to be shared.

What if we choose not to share our unique Spiritual Gifts, Talents, or Creativity, keeping everything for ourselves? In Earthen Vessels, we have free will to share or not to share, to use or not to use, and to consume or not to consume. But suppose we choose not to share or use our Spiritual Gifts and Blessings to help others, *As It Pleases God*. In this case, we can knowingly or unknowingly place a plug in our multiplying factors associated with Seedtime and Harvest. In addition, as a Temple of God, we can also block our Spiritual Growth, Discernment, and Development according to Kingdom Standards.

Why are we Spiritually Blocked as Believers? God uses people like us in Earthen Vessels to feed His precious sheep. Now, as we align ourselves with His Divine Will, if we have the heart and mind posture to starve His sheep, especially from what we have been given freely, then we are Spiritually Blocked until we awaken from our slumber.

Furthermore, when opting not to enrich the lives of others while taking all the Spiritual Benefits for ourselves, it is also possible to become a functioning Believer and still be Spiritually Blocked. How do we make this make sense? Unfortunately, TOXIC Believers are real! The funny thing about it is that amid their divisive rhetoric, judgmental attitudes, corrupt character traits, guilt or shame tactics, and a lack of empathy, they do not realize they are toxic. Really? Yes, really!

In the Eye of God, we must become Spiritual Vessels of positivity and change, spreading light while strategically building and inspiring those around us. If we are Spiritually Blocked, causing emotional distress, bullied anxiety, traumatizing abuse, or diminishing someone's sense of belonging in any way, a *Soul Cleansing* must occur. Doing so will help to get rid of toxic sludge, Mentally, Physically, Emotionally, and Spiritually, getting us unblocked and usable *As It Pleases God*.

Soul Cleansing

Cleansing the soul involves connecting with our inner selves, fostering self-awareness, and ultimately achieving a timely and harmonious balance within the psyche. At the core of the concept of *Soul Cleansing* is the acknowledgment of the Soul as the Divine Essence of our being.

The Soul is the most vital aspect of the Body. Though the Soul is unseen, it is as real as the air you are breathing right now. For example, you cannot see the oxygen you breathe, but the Breath of Life is so real, right? It is the sustaining life force for our earthly endeavors.

Theoretically, the Soul is to the Body like the marrow is to the bone. The bone dwells on the outside, and the marrow, the lifeline of the bone, dwells on the inside. No marrow, no bone! What does all of this mean for us? The Body cannot exist without a Soul, and the Soul cannot exist without a Body. It is the SPIRIT that operates apart from the Body.

The Soul is the vital INPUT epicenter of all your intellect, emotions, feelings, and beliefs, forming your character. Often, it is referred to as the heart, inner man, human psyche, or inner child, among many other names. In *Divine Etiquette: As It*

Divine Cleansing

Pleases God®, the heart I will be referring to will not be the heart pumping blood to the body, but the innermost being, center, or core of a human being.

I consider the Soul to be the invisible STOREHOUSE of your emotions, revealing your positive or negative feelings of happiness or sadness, affection or rejection, fear or courage, gentleness or harshness, love or hate, pleasure or pain, and desire or disgust. Your Soul governs you, and it has direct control over your will as well as your intellect, character, and personality. The Soul is the part of you who rebels against God out of the desire for control.

According to the Heavenly of Heavens, the Soul has the free will to choose what it wants to do, when it wants to do it, and how it wants to do it. How is this possible? Frankly, it is achieved by linking up to the satellite dish of your Mind in unison with your Will, Emotions, Desires, and Senses, channeling your every thought, choice, decision, or idea into what appears to be reality, based upon your perception. All in all, this gives birth or expands our lives to the lust of the eyes, the lust of the flesh, and the pride of life. How so? Unbeknown to most, it feeds our SOULISH NATURE. Plus, from the Garden of Eden Experience with Adam and Eve, the Soul naturally hides the SECRETS or ACCESS to our Spiritual Being.

Man's Heaven on Earth Experience has become real Spiritual Warfare from the inside out. This ripple effect and psychological toll come with a tug-of-war between our authentic self through our (Spirit Man) and the persona projected to the world through our (Soulish Nature). This analogy may sound a little insidious, but it is an all-too-real battle that emerges within the human psyche, shaping our thoughts, experiences, decisions, demeanor, and interactions with the world around us.

When dealing with the Soul of Mankind, internal warfare is not a battle fought with guns or swords. Instead, they are

Divine Cleansing

waged with words, thoughts, emotions, desires, and beliefs, positively or negatively.

Why does Spiritual Warfare occur, especially when we are sold out to the Kingdom of God? No one is exempt from Spiritual Warfare because it is indeed our Spiritual Training Ground. We simply need to know what to do when it occurs, why we are doing so, and GLEAN the Spiritual Training, *As It Pleases Him*.

What if we choose not to Spiritually Glean from our Spiritual Warfare? Once again, we have free will to participate or do our own thing. But know this: Spiritual Warfare does not remain isolated within the psyche; it radiates outwardly, influencing others, positively or negatively, with or without our permission. Moreover, regardless of our free-willed decisions, unresolved internal battles do not lose their get-up-and-go, even if they are suppressed. They can still manifest as irritability, anger, hatred, aggression, resentment, rejection, unforgiveness, or withdrawal, releasing too much Cortisol into our bodies and affecting our well-being. So, it is only wise to become a work-in-progress, resolving the resolvable, using the Fruits of the Spirit, and behaving Christlike at all times because most of our battles will be fought from within.

As *Divine Etiquette* is on the Divine Table of God, in this comparison and competitive culture, we will be TESTED to see what we are made of. Spiritually Speaking, if, for some reason, we are made of unwarranted anxiety, depression, fear, guilt, and a ceaseless quest for validation and purpose, we will 'get got' by the wiles of the enemy due to an underlying identity crisis or distorted self-worth.

According to the Heavenly of Heavens, if we are operating with jealousy, envy, pride, greed, or coveting when we are TESTED, stigmatic shame will be attached to our wiles, fostering intense feelings of inadequacy or internal conflict. Picturesquely, this oppressive feeling within the psyche

Divine Cleansing

makes us want to hide under a rock, not show our faces, or pass the blame through multiple forms of negative projection.

How can a Believer reverse an underlying identity crisis or a distorted self-worth? In the Eye of God, it is always best to get an understanding of all things, *As It Pleases Him*, while developing a *Spirit to Spirit* Relationship to sharpen our discernment faculties.

What does discernment have to do with anything? Without Spiritual Discernment, *As It Pleases God*, we can know the Word and still miss it. We can be sold out to the Kingdom and still miss it. We can operate in emotional intelligence and still negate Spiritual Intelligence while ending up looking like boo-boo the fool. Is this not the reason why the enemy (the wolves in sheep's clothing) laughs at Believers who cannot discern who they are or their false teachings? Then again, is this not why we are being deceived? Absolutely.

In a world overflowing with biases, information, opinions, and conflicting messages, Spiritual Discernment has become an invaluable commodity in our *Soulful Cleansing* Phase. Why do we need Spiritual Discernment when engaging in *Soul Cleansing*? Spiritual Discernment is a GIFT within the consciousness and senses of mankind. Once embraced for our Heaven on Earth Experiences as a Divine Birthright, it keeps on giving from the Heavens Above once we Spiritually Align ourselves, *As It Pleases God*.

The Divine Gift and Birthright of Spiritual Discernment has a snooze-you-lose concept attached to the Soul of Mankind. How so? It is designed to keep us Spiritual Awake or put us to sleep in a state of slumber through our willful choices, similar to a rooster faithfully crowing at a certain time of morning. In my opinion, it has a cock-a-doodle-doo time clock hidden within the psyche designed to alert us about anything or anyone that could affect our well-being,

Divine Cleansing

Mentally, Physically, Emotionally, Spiritually, or Financially. Is this a joke? Absolutely not!

There was a reason why, in Matthew 26:34, *Jesus said to Peter, "Assuredly, I say to you that this night, before the rooster crows, you will deny Me three times."* When it happened, Peter's *Soulful Cleansing* came forth. Here is what Matthew 26:75 says, *"And Peter remembered the word of Jesus who had said to him, 'Before the rooster crows, you will deny Me three times.' So he went out and wept bitterly."*

The symbolic crowing of the rooster or Spiritual Discernment serves as a wake-up call for denial, repentance, and the fulfillment of Jesus' Divine Prophecies, helping us through our human frailties. Unfortunately, we do not know where our loyalties lie until we are tested or put under immense pressure.

Faltering under duress is common for most, but it can become training for us all through the Power of our Testimonies. However, to make this process effective according to the Heavenly of Heavens, we must begin to PERCEIVE and UNDERSTAND *As It Pleases God* and not to please ourselves. Here is the deal in a Divine Call to Remembrance: The Soul stands between two worlds:

- ☐ The SPIRIT WORLD is linked through the Spirit and driven by Spiritual Absolutes such as Spiritual Principles, Laws, Systems, and so on.

- ☐ The MATERIAL WORLD is linked through the Body with our Thoughts, Will, Emotions, Desires, Lusts, Habits, and Senses.

Nevertheless, the Soul cannot have the SPIRIT WORLD and the MATERIAL WORLD at the same time. Why can we not

Divine Cleansing

have our cake and eat it too? *"No one can serve two masters, for either he will hate the one and love the other, or else he will be loyal to the one and despise the other. You cannot serve God and Mammon."* Matthew 6:24.

In my younger days, when I lacked understanding, I assumed for many years that the word Mammon meant Satan, but this was so far from the truth. Mammon means material gain or riches; therefore, the scripture states you will worship God the Creator or material gain.

The Soul of a human is given life at the first birth when born from the womb, which is considered the 'milking' stage of your life. No one tells us that if our milk is contaminated during this stage, then so are we! How is this possible? This phase prepares us Mentally, Physically, and Emotionally to face the world in Earthen Vessels. But we are not usually taught that we become a direct reflection of what we see, hear, speak, and consume.

How you were raised during your childhood is a direct revelation or mirror image of who you are today, positively or negatively. In so many words, the hidden person of the heart reveals your attitude, values, beliefs, desires, education, essence, character, traumas, and habits.

In fact, this explains why the Soul is often referred to as your inner child. What is planted within the soul will come out sooner or later, exposing the real you. It does not matter how many masks you put on or how many personalities you assume; your character cannot be fooled. The moment you are put under pressure, what is inside your Soul will come out; therefore, you must come to a true understanding of who you are from the inside out and not from the outside in.

As you continue in *Divine Etiquette: As It Pleases God*®, I will show you how your life will come together by knowing what you feel, why you feel, how you feel, where you feel, and when you feel through the nudging of your SPIRIT-MAN.

Divine Cleansing

How can we change the trajectory of our negative Soulish conditioning, traumas, or past hurts? First, we must repent, forgive, and decide to change for the better, creating a win-win out of everything. Secondly, we must be born again in the Realm of the Spirit using the Fruits of the Spirit and Christlike Character. Thirdly, in readiness, we must develop a *Spirit to Spirit* Relationship with the Holy Trinity while inviting Divine Wisdom, Clarity, Understanding, Purpose, and Connection to come forth for the *Spiritual Cleansing* and Self-Awareness Process.

Why do we need God in the *Spiritual Cleansing* Process to build authentic Self-Awareness, *As It Pleases Him*? Once again, we have a free will choice to allow God to do it, which involves introspection, understanding our emotions, and recognizing our patterns of behavior from a Divine Perspective. Doing so allows introspection and an understanding of our emotions to unlock layers of our psyche. Then again, we can attempt to do it for ourselves with self-satisfaction, selfish perspectives, and playing by our own rules with a superficial sense of satisfaction. Wait, wait, wait, before making a decision, let us go deeper.

Spiritual Cleansing

While it is possible to engage in a cleansing process unaided, needing no one. Doing so without incorporating God, *As It Pleases Him*, this significant caveat can lead to a reinforcement of our self-centered perspectives, with Him nowhere in the equation. Relying solely on our own understanding, know-how, how-to, and strength, we often risk becoming trapped in a cycle of self-absorption, malnourished dullness, and stiff-necked pompousness. As a result, we distance ourselves from the Greater Purpose, the Greater Good for mankind, and the

Divine Cleansing

Divine Interconnectedness that comes from a faith-based, Pleasing God or Oneness Perspective.

Here is the deal, according to the Heavenly of Heavens: *Spiritual Cleansing* allows us to explore our belief systems, heart and mind postures, and known and unknown habits with Divine Introspection. This process assists us in getting rid of our false ideologies, mindsets, and biases contradicting the Kingdom of God while helping us to connect to our Heavenly Father, *Spirit to Spirit*. In addition, it also helps us recognize patterns of behaviors, thoughts, or traumas from a Divine Perspective, bringing Divine Clarity and Understanding to our paths.

In the Eye of God, before committing to our Predestined Paths, we must undergo a vital process called Spiritual Pruning. Essentially, this transformative experience is essential in helping to get rid of the negative, debauched, or deplorable debris hanging out within the Mind, Body, and Soul that no one is exempt from having.

What if we are perfect, having no debris? You and I know it is not humanly possible to be 100% perfect in the Eye of God, especially when it comes to our internal thoughts, feelings, biases, and desires while living in a worldly environment. For this reason, self-deception and projection are on the rise, consuming the Mind, Body, and Soul, making us delusional. How so? The ideas, thoughts, and beliefs evoking images of flawlessness, zero judgment, unerring motivations, and a perfect existence where negativity, bias, and conflict cease to exist are erroneous. Perfection, as defined by human standards, often leads us into a deceptive trap to the point where we begin to believe our own lies.

In reality, debris hanging out in the psyche can come from negative thought patterns, unhealthy relationships, negative chatter, outright disobedience, unresolved or underlying traumas, and even destructive habits or lies. Here is what John 15:1-2 shares with us about the *Divine Cleansing*: "*I am the*

Divine Cleansing

true vine, and My Father is the vine dresser. Every branch in Me that does not bear fruit He takes away; and every branch that bears fruit He prunes, that it may bear more fruit."

So, if you think you are perfect, in need of no repentance, stop with the lies and opt to become a work-in-progress, *As It Pleases God*. In recognizing your shortcomings, it saves time and energy, preventing you from fighting against yourself and the Will of God. Allowing you to learn, adapt, grow, and sow back into the Kingdom when called upon.

What does the pruning consist of? With God Almighty, it may vary from person to person, situation to situation, trauma to trauma, and so on. However, I will say this: We must engage in confronting uncomfortable truths, facing fears, or letting go of relationships and habits that hold us back. Then again, He will often use affliction and rejection to develop, discipline, and grow us according to our Predestined Blueprinted Purpose. To Spiritually Align this, here is what Isaiah 48:10 says, *"Behold, I have refined you, but not as silver; I have tested you in the furnace of affliction."*

Let us talk for a moment: The word Spirit has always sparked my curiosity since childhood. I knew that it was something sensitive and misunderstood by many. As the Spiritual Seeker of the WHY, I began to ask questions. I was told countless times that the Soul and the Spirit were the same, but my Spiritual Intuition told me otherwise.

What is the Spirit? I am so glad you asked. Your Spirit dwells within the innermost depths of your Soul. It is a SUPERNATURAL SOURCE that cannot be seen or touched, but produces Spiritual Guidance and Discernment from within. In all simplicity, this is commonly referred to as the Higher Self. Once AWAKEN to become ONE with the Holy Spirit, your Spirit allows you to communicate with, comprehend, contact, and worship God, *Spirit to Spirit*. It allows you to extend yourself beyond the material world as

Divine Cleansing

well as the limits of your own mind, tapping into the true essence of Divine Wisdom, Courage, Love, and Compassion for God, oneself, and others through and because of the Blood of Jesus.

The day Adam and Eve sinned in the Garden of Eden, they died Spiritually, passing Spiritual death on through all generations until the end of time. As a result, we are all born incomplete, missing this vital link, requiring us to be born again. We cannot be born again in the Mind, Body, or Soul, ONLY in Spirit. Through your Spirituality, your sense of consciousness is developed, giving you the Spiritual Eyes to see things differently and the Spiritual Ears to hear the Voice of God. The Human Spirit is not the same as the Holy Spirit. The Holy Spirit is the Spirit Himself bearing witness with your Spirit, and your Spirit is the channel through which the Holy Spirit will flow.

The Holy Spirit is the Third Person of the Holy Trinity, including the Father and Son. The Holy Spirit revives your Spirit and fills you with the abundance of life, love, and eagerness. Adam lost the Spirit in the beginning, but Jesus brought back the Holy Spirit and released Him to us once again, giving us the Bread of Life, saying: *"I am the bread of life: he that comes to me shall never hunger; and he that believes on me shall never thirst."* John 6:35.

As It Pleases God, I am now introducing this way of life as well. Nevertheless, it takes the acceptance of Jesus, the Lamb of God, who had no sin or blemish, to activate your Spirit. For the record, God will Spiritually Lead, Teach, and Regenerate through the Holy Spirit. He will also ACCUSE or EXCUSE an individual whose life does not line up with their Divine Blueprint.

What about free will? Unfortunately, free will has nothing to do with our reason for being. Picturesquely, it is like apples (earthly) and oranges (Heavenly); they are not the same. Now, free will does give us the opportunity to engage or disengage with our reason for being...still, it does not change it. Why not? Before we took our first breath of life, there was an AGREEMENT made with our Heavenly Father for our Heaven on Earth Experiences. Blasphemy, right? Wrong. Jeremiah 1:5 says, *"Before I formed you in the womb, I knew you; before you were born, I sanctified you; I ordained you a prophet to the nations."*

Frankly, just because we do not remember the Divine Agreement does not mean it is not enforceable, nor does it mean it has been voided. Actually, it is waiting for us to AWAKEN from our slumber. Plus, this is why we have the Holy Spirit to GUIDE us back to the Divine Blueprinted Reason and the Blood of Jesus to COVER us and our reason for being.

How do we get the ball rolling on discovering the reason for our being? Being that we are all different with our own unique experiences and traumas, there is no way set in stone. Nonetheless, in our *Spirit to Spirit* alone time with our Heavenly Father, if we repeat Psalm 139:13-16, it will begin to stir up something inside of us. Here is what it says: *"For You formed my inward parts; You covered me in my mother's womb. I will praise You, for I am fearfully and wonderfully made; marvelous are Your works, and that my soul knows very well. My frame was not hidden from You, when I was made in secret, and skillfully wrought in the lowest parts of the earth. Your eyes saw my substance, being yet unformed. And in Your book they all were written, the days fashioned for me, when as yet there were none of them."* And then say, 'Speak Lord, your servant is listening,' while documenting what is being said.

What is the purpose of documenting? Often enough, it is a test of our willful obedience, determining our level of usability. Hypothetically, if God's Divine Words are lost in the corresponding phase, surely they will become lost in the conveying.

What does corresponding and conveying mean for a Believer? First, with vigilance and integrity, we must speak truthfully and faithfully when representing or re-presenting God's Divine Words. Secondly, we must become ever so careful about false teachings, distractions, contradictions, and misrepresentations while guarding what has been entrusted to us. Thirdly, we should not get lost in debates and discussions that do not contribute to our Spiritual Growth.

For these corresponding and conveying reasons, and with heightened responsibility and stewardship, *Spiritual Cleansing* plays a vital role in keeping the Divine Portals of Communication open and uninterrupted with our Heavenly Father. Here is how 1 Timothy 6:20 advises us about this matter: *"O Timothy! Guard what was committed to your trust, avoiding the profane and idle babblings and contradictions of what is falsely called knowledge."*

What if we cannot handle all the moving pieces of God on our own? The Holy Spirit gives you the power to do what you cannot do in your own strength while Spiritually Illuminating the power of change. For this reason, *As It Pleases God*, you must master these four aspects (Mind, Body, Soul, and Spirit) of who you are, and you will then find that making the appropriate adjustments with the use of the Fruits of the Spirit and exhibiting Christlike Character will become a piece of cake, Guaranteed!

From the Ancient of Days, as a part of the *Spiritual Cleansing* Process, there are times when we are required to fast. Really? Yes, really! Above all, in *Divine Cleansing* and overcoming life's most difficult challenges, Matthew 17:21 says: *"However, this kind does not go out except by prayer and fasting."*

What is our kind? In a world filled with challenges and obstacles, our kind can be anything. Truthfully, we often find ourselves grappling with various forms of strongholds without realizing what they are. In reality, whatever kind of stronghold we are faced with can possess a known or unknown yoke, manifesting as emotional struggles, mental barriers, hidden trauma, or even Spiritual Yokes that weigh us down from the inside out. Regardless of the nature or its kind, it is getting to *The Fasting Part* that really matters the most.

Furthermore, to confront and overcome the challenges we face with a deep commitment to seeking Divine Clarity, Supernatural Strength, and Foolproof Help, it is only wise to use our hidden Superpower of fasting to break bonds, sever yokes, confront strongholds, break chains, and cut ties. Unfortunately, this Spiritual Commitment is not a one-time efforting occurrence but an ongoing process, *As It Pleases God*.

The Fasting Part

In connecting to the Heavenly of Heavens for *Divine Etiquette* the way God intended, we must incorporate some type of Spiritual Fast on occasion with our prayer and meditation edifices. We will discuss prayer and meditation in depth in the next chapter, but for the *Divine Cleansing* Process, we must include *The Fasting Part* in this one, sprinkled with a little prayer.

How do we make prayer make sense? It is often viewed as a direct line of communication with God, *Spirit to Spirit*. Often, it can become a begging, griping, bossy, manipulative, or complaining session. However, *Divine Etiquette: As It Pleases God*® wants us to understand it should be used as a time of expressing gratitude, seeking guidance, confessing sins, forgiving ourselves and others, repenting for known and unknown issues, and requesting help. In our *Spirit to Spirit* alone time with our Heavenly Father, *As It Pleases Him*, is indeed our reflection, growth, and time of unfiltered intimacy that we will discuss in the next chapter.

Now, the question is, 'What is *The Fasting Part* for a Bloodwashed Believer all about?' Fasting is voluntarily

Divine Cleansing

sacrificing (giving up something) before God, our Heavenly Father, especially when praying and meditating or doing a Soulful or *Divine Cleansing*.

In the Eye of God, fasting is a way to transformatively purify the Mind, Body, and Soul, focus on Spiritual Growth, and become closer to Him and *As It Pleases Him*. Spiritually Speaking, it is a time of self-reflection, self-discipline, self-control, self-mirroring, and self-denial, where individuals abstain from foods, drinks, or other earthly pleasures for a certain period of time. The act of fasting is seen as a way to strengthen one's faith, power, or anointing, demonstrating obedience and devotion to God. Then again, it is also used to gain a deeper understanding or break down one's weaknesses, soul ties, yokes, and limitations.

Fasting is to be used to receive the fullness, guidance, and power of the Holy Spirit flowing through you. As a forewarning, it is not to be used as a weapon to get money, houses, cars, or other worldly possessions. These things may come as a result of a fast, but fasting primarily for material gain is considered a fast for the wrong reason.

Although there are many different types of fasts, you must choose what works for you, your body type, or your health condition. The *Divine Etiquette*: Type of Fast List will help you decide what works best for you. While fasting can offer certain Spiritual Advantages, it is crucial to approach this practice with caution and responsibility. As a FORMAL DISCLOSURE for *Divine Etiquette: As It Pleases God*®, please consult your physician or a healthcare professional before engaging in any fast.

With *Divine Etiquette: As It Pleases God*®, we believe that approaching every aspect of our lives with grace, respect, and kindness is fundamental to living in alignment with Divine Principles, *As It Pleases God*. Our mission is to cultivate an environment where love, compassion, and understanding guide our actions, thoughts, beliefs, and interactions with

Divine Cleansing

others. We do not diagnose or treat health conditions under any circumstances; therefore, the fasting period is a personal choice and is not intended as a substitute for medical treatment.

Listed below are the acceptable types of fasts that we can engage in for a *Divine Cleansing* of the Mind, Body, Soul, and Spirit, but not limited to such:

- ☐ **WATER FAST**: This involves consuming only water for a certain period of time, usually ranging from 24 hours to several days.

- ☐ **JUICE FAST**: This involves consuming only fruit and vegetable juices for a certain period of time, usually ranging from a few days to several weeks.

- ☐ **LIQUIDS ONLY FAST**: This involves consuming only liquids such as water, tea, and broths for a certain period of time, usually ranging from several days to a week.

- ☐ **FRUIT FAST**: This involves consuming only fruits for a certain period of time, usually ranging from a few days to a week.

- ☐ **VEGETABLE FAST**: This involves consuming only vegetables for a certain period of time, usually ranging from a few days to a week.

- ☐ **PARTIAL FAST**: Eating one meal a day or sacrificing a meal a day. This fast involves cutting out certain foods or food groups for a certain period of time, usually for personal, Religious, or Spiritual Reasons.

Divine Cleansing

- ☐ **COMPLETE FAST**: This involves abstaining from all food and drink for a certain period of time, usually for personal, Religious, or Spiritual Reasons.

- ☐ **MEAT FAST**: Refraining from eating meat only. This involves abstaining from meat, fish, and other animal products on certain days of the month, usually ranging from a few days to a week.

- ☐ **MASTER CLEANSE FAST**: This involves drinking a mixture of real lemon juice, organic maple syrup, real ginger (optional), and cayenne pepper for a certain period of time, usually ranging from several days to a week.

- ☐ **INTERMITTENT FASTING**: This involves alternating periods of eating and fasting, usually on a daily or weekly basis.

- ☐ **DANIEL FAST**: This involves consuming only fruits, vegetables, and grains for a certain period of time, usually for personal, Religious, or Spiritual Reasons.

- ☐ **DRY FAST**: This involves abstaining from all food and drink, including water, for a certain period of time, usually ranging from 12 to 24 hours.

- ☐ **TECHNOLOGY FAST**: Sacrificing or abstaining from Television, Social Media, Phone Engagements, and so on.

- ☐ **ACTIVITY FAST**: Sacrificing or abstaining from extracurricular activities, hobbies, or habits.

Divine Cleansing

☐ **SEX FAST**: Sacrificing or abstaining from sexual relations or used when breaking soul ties, bad habits, and prolonged lusts from the inside out.

Which type of fast should we choose? If one is 100% healthy and physician-approved to embark upon a fast, one must also take it to God, our Heavenly Father, in prayer, *Spirit to Spirit*, to determine which one is appropriate.

In short, fasting is a proven practice that can lead to profound *Spiritual Growth* and Divine Transformation, *As It Pleases God*. Where is the proof? The enforceable foolproof is located in Isaiah 58:6: *"Is not this the fast that I have chosen: To loose the bonds of wickedness, to undo the heavy burdens, to let the oppressed go free, and that you break every yoke?"*

Can fasting really help Believers break Spiritual Yokes? Absolutely. Now, according to the Heavenly of Heavens, we cannot limit our fasting privileges or capabilities to breaking Spiritual Yokes only. Although our burdens, sins, or oppressive forces can weigh heavily on us with emotional turmoil, recurring traumas, or negative thought patterns, we still have a Spiritual Tool called fasting that can help us, especially if we wholeheartedly allow it to do so while getting ourselves out of the way.

In addition to drawing closer to God, seeking clarity, and breaking Spiritual Bonds, fasting helps us develop Spiritual Discipline, Humility, Growth, and Awareness Mentally, Physically, Emotionally, and Spiritually. If we are in doubt when doing our part in fasting, repeat Matthew 11:28-30 back to God, *Spirit to Spirit*, saying: Father, my God, Who Art in Heaven, You said in Your Word, *"Come to Me, all you who labor and are heavy laden, and I will give you rest. Take My yoke upon you and learn from Me, for I am gentle and lowly in heart, and you will find rest for your souls. For My yoke is easy and My burden is light."* For this,

Divine Cleansing

O Lord, I place a Spiritual Demand on this Scripture with the *Spiritual Growth* necessary, in the Name of Jesus. Amen.

Are we really demanding God? No, we are not demanding Him to do anything as a form of entitlement. We are only coming to a realization, placing a Spiritual Demand or taking Divine Possession of what is already ours, similar to a diamond in the rough. Just as a diamond, hidden within layers of dirt, rocks, and debris, requires skilled hands to extract it, our Spiritual Gifts, Potential, and Blueprint necessitate an active engagement with them as well.

If we do not place a demand, then who will? Tapping into the Divine Resources is nothing new; the TREASURES that lie beneath the surface are waiting for our Divine Awakening and to be Divinely Unveiled.

According to the Heavenly of Heavens, overlooking the vast treasures that lie just beneath the surface is not going to cut it anymore. We are being Divinely Called to tap into the Divine Resources that are readily available to us instead of sobbing and thinking everyone else is better than us or whitewashing the truth. What is the truth? *"You are a chosen generation, a royal priesthood, a holy nation, His own special people, that you may proclaim the praises of Him who called you out of darkness into His marvelous light."* 1 Peter 2:9.

For the record, everyone is given a GIFT or SOMETHING to work with. It is our responsibility to find it, proactively work on it step by step, and then present it, *As It Pleases God.* In my opinion, if we are incorporating a fast amid doing so, it can indeed help the unveiling process and demand more from ourselves than what we are getting. Here is the Spiritual Seal to use: *"For we are His workmanship, created in Christ Jesus for good works, which God prepared beforehand that we should walk in them."* Ephesians 2:10.

Why must we demand more from ourselves and place a Spiritual Seal as Believers? We often expect God to drop everything in our laps while not realizing He has already given us what we need in Earthen Vessels. Simply put, there are HIDDEN TREASURES within each of us, and they are not going to come forth without us extending the extra effort or putting in the work. What does this mean? Let us take it to Scripture: *"But we have this treasure in earthen vessels, that the excellence of the power may be of God and not of us."* 2 Corinthians 4:7. When they are PLEASING to God, He will give us Divine Access to more of whatever we need according to our Predestined Blueprint. Still, we must do our part!

To bring our Hidden Gems to light or unearth them, they need positive awareness, intention, nurturing, selflessness, and action, *As It Pleases God*. Once we begin to operate in this manner, we will find that we will naturally want to function in the Spirit of Excellence, even amid our imperfections, when redefining our narratives, or when releasing our limited belief systems to become a work-in-progress. Here is the Divine Secret that is no longer a secret, according to Colossians 3:2: *"Set your mind on things above, not on things on the earth."*

What is the big deal about the above factors for Believers? In *Divine Etiquette*, this is the expected heart posture God is looking for in each of us, according to Matthew 13:44. It says, *"Again, the kingdom of heaven is like treasure hidden in a field, which a man found and hid; and for joy over it he goes and sells all that he has and buys that field."* What field is this? YOU, the real Spiritual You, to be exact.

The GREATER VALUE in the Eye of God lies within each of us; therefore, we must invest in our *Spiritual Growth* Process to ensure we extract all that He has placed within us in Earthen Vessels.

Chapter Ten

Spiritual Growth

When we merge *Spiritual Growth* with *Divine Etiquette: As It Pleases God*®, we open the Divine Gateway of the EXTRA and the SUPER. In the Eye of God, the Extra pertains to the Extraordinary, Extra Favor, Extra Power, Extra, Extra, Extra Everything. The Super is related to the sneak peek into the Supernatural Realm (the beyond human experiences) without having Spiritual Violations or Consuming Fears.

In the Eye of God, this POWERHOUSE COMBINATION is top-notch and unmatched for our Heaven on Earth Experiences. One of which self-discovery and enlightenment, *As It Pleases God*, are designed to illuminate the Divine Pathway of Greatness, allowing us to embody the Divine Harmony and Love needed to bring us into Divine Oneness. In my opinion, it makes our Spiritual Fruits authentically palatable in all of our interactions while helping us to self-correct at the drop of a dime.

Spiritual Growth

In honoring a Sacred Life, this type of *Spiritual Growth* also grants us a deeper understanding of ourselves, others, and our Divine Purpose, allowing us to Spiritually Till our own grounds. More importantly, it also assists with our connection to the Kingdom of God and His Spiritual Perspectives, Secrets, Treasures, and Wisdom. All of which makes us the Crème de la Crème in *Divine Etiquette: As It Pleases God*®.

What makes *Spiritual Growth* and *Divine Etiquette* so different for Believers? When God is involved in our respectful interactions, *As It Pleases Him*, such as with kind mindfulness in communicative people skills, things change for the better. Also, there is an appreciation and reverence for the Divine Innerworkings of the Holy Spirit in ourselves and those around us. Lastly, when the Blood of Jesus covers us, we can embrace this Powerhouse Combination.

This dynamic duo not only enhances our Spiritual Journeys, but it also brings us closer to manifesting our Heaven on Earth Experiences in Earthen Vessels, *As It Pleases God*. How so? In all simplicity, it is with one mindful interaction or step at a time with a work-in-progress mindset using the Fruits of the Spirit. At the same time, it incorporates us self-checking or self-governing *Our Attitudes* along the way to ensure we are behaving Christlike.

Our Attitudes

In today's fast-paced and right now world, we often look for quick fixes to life's complex problems, forgetting that *Our Attitudes* can really make, create, de-escalate, or resolve problems. When dealing with intangibles like attitudes,

Spiritual Growth

emotions, and mindsets, the answer to *Our Attitude* is not found or sold in a pill bottle.

Many things can be purchased with the right amount of money, but a Righteous Attitude or Character cannot, not even for a TRILLION DOLLARS or more. In the Eye of God, it takes awareness, work, introspection, practice, and genuine effort.

What does all of this attitude jargon mean for Believers? All it means is that your attitude is developed. Suppose you want all that life has to offer you, or you desire to become the Crème de la Crème of Kingdom Poshness. In this case, you must get with the program and adjust your attitude accordingly, especially if you desire for an overabundance of Spiritual Provisions to come flowing your way.

Why must we adjust our attitudes, *As It Pleases God*? It is indeed a Spiritual Magnet based upon your self-talk, self-perception, thought process, and how you treat others, especially when no one is looking. In addition, *Our Attitudes* shape our perceptions and interactions with the world around us, be it good, bad, or indifferent. Above all, it influences our biological processes of how we respond to challenges, setbacks, rejection, fear, and failure.

However, medication can treat the symptoms stemming from our biological responses or neglectfulness. Still, it does not address the underlying attitudes, root causes, or negative patterns that contribute to our conditions. As a part of our *Spiritual Growth*, it is our responsibility to take whatever it is or is not to the Lord, *Spirit to Spirit*, for self-reflection and how to reverse negatives into positives properly.

Contrary to what most would think, the UNVEILING of your Divine Blueprint will depend on your attitude, not your aptitude. What do *Our Attitudes* have to do with anything, as long as we are Believers? In the Kingdom, it plays a vital role. Have you ever had someone approach you, claiming to be a Messenger of God, and they treated you worse than someone you know sent straight from the Pits of Hell? Only to have you left scratching your head in dismay or feeling like the scum of the earth. Personally, I know I have, and this is WHY I am NOT sugarcoating the truth. Fortunately, this is another reason why a good, positive attitude is essential for becoming and remaining a Divinely Appointed Representative of the Kingdom.

Why is Kingdom Citizenship so conciliant regarding *Our Attitudes* as Believers? Please allow me to break it down for you: Your attitude is the way you act or behave, displaying what you feel, think, and believe, as well as your biases, sometimes without having to say one word. It is also a direct compilation of your emotional state, reflected in your image, thoughts, actions, reactions, and how you speak. It is nothing more than your character covered by your personality traits, governing your Divine Destiny, or the chains holding you back from it.

It is common in today's world to have your personality differ from your character. Your character is a distinctive trait or quality, setting a pattern of behavior related directly to your morals. A positive attitude attracts people, and a negative attitude will repel them, even if they do not admit it. Frankly, this is how we get those in a committed relationship blocking, avoiding, or outright developing a deaf ear to each other.

The Emotional, Mental, Physical, and Spiritual battles begin when there are inconsistencies between your character, personality, or superficial masks. Inconsistency gives room for your attitude to change depending on the situation, conditions, or circumstances. Unfortunately, this usually will lead to you scaring people off before they get too close, discovering who you really are behind closed doors.

Spiritual Growth

When attitudinal inconsistencies are present, you can assume three, four, five, or as many faces as your soul needs to cover up the real you. Why do we need so many faces? One would often assume another face to protect oneself from shame, fears, and insecurities or to cover up embarrassments, failures, or defeats, leading to self-hatred or issues with esteem.

Unbeknown to most, each face takes energy, so the more faces we assume, the more exhausted we are at the end of the day. Is this really happening? Absolutely! Why should we become aware of each mask assumed? First, a mask is no more than a cover-up or whitewash. Secondly, it determines how we treat others, especially when no one is looking or when we think we can get away with our behaviors.

Listen, and listen to me well; if someone throws anything together or makes a conscious attempt to serve me shambles, all types of RED FLAGS go up. Why the red flags? It is a sign of deceit, contempt, or debauchery, especially when they know what they are doing and do not inform me in advance regarding their intentions.

Is issuing red flags not considered judging? Absolutely not! It is called paying attention to their fruits, for they bring forth the Tree of Life or Death to the human psyche. For example, if someone knowingly SERVES you rotten fruits, vegetables, or meat, Mentally, Physically, Emotionally, or Spiritually, it is a sign of charactorial trauma or lack of integrity. So, beware!

More importantly, the moment we step into a phase of spying on others or violating their privacy, it takes the trauma of the human psyche up a notch, escalating our charactorial flaws. Why is the escalating occurring within the human psyche? In an age marked by unprecedented technological advancement, social unrest, and backhanded insults, we leave ourselves open to consuming negativity without Spiritual Boundaries. Therefore, it becomes increasingly critical to examine the Spiritual Dimensions of our current condition through our Spiritual Lenses, *As It Pleases God*.

Why do we need to add God into the equation? The Spiritual Violation of man's free will is one of the reasons we are in the sensitive state that we are in now! Really? Yes, really. Although God knows everything about us, He still does not violate our Spiritual Rights or *Free Will*. So, what makes us think for a minute we can sum up a person's life with our thwarted perceptions and get away with it? We cannot! *Free Will* is *Free Will*, and we as Believers must respect this fact, even if we do not agree with God's Method of Operation or His ways of Spiritually Training His sheep.

Free Will

For the record, *Free Will* in the Eye of God is considered a CORNERSTONE of our human existence. It represents our ability to make choices unencumbered by people or any external forces, allowing us to forge our paths in life, pursue dreams, engage in relationships of choice, and so on. Nevertheless, when the *Free Will* of mankind is compromised, it invokes a Spiritual Uprising from the Heavenly of Heavens. Let me say this before moving on: When the Heavens are against us for whatever reason, the Vicissitudes and Cycles of Life will begin to do a number on us from the inside out with disconnection, disillusionment, and despair.

Understanding the severity of *Free Will* violations is often overlooked because we seem to get what we want through control and authoritarianism. Still, in the Eye of God, He will begin to view us as an enemy when attempting to disrupt the Divine Blueprint of another without permission. Even Satan gets permission from God to afflict us. Take a look at the Book of Job in the Bible; this is all the proof we need. Yet, we as humans seemingly attempt to override the Divine Will of

Spiritual Growth

God for mankind, doing whatever, whenever, however, whyever, and with whomever without consulting Him whatsoever.

Unbeknown to most, *Free Will* is tied to our Divine Purpose, Predestined Blueprinted Mission, Sense of Identity, rational choices, and decision-making faculties.

The price of disobedience or violating someone's *Free Will* usually entails traumatizing ourselves further with some form of an identity crisis, uncontrollable habits tied to the lust of the eyes and flesh, or a superfluous hunger for power, money, or sex. Plus, if our math is not mathing with our efforts in life, this is usually the calculations that are debauched.

In addition, when *Free Will* is muffled or hijacked by another, the repercussions can be profoundly yoking in more ways than one. How so? Unfortunately, this is why we overlook the God-Given treasures hidden in plain sight. Through silent acts of idolatry, we unknowingly pick up trash, destroying us rather than building us. And then, we have the nerve to blame God. Better yet, we ask Him to clean up our messes without truly understanding WHY we got ourselves in a mess in the first place.

Can we really pick up trash and debris as Believers? Absolutely. No one is exempt from this process, and this is how we learn the Spiritual Duality between trash and treasures, good or bad fruits, building and destroying, and so on. Plus, it happened to me, and this is how I am able to bring forth such Divinely Relevant Information for a time such as this. Above all, I learned how to mind my business without violating the *Free Will* of another, allowing people to choose for themselves without beating them over the head with the Bible.

How can I say such a thing, right? If we are consumed by snooping, outing people, or controlling God's precious sheep, there is a problem with the Attitudinal Values, Character, and Perception in the Eye of God.

Spiritual Growth

What do our attitudes have to do with snooping? From a Spiritual Perspective, they are both grouped into the Spirit of Defiance. And, if we are bold enough to play god or become a demigod, then we are bold enough to accept the consequences and repercussions of violating someone's *Free Will*.

What is the purpose of knowing this information? When dealing with *Spiritual Growth* while obtaining the work-in-progress mindset, *As It Pleases God*, we cannot become caught up in *Free Will* violations as such.

Listen, if someone offers the open book of their Testimony, then we are free to partake of the willfully given information. But if we are developing or concocting a testimony and attaching a name to it based on our insecurities, traumas, downfalls, biases, perceptions, and so on, for clickbait, social status, or to destroy lives or hurt someone, we change the rules of the game. Is this Biblical? I would have it no other way: *"These six things the LORD hates, Yes, seven are an abomination to Him: A proud look, A lying tongue, Hands that shed innocent blood, A heart that devises wicked plans, Feet that are swift in running to evil, A false witness who speaks lies, And one who sows discord among brethren."* Proverbs 6:16-19.

The Expectations of the Kingdom are set in motion to work for us, not against us; therefore, it is imperative to get a proper understanding of our *Spiritual Power Tools*.

Spiritual Power Tool

In understanding the *Real You*, the true power of your Divine Blueprint or DNA is wrapped up in your ability to PRAY. Prayer has been the most POWERFUL key to my survival, not just in the bad times or moments of desperation, but in the good times as well. It has been a great *Spiritual Power Tool* that has changed my life tremendously. I thank God for the Power of Prayer and my ability to share this information with you.

Spiritual Growth

Prayer is the communication of a sincere, humble request to God. Praying intensifies your ability to face life, make the right decisions, and have the *Spiritual Growth* to keep you on a straight and narrow path in seeking the Righteousness of God.

In addition, prayer gives you Spiritual Access to Spiritual Gifts, Divine Answers, Heavenly Strategies, Kingdom Mysteries, and *Spirit to Spirit* Downloads. It is also the Spiritual Key to your Divine Blessings, Birthrights, Predestined Blueprint, and Spiritual Freedom from bondage, yokes, and blockages. However, the essential ingredients in the Edifices of the Kingdom must be used in conjunction with Unwavering Faith, Spiritual Fruits, and Christlike Character.

When using prayer as a *Spiritual Power Tool*, it gives you the ability to confess your thoughts, troubles, weaknesses, sins, strengths, idiosyncrasies, desires, thanksgivings, faithfulness, and dependency on someone other than yourself. You do not have to go to college, acquire a particular skill, or get a license to attain dynamic praying abilities. With Him, you can go for what you know. In a sense, from my perspective, talk to God like you are speaking to your best friend, but as an ARCHITECTURAL FRIEND.

Why should we speak to God as an Architectural Friend? Is this not blasphemy? Absolutely not! Your Heavenly Father has your Divine Blueprint with all of the intricate details given to no one outside of the Holy Spirit. Plus, your Predestined Blueprint is covered under the Blood of Jesus, giving you Divine Access once the Spiritual Criterias are met, *As It Pleases God*!

Moreover, with a work-in-progress mindset of seeking Divine Guidance with intentionality, we have the Divine Right to approach God with a creative brainstorming session. The only thing about this is that we must come with pen and paper ready to document regarding whatever, whenever,

Spiritual Growth

however, whyever, and about whomever. Need I say more? Of course, there is more; let us talk about it.

Picturesquely, this is similar to Noah building the Ark with instructions. Here is how to approach Him with an Architectural Posture:

- ☐ Question about What, When, Where, How, Why, and with Whom.
- ☐ Question about form, style, system, and conveyance.
- ☐ Question about materials, uses, and avoidances.
- ☐ Question about who or what to use.
- ☐ Question about who is included or excluded.
- ☐ Question about start-up and conclusion.
- ☐ Question the purpose of whatever with whomever.
- ☐ Seek feedback on form and structure.
- ☐ Ask for clarity and understanding.
- ☐ Ask the question, 'How can I make this better?'
- ☐ Ask the question, 'What do I need to do to improve the strength of _____?'

In your *Spirit to Spirit* alone time to develop your *Spiritual Superpower Tools*, approach your Spiritual Discussions with an open mind, ready to receive constructive feedback for Divine Refining.

On the other hand, with all due respect, when you go to a friend or foe about your issues before going to God, expect to become misled or misdirected, especially if He is nowhere in the equation. For this reason, always take whatever it is to God FIRST in prayer before attempting to take it to someone else.

What is the purpose of seeking God before sharing with others? First and foremost, to follow proper Spiritual Protocol. Secondly, giving Him time to go before you to prepare the way or send confirmation through someone else.

Spiritual Growth

Thirdly, it helps to place a Spiritual Seal on your trust in the Holy Trinity. As Mark 11:24 says, *"Whatever things you ask when you pray, believe that you receive them, and you will have them."*

Here is where most go astray; they may repent and pray about whatever they are experiencing, but they do not replace the negative emotion, act, word, or habit with a positive one. Unfortunately, they leave it open. Open to what? Anything! For example, anything or anyone can come into your house if you leave the door open long enough, right? Well, the same principle applies to our prayers as well.

Unfortunately, this is one of the reasons we have *Unanswered Prayers*, stunting our *Spiritual Growth* while appearing to do everything right with the powerful conduit of prayer. To say the least, the disheartening reality of feeling as if we are not getting through or breaking ground with God really affects us. How so? We tend to secretly give up due to feelings of being utterly confused, disillusioned, and seemingly stagnant, as we are sometimes mocked or shamed for praying and believing in Him. As a unique catalyst for *Spiritual Growth*, it is time to stop lying to ourselves about this matter and get to the introspective root cause, *As It Pleases Him*.

Unanswered Prayers

Amidst this whirlwind of change and transformation, many find themselves grappling with *Unanswered Prayers* that can hinder *Spiritual Growth* and Development. The feelings of stagnation and disappointment are real, stemming from our unmet needs, desires, and expectations. Which, in my opinion, can sometimes appear like yokes and roadblocks on our Spiritual Journey.

Regardless of real or imagined blockages, we all have had unanswered prayers hindering our *Spiritual Growth*, causing us to question our faith, feel abandoned, or struggle with feelings of inadequacy. If not, just live a little longer. The growing pains of life are not for the weak; it has a way of trying us until we decide to become stronger, wiser, and more astute in the Eye of God.

Is it by force? Absolutely not. When we make free will choices, there are always positive or negative consequences or repercussions associated. Due to the natural elements of Spiritual Dualism involved, we must begin to examine our motives, postures, and desires.

Nevertheless, once we begin to reap the consequences of our not-so-good decisions, we sometimes feel that we have been dealt a bad hand or that life is really brutal. When, in all actuality, it was indeed our choice made out of willful disobedience, negligence, or selfishness. As a matter of fact, when we act out of impulsiveness or self-interest, the consequences may reveal themselves slowly, often taking us by surprise and appearing out of nowhere. Although it is sometimes hard to admit, most often, this is one of the reasons for Godly silence.

Why would God not answer us? The reasons may vary from person to person, situation to situation, mindset to mindset, lesson to lesson, and so on. In the reflecting process, James 4:2-3 may have a valid point here: *"You lust and do not have. You murder and covet and cannot obtain. You fight and war. Yet you do not have because you do not ask. You ask and do not receive, because you ask amiss, that you may spend it on your pleasures."*

How can we pray amiss, especially when it is a heartfelt prayer? When dealing with the heart, unforgiveness has held more people back from receiving than anything known to mankind. Here is how God feels about this matter: *"And whenever you stand praying, if you have anything against anyone, forgive him, that your Father in Heaven may also forgive you your trespasses. But if you do not forgive, neither will your Father in Heaven forgive your trespasses."* Mark 11:25-26.

Spiritual Growth

The bottom line is that when dealing with *Unanswered Prayers*, it is imperative to check our level of repentance. Then again, we must also deal with a few things that have an undertone of UNFORGIVENESS residing from within, but not limited to such:

- ☐ The lust of the eyes, the lust of the flesh, and the pride of life.
- ☐ Murdering others Mentally, Physically, Emotionally, Financially, or Spiritually.
- ☐ Coveting and competitiveness.
- ☐ Jealousy and envy.
- ☐ Fussing, fighting, and chaos.

Can these things really facilitate *Unanswered Prayers*? Absolutely. When seeking comfort, guidance, or intervention from our Heavenly Father, negative charactorial traits, such as bitterness, hatred, anger, lack of empathy, untamed lusts, outright disobedience, and boastful pride, are the most prominent hindrances known to mankind. In addition, they are also the most ungoverned and unchecked hindering factors in PRAYER SABOTAGE as well. Unfortunately, this goes beyond self-sabotage into Spiritual Sabotage, clouding our Divine Access to certain Promises, Wisdom, and Treasures of the Kingdom.

According to the Heavenly of Heavens, we often look for our prayer obstacles outside of ourselves, but in the Eye of God, it begins from within the human psyche. Being that the psyche is unseen, it often gets overlooked or downplayed, erecting formidable barriers in our *Spirit to Spirit* Relations with our Heavenly Father. While simultaneously tainting our mind and heart postures, intents, or openness with all forms of divisiveness and lies, while appearing right in our own eyes. Is this really happening? Absolutely. It is taking place right

Spiritual Growth

before our very eyes, from the pews to the pulpit, with a grace justification that will make us hang our heads down in shame.

Why the shame and unease among Believers? We are bringing the pimp and prostitute mindsets and heart postures into God's face to control the narratives of ourselves and others as if He does not know what is going on from within. The manipulative infiltration of our places of worship has God giving us a major side-eye, especially when we are silently helping others to control God's Divine Narrative to satiate our hidden agendas. What is the big deal here? Instead of seeking God for who He is and what He wants, we risk approaching Him as if He were merely a means to an end, a provider to fulfill our self-serving needs, wants, desires, and agendas.

What is God requiring of us to get our prayers answered? He needs authenticity, humility, deep introspection, integrity, and surrender to His Divine Will and our Predestined Blueprint, leading all things back to Him, *As It Pleases Him*. As congregants, leaders, sheep, shepherds, or whatever we call ourselves, we should not be leading all things back to ourselves with entitlement or transactional faith. Nor should we build our arsenals to character assassinate or thumb our noses at God's precious sheep, even if we feel as if we have one up on them or feel as if they are beneath us.

Due to unsettling realities and inappropriate mindsets, the *Unanswered Prayer* Chart is designed to get your wheels turning in the right direction when it comes down to praying. Here are a few other items that lead to *Unanswered Prayers* in the Eye of God, but not limited to such:

- ☐ God wants you to wait.
- ☐ You are wayward in your approach.
- ☐ You are in an unrepentant state.
- ☐ You already know the answer is 'No.'

Spiritual Growth

- ☐ You are in a Spiritual Classroom.
- ☐ You have not done your homework or research.
- ☐ You know better, but choose NOT to do better.
- ☐ You have not taken the time to search the scriptures for the answer.
- ☐ You have developed a deaf ear to God.
- ☐ You are asking amissly.
- ☐ You are violating the free will of another.
- ☐ You already have the answer that you did not accept.
- ☐ You are not exhibiting the Fruits of the Spirit.
- ☐ You are outright contradicting Spiritual Protocol, Principles, or Laws.
- ☐ You are using God as a psychic reader.
- ☐ You lack faith.
- ☐ You are complaining.
- ☐ You are operating in an UNGRATEFUL SPIRIT.
- ☐ You have forgotten about or have not given THANKS for your previous Blessings.
- ☐ You are unwilling to learn or resolve your brokenness, mistakes, or mishaps.
- ☐ You are negatively cynical and judgmental.
- ☐ You are stuck in a slave, excuse, or victim mentality.
- ☐ You are stuck in the past and unwilling to move forward.
- ☐ You are very combative while locked on being reactive, responding to everything or anyone.
- ☐ You are extremely divisive, playing slick.
- ☐ You are abusive or destructive.
- ☐ You are lazy, uninspired, or unmotivated.
- ☐ You lack the commitment to the Will of God.
- ☐ You are constantly lying to yourself, others, and God.
- ☐ You are behaving like a stiff-necked person, being lukewarm or dull.
- ☐ You are engaging in idolatry.

Spiritual Growth

- ☐ You are a wolf in sheep's clothing, dabbling in unrighteousness.
- ☐ You are looming curses over the innocent.
- ☐ You are wallowing in a pool of unforgiveness.
- ☐ You are prostituting God or His Kingdom.
- ☐ You are being manipulative, conniving, or scheming.

While *Unanswered Prayers* can leave you questioning your faith, it does not have to remain so. If you are praying amiss, God is bigger than any problem you are facing. Do not be afraid to go to Him, for He knows all, and He will guide you. If there is a situation with you, your relationships, your children, or on the job, whatever it is, place it in His hands and leave it there. There is no need for complaints if you put Him in control. Just REPENT, FORGIVE, give THANKS, learn, prepare, and consider it done. Frankly, this is where your faith comes in! *"Yet if anyone suffers as a Christian, let him not be ashamed, but let him glorify God in this matter."* 1 Peter 4:16.

Is praying difficult? Only if you make it. Here is how to keep it simple: When praying, include this checklist:

- ☐ Find a quiet space with little or no distractions.
- ☐ Greet God, *Spirit to Spirit*.
- ☐ Direct the prayer specifically to your 'Heavenly Father.'
- ☐ Usher in the Divine Presence of the Holy Spirit.
- ☐ Cover yourself, your family, your home, your job, or whatever with the Blood of Jesus.
- ☐ Proactively repent for known and unknown sins, thoughts, behaviors, desires, habits, or words.
- ☐ Forgive yourself and others.
- ☐ Ask God for what you need or make a petition.
- ☐ Rebuke or cast down evil or negativity while replacing it with scriptures or positive affirmations.
- ☐ Pray for others.

Spiritual Growth

- ☐ Ask for guidance, strength, and understanding.
- ☐ Document requests, instructions, advice, or answers in your Spiritual Journal.
- ☐ Give THANKS.
- ☐ Spiritually Seal the prayer with 'In Jesus' Name, AMEN.'

Is this checklist foolproof? Nothing is foolproof with God if you do not activate your faith in Him or operate *As It Pleases Him*. Nonetheless, if you follow the instructions in this book, *Divine Etiquette*, you will be well on your way to making this checklist Divinely Foolproof.

Now, if you opt not to use this checklist, you can always ask God to teach you how to pray, *As It Pleases Him*. Here is the Spiritual Leverage you need: "Likewise the Spirit also helps in our weaknesses. For we do not know what we should pray for as we ought, but the Spirit Himself makes intercession for us with groanings which cannot be uttered. Now He who searches the hearts knows what the mind of the Spirit is, because He makes intercession for the saints according to the will of God. And we know that all things work together for good to those who love God, to those who are the called according to His purpose." Romans 8:26-28.

Additionally, if you do not have wisdom, courage, or strength, ask for it! You may say at times, 'God knows what I need,' and you are right. He knows what you need before you ask. But He wants you to know and understand what you need as well, with a willful *Spirit to Spirit* AGREEMENT between you and Him.

What if we are not ready for a *Spirit to Spirit* Agreement with God? He adds no pressure; simply include Him in the equation of all things with a work-in-progress mindset.

When operating with a righteous heart and mind posture when praying, keep asking for God's Divine Will to be done,

Spiritual Growth

and you will be given what you ask for when the time is right. Here are the Spiritual Seals that are Divinely Enforceable: *"Therefore I say to you, whatever things you ask when you pray, believe that you receive them, and you will have them."* Mark 11:24. *"For everyone who asks receives, and he who seeks finds, and to him who knocks it will be opened."* Matthew 7:8. Make sure you incorporate the Fruits of the Spirit and Christlike Character while aligning it with the Word or Will of God.

Why must we pray with the Fruits of the Spirit in mind while behaving Christlike? Praying amissly with debauched motives will get us in trouble in or out of the Kingdom.

When canceling, replacing, and sealing the COVENANT AGREEMENT with God through Scriptures, it is okay to personalize them to fit our *Spirit to Spirit* Conversations with Him. However, when canceling a negative trait or attribute, we cannot just cancel it without replacing it. If we cancel without replacing it, then what is going to take the place of what we canceled? My point exactly...NOTHING!

If we do not fill in the blank when canceling, casting down, or rebuking, we leave this blank open for another negative trait or attribute to take its place, defeating the purpose. Therefore, we must complete the process...when we remove or cancel, we must replace it with positive affirmations or scriptures to back it up. This sort of replacement is crucial; we do not want to leave ourselves open to an attack from the enemy. Here is the sample format:

"I cancel out the Spirit of _____; I send it back into the pits of Hell from whence it came. In the Name of Jesus, I usher in the Spirit of_____, SCRIPTURE_____."

As a part of our Spiritual Birthrights, we have the authority and the POWER to cast down or cast out any and all negative

Spiritual Growth

attributes. We do not have to depend upon anyone to do it for us; we simply need the right Spiritual Power Tools and use the proper Spiritual Protocol.

Do not forget that the Word of God is our AMMUNITION. From this point on, it is time out for the 'Woe Unto Me' mentality. We have everything we need inside of us. There is no need to delay or put off anything that needs our attention. Our goal is to make our lives better by owning our issues and creating a win-win situation out of them.

No matter what you are going through, it is best to work it out in a *Spirit to Spirit* Relationship with your Heavenly Father before involving negativity of another kind. Why must we work it out, seeking our own Salvation as a Believer? If you are not well-versed in reversing negatives into positives, God expects you to at least do your homework to get an understanding of whatever or with whomever.

By letting go of your fixed expectations, if you do not know the opposite of something, Google can become your best friend in Spiritually Converting a word. In addition, it can also help you pinpoint Biblical Scriptures to proactively reverse negativity or debauchery before praying. Remember, the Blood of Jesus still works on your behalf, so you may as well use it!

On the other hand, if you find yourself continuing to complain about a situation, circumstance, event, or condition, it indicates you have not placed it in God's hands or have lost faith in Him. Listed below are a few tips on prayer:

- ☐ Never pray to harm someone.
- ☐ Never pray for evil against someone.
- ☐ Never pray for the death of someone.
- ☐ Never pray for total control over someone.
- ☐ Never pray for another person's possessions (coveting).

Spiritual Growth

- ☐ Never pray to force someone to love you or fall in love with you.
- ☐ Never pray to break up someone's home.
- ☐ Never pray to show off your talents to boost your ego.
- ☐ Never pray out of selfishness, pride, or greed.
- ☐ Never pray for someone to do anything against their will.
- ☐ Never pray unwarranted or selfish curses.
- ☐ Never pray for hatred over another.
- ☐ Never pray sadness, sickness, ill will, or debauchery into the life of another.

All of these are negative prayers! If you send out negative prayers, you will reap negativity based on the Law of Reciprocity. What does this mean? In simplicity, the energy you send out through your thoughts, words, and prayers can significantly influence your experiences and the world around you.

Plus, if your prayers are rooted in negativity, resentment, revenge, anger, hatred, or fear, those negative prayers can backfire, landing in your close circle and missing the intended target. For instance, if you pray for someone's downfall out of jealousy, revenge, or anger, you may inadvertently invite misfortune into your own life. So, be very careful about your heart posture and motives while keeping your prayers positive, forgiving, thankful, and merciful.

How do we know if we are wrestling with the potential to send out negative prayers? Truthfully, we all know when our hearts and minds are not right or when there is a stench of envy, jealousy, or pride; we are just in denial. However, as a reminder, listed below are a few indicators, but not limited to such:

- ☐ When we are dealing with negative emotions.
- ☐ When we have a constant bout with bad behavior.

Spiritual Growth

- ☐ When we have uncontrollable, negative mental chatter.
- ☐ When our tongue is abusive, harmful, or untamed.
- ☐ When we are very defensive or resistant.
- ☐ When we are waiting for the worst to happen.
- ☐ When we push our insecurities off on others.
- ☐ When we are very reactive, like a time bomb.
- ☐ When we feel imprisoned, trapped, or blocked.
- ☐ When we are outright, consciencelessly abusive with no regard for human life.
- ☐ When everything revolves around us.
- ☐ When everything is for our benefit only.
- ☐ When we are always feeling sorry for ourselves.
- ☐ When we are wallowing in unresolved trauma.
- ☐ When we create untruths about ourselves or others.
- ☐ When we do everything in our power to avoid loss.
- ☐ When we cannot deal with lack or rejection.
- ☐ When we are addicted to drama or chaos.

God has created everyone with a will of their own; do not attempt to violate another person's ability or free will to choose when you are praying. Always pray for God's Divine Assistance when facing the struggles of others. Whether someone is grappling with personal issues, health problems, financial issues, or emotional turmoil, taking a moment to pray for their well-being can be a transformative act as an intercessor.

As we lift others in prayer with *Divine Etiquette*, there is a difference between interceding with compassion, faith, and empathy with Higher Beliefs, and praying against someone with anger, hate, spitefulness, and deceit with lower intentions. All of which determines if we will become a Healer in the Eye of God with peace and hope, or a destroyer

Spiritual Growth

common to man, evoking chaos, confusion, deceit, and unrighteousness. Does it make a difference? Absolutely!

Suppose the negativity is affecting you personally. In this case, you do have the right to cast down the negative Spirit or Energy of whatever while ushering in positivity and Scriptural Truths. Here is my sample prayer for canceling and replacing: *'I cast down and cancel the Spirit of Deceit, and I usher in the Spirit of Righteousness and Divine Illumination in the Name of Jesus.'* Then, ask for God's will to be done, not yours! *"Nevertheless not My will, but Yours, be done."* Luke 22:42.

Whether we get our prayers answered or not, Spiritual Dualism will still exist to build or tear down. In addition, they are the elements of our sweet-smelling perfumed prayers, fragranced with our deepest desires and intentions, often laced with what we put in them, positively or negatively.

Here is what King David left for us to glean in Psalm 141:2: *"Let my prayer be set before You as incense, the lifting up of my hands as the evening sacrifice."* When our prayers are encompassed with beauty, sweetness, and pleasantness in the Divine Presence of God, we can get His ATTENTION, *Spirit to Spirit*. Really? Yes, Really!

We often grapple with the nature of Spiritual Dualism without having a clue about what we are dealing with or how to move God on its behalf. At its core, Spiritual Dualism is a concept that suggests the coexistence of opposing forces within the Spiritual Realm. Basically, it emphasizes the constant interplay between light and darkness, good and evil, right and wrong, unity and division, and so on. Knowing the difference, *As It Pleases Him*, gives us the upper hand in our prayerfulness and Spiritual Covering. In addition, it enhances our discerning faculties, prompting us to know when to capitalize, hold, fold, reject, or walk away.

How do we get the lower hand as Believers? If we know nothing about Spiritual Dualism while behaving like the

Spiritual Growth

enemy, then how powerful do we become using evil to contend with bad thoughts, words, behaviors, desires, and habits? Unfortunately, we diminish our power, becoming weaker vessels in the Eye of God. Also, we are subjected to the side effects of mockery, rejection, and shamefulness, similar to the Garden of Eden Experience with Adam and Eve.

The lack of understanding about applying Spiritual Dualism to our prayers is how we 'get got' through deceptive measures over our Spiritual Dominion. When dividing ourselves and others for selfish gain or control instead of unifying, *As It Pleases God*, we can sometimes void our ability to become FRUITFUL and MULTIPLY, Mentally, Physically, Emotionally, Spiritually, and Financially for the Greater Good.

In this dualistic framework, positive prayers consist of a few items but are not limited to such:

- ☐ Addressing the prayer with praise to God as the Heavenly Father.
- ☐ Repentance and Forgiveness.
- ☐ Reverence.
- ☐ Asking for God's Divine Will to be done in all aspects of your life.
- ☐ Requesting your provisioning or needs for that day, such as food, strength, wisdom, petition, supplication, and intercession.
- ☐ Thanksgiving. Give thanks for all things.
- ☐ Confession of sins, known and unknown.
- ☐ Protection and deliverance from all temptations.

Conversely, on the opposite side of this dualistic framework, negative prayers consist of a few items, but are not limited to such:

Spiritual Growth

- ☐ Asking the 'Why' questions that violates the free will of another person.
- ☐ Giving God an ultimatum.
- ☐ Payback prayer: 'They hurt me, so, God, show them how it feels.'
- ☐ Placing curses on people using an evil tongue.
- ☐ Hidden agendas or pimping God.
- ☐ Pride and arrogance.
- ☐ Placing non-repenting, unforgiving, or ungrateful requests or decrees.
- ☐ Whining, fussing, condemning, and complaining.

Our lives are Spiritually Marked for *Spiritual Growth* and Abundance, and it is our responsibility to do our part in the matter, Spiritually Tilling our own ground. Unfortunately, we cannot delegate this part of our Heaven on Earth Experience; we must put our hands to the plow and not turn back.

For example, when farmers begin to plow, their attention must be on the channel in front of them. If they frequently look back, the lines they create will be crooked and ineffective, making a mess. Thus, in Earthen Vessels, we must avoid distractions from past experiences or regrets that cause our minds to jump the track or trigger unrest within the psyche.

Are we not supposed to deal with our issues? Yes, we are, but not when plowing! In our moments of rest, we can deal with our issues. Until then, we should check our problems at the door, especially when it is time to put in the work.

Why is putting in the work so important in the Eye of God? The essence of dedication, focus, and obedience is necessary for our Spiritual Journey, *As It Pleases God*. Even Jesus said in

Spiritual Growth

Luke 9:62, *"No one, having put his hand to the plow, and looking back, is fit for the kingdom of God."*

Now, this type of commitment and focus may require us to understand *The Power of Meditation*, but I am sure it will be well worth the endeavor.

The Power of Meditation

In connecting to the Heavenly of Heavens with *Divine Etiquette: As It Pleases God*®, meditation is usually the one vital ingredient missing from the Spiritual Equation. In addition, it is also a possibility that this is one of the reasons *Divine Etiquette* is not a the forefront of a Believer's Repertoire.

A calm and peaceful Spirit is required to maximize the benefits of having the Holy Spirit at our beck and call. In addition, it is also mandated when correctly using the Blood of Jesus as a Spiritual Covering from head to toe. Here is the Spiritual Decree of Consideration: *"Give ear to my words, O LORD, Consider my meditation. Give heed to the voice of my cry, My King and my God, For to You I will pray. My voice You shall hear in the morning, O LORD; In the morning I will direct it to You, And I will look up."* Psalm 5:1-3.

In today's day and age, we are unawaringly taught as a form of deception to live without meditating on the Word of God, or we do not need to do it. However, when *Connecting to the Heavenly of Heavens* on a Divinely Elite Level or partaking of Spiritual Meat, *As It Pleases God*, we must sit ourselves down to quiet the human psyche.

Why must we quiet the psyche? It is fighting for control, and if we do not put it on a short leash, it will begin to run the show, Mentally, Physically, Emotionally, and Spiritually.

We both know that in this fast-paced society in which we live, our minds are bombarded by thoughts, distractions, and external stimuli that can create inner and external turmoil with or without our permission. If we do not learn to bridle our psyche, *As It Pleases God*, it can dominate our lives, running the show in ways that undermine our well-being and releasing a cascade of hormones, including cortisol. And, when too much cortisol is released into our system, it can override the body's 'fight or flight' response with a continual dumping system. Unfortunately, prolonged elevations of cortisol will make us sick.

What does cortisol have to do with the psyche of mankind? Cortisol, often referred to as the 'stress hormone,' plays a significant role in how our body responds to stress and danger. In addition, it regulates a variety of functions, including our metabolism, immune response, and blood pressure. All of which are derived from what is going on within the psyche of mankind.

The psyche, often seen as the seat of our known and unknown thoughts, beliefs, and emotions, has a natural tendency to seek control through varying fears, worries, and traumas. As a result, cortisol is released when we are faced with stress, anxiety, or overwhelming challenges or feelings.

If we leave our psyche unchecked or ungoverned, it can lead us down a path of despair, confusion, and imbalance, even if we think we have it going on. Above all, it can cause us to react impulsively, erratically, waywardly, unwisely, or defensively, creating a Spiritual Disconnect. Conversely, in the Eye of God, we should operate thoughtfully, strategically, or Christlike to release tension and good hormones to promote a Spiritual Connection, *Spirit to Spirit*.

Understanding the Science behind *The Power of Meditation* can help us understand that the hormonal release of Endorphins, Serotonin, Gamma-Aminobutyric Acid (GABA), Oxytocin, and Melatonin can illuminate why meditation is an effective tool for achieving peace, clarity, and balance in our lives. By opting out of meditating, we may need to engage in other activities to release these hormones into our bodies.

Is this meditative hormonal balance hoopla some sort of joke? I do not play around with the well-being of any man! I UNVEIL the Divine Truth, and what you do with it is on you! Biblically, here is what *The Power of Meditation* can do for us: *"But his delight is in the Law of the LORD, and in His law he meditates day and night. He shall be like a tree Planted by the rivers of water, That brings forth its fruit in its season, Whose leaf also shall not wither; And whatever he does shall prosper."* Psalm 1:2-3. The remarkable hormonal shifts that meditation can instigate will indeed blow your mind!

On the other hand, if we are running around like hellions on wheels and think the Holy Spirit will uphold us in our debaucherous state, we are sadly mistaken. Really? Yes, really! *"The ungodly are not so, but are like the chaff which the wind drives away. Therefore the ungodly shall not stand in the judgment, Nor sinners in the congregation of the righteous."* Psalm 1:4-5.

What is the difference between prayer and meditation? We often try to complicate the two due to a lack of understanding. Simply put, prayer is our way of TALKING, sharing, invoking, decreeing, or conveying, making our requests known to God. Meditation is our way of LISTENING to Him as we review, purge, and manifest what we want and do not want while giving thanks and reverence in all things. In addition, it is a process of thinking, pondering, hearing, understanding, digesting, and releasing for our Heaven on Earth Experience based upon the Word or Promises of God.

If we spend all of our prayer time talking, begging, or giving orders, then we have God all wrong! Unbeknown to most, meditation is a process that gives us the ability to think through what we are doing, why we are doing it, how we are doing so, when we are doing it, where we are doing it, and with whom.

Often enough, the thought of sitting still creates more unrest than the process of meditation itself. For this reason, we will find people avoiding this because their mental chatter drives them insane. So, they prefer to stay busy or exhaust themselves to avoid this temporary feeling of loss of control from the inside out.

How do we meditate? Although there are many different forms of meditation, you must develop what works for you, *Spirit to Spirit*. What does this mean? The *Spirit to Spirit* Relationship is between you and God, and to truly master a particular area of your life, you will need to MASTER the ability to follow the Inner Guide from within through the process of meditation, but not limited to such.

The *How To* Meditate *Chart* is available to assist you in trusting God's plan for your life. Once again, this is not set in stone; these are tips to get the ball rolling on your *Spirit to Spirit* Communion with your Heavenly Father.

Why do we need a chart, especially if our *Spirit to Spirit* Communion is not set in stone? Everyone is designed differently and has varying wants, needs, desires, and traumas. So, what works for one person may not work for another.

However, for beginners, it can be challenging to figure out where to start or what to do. Meanwhile, this chart pinpoints Divine Expectations to glean from, with an overview of mindfulness, concentration, and visualization. The goal is to experiment with each technique and see which ones work best for you because it is not a quick fix; it requires patience, dedication, and practice.

- ☐ Determine the location in which you feel comfortable meditating *Spirit to Spirit* with God.

Spiritual Growth

- ☐ Decide what time you are going to meditate daily in the Word of God.

- ☐ Decide how long you are going to meditate, breathing in the Breath of Life.

- ☐ Meditate every day, filtering out negativity while ushering in Positivity.

- ☐ Always sit in an upright position to prevent yourself from falling asleep.

- ☐ Slowly take deep and long breaths, filling your lungs and then exhaling.

- ☐ This is your personal QUIET TIME with the Holy Trinity. Make sure you are not disturbed.

- ☐ You can meditate on a Biblical passage or over an issue.

- ☐ Do not over analyze or complicate your meditation. Just keep it simple.

- ☐ Keep an open mind and let go of everything.

- ☐ Allow yourself to become relaxed, only using your **INSIDE VOICE** to commune *Spirit to Spirit*.

- ☐ Cultivate the inner zone of peace by going over the Fruits of the Spirit with 'I Am' statements.

- ☐ Reflect on the qualities of God that you want to emulate.

- ☐ Release stress, thoughts, desires, or whatever to God.

Spiritual Growth

- ☐ Repent, Forgive, and give THANKS.

- ☐ If your mind wanders off, do not judge. Gently bring your attention back to the Breath of Life.

- ☐ When any negative thoughts or emotions arise, release them and replace them with positivity.

- ☐ Repeat: The Blood of Jesus, Speak Lord, Holy-Ghost Fire, or Peace Within My Walls.

- ☐ Recite Biblical Scriptures or Affirmations that resonate with you.

- ☐ Ask God for guidance, understanding, and wisdom.

- ☐ Listen for any messages, nuggets, or insights that God may be sending you.

- ☐ End your meditation with a prayer of GRATITUDE.

- ☐ Journal about your experiences and insights during your *Spirit to Spirit* meditation with God.

- ☐ Review your notes often because you will tend to forget without realizing what you have forgotten.

- ☐ Rinse and Repeat (Cleanse your mind and repeat the next day).

What if one has a hard time relaxing? It means they are human! However, you need to know what to tell your Mind,

Spiritual Growth

Body, Soul, and Spirit. Here is how I do it...still, you must find what works best for you.

- ☐ Take control over your Mind, Body, Soul, and Spirit. How? Say it to yourself!

- ☐ Tell each part of your body to relax. Call each body part out, one by one, saying I relax my head, I relax my eyes, I relax my nose, I relax my mouth, and so on.

- ☐ Relax your breathing. It should begin to slow down, giving you an opportunity to continue.

- ☐ Relax your mind. Let go of all the clutter, giving it all to God without hesitation.

- ☐ Relax your muscles from head to toe.

- ☐ Allow all the pressures of life to be released through the soles of your feet.

- ☐ Every time you breathe in, imagine breathing in the Breath of Life.

- ☐ When you exhale, imagine releasing stress and pressure.

- ☐ Imagine surrendering your body to its Divine Blueprint.

- ☐ Repeat this process until you MASTER it!

Spiritual Growth

Can we succeed without meditating? Absolutely, we can succeed without it, but we must consider whether or not it is going to last. When our outer man wants to dominate, we must determine whether our success will fade, whether our peace will remain, whether our mental stability will sustain us, and so on.

In a world plagued with unpredictability, the overwhelming stress of the unknown will cause the best of us to create self-sabotage or booby-traps in other areas of our lives. The moment we think we are exempt from stress, it has a weeding effect, sprouting out of nowhere through our known and unknown cracks, obscuring our sense of good judgment, relatability, or rationale.

The Power of Meditation provides us with a Spiritual Safety Net or Pathway to calm the psyche, allowing us to operate in clarity instead of fear and doubt. Even if we do not understand what the psyche is or is not, or what is taking place within it, meditation allows us to acknowledge our feelings while not becoming ruled by them.

Although some may attempt to make meditation spooky or an unhinged practice through elements of deception; however, it is essential to approach meditation with clarity and understanding, *As It Pleases God*. What is the purpose of deceptive measures? It is designed to get us to avoid what we desperately need in Earthen Vessels while remaining in the Milking Stages of Spirituality.

In the Eye of God, for our Heaven on Earth Experiences, when we are presented with a false sense of progress or success, we can indeed miss the vital lessons and experiences designed to PREPARE us for the unveiling of our Predestined Blueprinted Purpose. In Earthen Vessels, the result of these proactive omissions leaves a gut-wrenching longing from within that we often cannot share with others.

For the record, before moving on, this sinking pit from within the psyche is nothing to joke around with, even on our

Spiritual Growth

best day. What is the big deal, especially when we all have longings from within? Unkempt, deceptive measures with God nowhere in the equation, only to please ourselves or satiate our agendas, will have us mentally and emotionally climbing the walls with our feet on the ground.

Why would a Blood-Washed Believer feel as if they are climbing the walls or their mind has jumped the track? Regardless of whether we are under the Blood of Jesus or not, if we are rebellious, contentious, resistant, stiff-necked, lukewarm, dull, disrespectful, selfish, prideful, or leave rotten fruits all over the place, we will become consumed with control over people, places, and things, violating the elements of free will to maintain the status quo. How so? We will begin playing a demigod role, concocting schemes to get what we want, seeking ways to manipulate others, or engaging in acts of idolatry while appearing right and justified in our own eyes.

Suppose we do not pay attention to deceptive measures while meditating. In this case, it will inadvertently deplete our power while thinking we have Divine Power or have it going on in the Realm of the Spirit. When, in all actuality, it is a low-burning flame of worldliness based on the lies that we are telling ourselves. How do we know if we are lying to ourselves? The subtle danger lurking beneath the surface is that we all have an inner knowing about the lies we tell ourselves and the illusions that we present. Suppose we deny the truth or have unexamined beliefs, thoughts, desires, words, or actions. In this case, it means we agree with the lie, permitting it to deceive us further, perpetuating the Spiritual Drainage to come forth, and zapping our power.

Whereas, when meditating, *As It Pleases God*, it calms the Mind, Body, Soul, and Spirit down, giving us an opportunity to reflect and self-correct, unmasking our underlying lies, fears, and insecurities. Once we remove the Spiritual Veneers, *As It Pleases God*, we can then move on to Spiritual

Spiritual Growth

Advancement, Training, or Preparation for our next with Divine Empowerment instead of justified Spiritual Depletion.

What is a Spiritual Veneer? It is a bogus covering that hides what lies within. An example of a superficial layer of Spirituality is when someone proclaims to be a Prophet of God, and they are 100% dependent upon their notes to say, 'Thus saith the Lord.' Now, if the computer goes down, the Voice or Prophecy of God stops...that, my friend, is a HOAX! Here is the deal when demystifying meditation: Keep it simple, use the Holy Trinity, the Word of God, the Fruits of the Spirit, and behave Christlike. And if there is any form of deception, the Holy Spirit will help us self-correct or filter, and the Blood of Jesus will cover us with Spiritual Atonement.

For our Heaven on Earth Experiences or to get the real Spiritual Meat in the Eye of God, meditation lays the groundwork for our *Personal Growth* and Unlimited Potential, *As It Pleases Him.* How do we make this make sense as a Believer? When used properly as a Spiritual Ally, meditation allows our inner man to speak, giving us the ability to understand our true GREATNESS and the unlimited potential we already possess from within. In addition, it also promotes healing, mental clarity, inner peace, and internal balance, enhancing our overall well-being amid chaos, confusion, or seeming defeat.

According to the Heavenly of Heavens, at the core of our being, if we cannot communicate effectively from the inside out, our Predestined Blueprint cannot come forth as it should. Why not? Divinely Accessing our Predestined Blueprint requires a deep level of self-awareness, humility, and authenticity, with the ability to communicate our inner thoughts, senses, and feelings effectively. All of these help us to understand our desires, fears, motivations, or postures, helping us to express them with clarity outwardly with *The Power of Kindness,* while being ready, willing, and able to work on our behalf, *As It Pleases God.*

Chapter Eleven

The Power of Kindness

In a world that often feels fast-paced, painstakingly confusing, and unawaringly disconnected, we need help. *The Power of Kindness* serves as a heartfelt reminder of the profound impact that simple acts of compassion, empathy, understanding, and sensitivity toward others' feelings and circumstances can have on our lives and those of others. According to the Heavenly of Heavens, kindness is multifaceted for the sake of all mankind.

According to *Divine Etiquette: As It Pleases God®*, not only is kindness a moral choice or display of integrity, converting harsh and demoralizing experiences into more respectful and humane ones. Kindness, at its core, is also a transformative force with the Divine Capability to internally change us positively, providing a sense of Spiritual Fulfillment and Divine Purpose.

Even Jeremiah 31:3 shared the Gravitational Power associated with lovingkindness: *"Yes, I have loved you with an everlasting love; Therefore with lovingkindness I have drawn you."* In the Eye of God, lovingkindness is more than just a fleeting

The Power of Kindness

gesture in challenging situations, when dealing with negative influences, or when engaging in personal struggles. It also bridges great divides, heals gouging wounds, and fosters genuine connections among us in Earthen Vessels.

By exploring the various dimensions of kindness with love, this concept invites us to reflect and to use self-corrective measures with our actions, thoughts, words, and beliefs, *As It Pleases God*. In addition, it is also designed to uplift us strategically, but also to illuminate the path of those around us positively.

The Power of Kindness is one of our Superpowers hidden in plain sight, giving us Divine Leverage with God and man. Although our kindness can sometimes be viewed as a weakness, we cannot allow the enemy to block this Divine Power given to us from the Ancient of Days. Nor should we become afraid to use it.

More importantly, when we are Divinely and Authentically Kind to others, we should not be afraid to ask for help when we need it. In the Eye of God, kindness is not merely about selfless giving all the time. The reciprocal Acts of Kindness also involve recognizing our own needs and gaining the strength needed to ask for help when we require it. Even if we are uncomfortable requesting help from others, have a negative stigma of the weakness associated with it, or fear judgment, we must Spiritually Reframe our narratives to both GIVING and RECEIVING.

According to the Law of Reciprocity, often encapsulated in the concept of 'Seedtime and Harvest,' the more we pour out, helping others and contributing to the cycle of goodwill, there will come a time when we need to be poured into. All of which is wrapped into this one word called INTERACTION. The moment we ENTER into ACTION, positively or negatively, the Law of Reciprocity and Duality kick into high gear to connect or disconnect, support or disengage, feed or starve, control or set free, reward or discipline, and so on.

What about those who proclaim to be Believers who refuse to help someone out of envy, jealousy, pride, spite, hatred, or fear? At the core of this dilemma, when operating in FAITH, *As It Pleases God*, regardless of how we feel about their refusal, they have free will to do whatever, whenever, however, whyever, and with whomever, especially if they are not our children. Above all, we are not God, nor do we have a Hell to put them in because they refuse to help us or others.

Everyone, and I mean everyone, has a right to choose their actions, thoughts, beliefs, and desires. The goal in the Eye of God is to live by example using the Fruits of the Spirit, behave Christlike, and inspire change positively for the Greater Good.

Now, on the other hand, suppose they are using mind games or manipulation to alter the narrative or selfishly deceive for the lesser good of mankind. In this case, with genuine love and support, we have the Spiritual Right to cast it down, cancel it, or refuse to engage. Rather than succumbing to anger, revenge, hatefulness, grudges, or judgment, we have options.

Still, with our free-willed options, we should never buy into the big bad wolf mentality, attempting to blow people's houses down when we cannot get what we want or have our way. Nor should we engage in huffing and puffing with all types of contention, lashing out, or making everyone's life difficult. When we become the bully or the aggressor, it becomes counterproductive and detrimental to our well-being, especially when revenge is involved. For this reason, Philippians 2:3 says, "*Let nothing be done through selfish ambition or conceit, but in lowliness of mind let each esteem others better than himself.*"

In *Divine Etiquette: As It Pleases God*®, asserting ourselves through forceful means disengages *The Power of Kindness*. According to the Heavenly of Heavens, it is HUMILITY that helps us stand our ground with anyone or anything designed to sift us negatively or unjustifiably. Therefore, if we desire to stand in POWER, *As It Pleases God*, with *The Funny Feeling* and all, 2 Chronicles 7:14 shares the Spiritual Seal on how to do so: *"If My people who are called by My name will humble themselves, and pray and seek My face, and turn from their wicked ways, then I will hear from heaven, and will forgive their sin and heal their land."*

What does humility have to do with kindness? They both work hand in hand. If we refuse to become humbly kind, here is what Luke 14:11 leaves for us to glean: *"For whoever exalts himself will be humbled, and he who humbles himself will be exalted."* So, with that being said: *'Choose Your Hard.'*

The Funny Feeling

The Power of Kindness, when used with *Divine Etiquette: As It Pleases God®*, can sometimes be classified as the uncomfortable, *Funny Feelings* that we experience when there are hidden triggers, longings, or deprivations, working positively or negatively.

For example, have you ever experienced a *Funny Feeling* when doing a good deed? I am referring to that feeling that warms your heart and puts a smile on your face. It is a feeling that is hard to put into words, but you know it when you feel it. Doing good deeds has been proven to have a positive impact on your well-being because it releases Endorphins, a God-Engineered natural feel-good chemical, which can reduce stress and increase happiness.

On the other hand, sometimes we can experience a *Funny Feeling* while doing good deeds that can leave us feeling ashamed. One of the leading causes of this negative, *Funny Feeling* is the fear of being seen as boastful, seeking attention, not living up to our moral standards, self-doubt, or our egos getting the best of us. The second cause could be our

The Power of Kindness

conscience warning or convicting us out of guilt, shame, a nudge to self-correct, we are lacking integrity, or we are engaging in a free will violation. All of these are examples, but not limited to such.

Unfortunately, we live in a society where we are often judged for our actions, and sometimes, doing good deeds can lead to unwanted attention and criticism, which can provoke a feeling of discomfort, rejection, and shame. In the Eye of God, we must acknowledge the feeling and understand where it comes from. Once we understand the root cause, we can work on changing our perspective and focus on the positive impact that our actions have on others.

The bottom line is that we are often our own worst critics, and we need the healing of our emotions, thoughts, fruits, and character. Why do we need healing as Believers? When we become too emotional or imbalanced, the Holy Spirit must lie dormant. The moment our Spiritual Wires become crossed with worldliness, we will feel it within the human psyche. From a Spiritual Perspective, this is DANGEROUS.

How is the danger presented to us when we are making a free will choice of doing our own thing? Regardless of whether we are healed or unhealed, we do not want to cross our wires with worldliness and Kingdom Business. When operating with one foot in the Kingdom and the other foot out, dabbling in worldliness, it is similar to getting water on a cord plugged into an electrical socket. And then, getting a shock or wake-up call from time to time, letting us know that something is not right or we are out of order. Therefore, we should not play around with what we do not understand, especially with Spiritual Means.

For the record, according to the Heavenly of Heavens, these unknown blockages or short circuits are one of the reasons we use less than ten percent of the brain. Ten percent? Yes, I said less than ten percent!

The Power of Kindness

How do we know if we are emotionally sensitive, short-circuited, or fragile? First, if you have a problem or a *Funny Feeling* when doing something positive, productive, righteous, and fruitful, there may be an issue that needs reckoning. Secondly, if you find yourself getting upset or overwhelmed easily, feeling like your emotions are controlling you, or you are experiencing strong reactions to minor events, you may be emotionally sensitive. Thirdly, when you leave God out of your equational efforts, in due time, a sensitivity will occur within the human psyche when you are triggered by something or someone.

Short-circuiting can occur when stress, anxiety, or other negative emotions cause your brain to become overloaded and unable to process information effectively. Therefore, it is essential to identify and manage emotional sensitivities to prevent them from negatively impacting your personal and professional life.

How do we counteract short-circuits? First, *The Power of Kindness* works extremely well when we place God first in our lives. Secondly, when using the Fruits of the Spirit and behaving Christlike will help us shed the traumatizing effects, rewiring the brain naturally and properly balancing our good hormones. Thirdly, when we cover ourselves with the Blood of Jesus, *As It Pleases God*, we can transform whatever it is or is not into a Testimony or a Story for Kingdom use. Lastly, when we become ONE with the Holy Spirit, our Spiritual Discernment will proactively prepare us for what is to come through our conscience and senses.

How do we know if we are depriving ourselves of *The Power of Kindness*? Listed below are a few examples, but not limited to such:

☐ Do you feel funny telling someone you love them?

The Power of Kindness

- ☐ Do you feel funny hugging someone?
- ☐ Do you feel funny saying, 'I'm sorry?'
- ☐ Do you feel funny saying, 'Please?'
- ☐ Do you feel funny saying, 'Excuse me?'
- ☐ Do you feel funny saying, 'I was wrong?'
- ☐ Do you feel funny saying, 'Thank you?'
- ☐ Do you feel funny saying, 'I understand how you are feeling?'
- ☐ Do you feel funny saying, 'Please forgive me?'
- ☐ Do you feel funny when expressing compassion?
- ☐ Do you feel funny saying, 'How can I help you?'
- ☐ Do you feel funny saying, 'Bless you?'
- ☐ Do you feel funny saying, 'You look nice today?'
- ☐ Do you feel funny saying, 'I am proud of you?'
- ☐ Do you feel funny saying, 'Let me know if you need something?'
- ☐ Do you feel funny saying, 'Yes or No, Ma'am, or Yes or No, Sir?'
- ☐ Do you feel funny saying, 'Congratulations?'
- ☐ Do you feel funny saying, 'I am happy for you?'

If the answer is 'Yes' for any one of these questions, you are an EXPERT on covering or hiding your emotions. If you answered 'No' to all of the questions, then congratulations, you are doing well for yourself...I am so proud of you.

We are pre-wired to experience a wide range of emotions, making them a natural and healthy part of the human experience, but there are times when it may be necessary to conceal or control them. Whether you are in a professional setting or dealing with personal issues, being able to manage your emotions at the drop of a dime can help you navigate challenging situations, achieve your goals, and enhance your people skills.

Although many find it challenging to control their emotional responses, especially when they are feeling overwhelmed or stressed...but, with practice and patience, it is possible to become an expert at covering or hiding your emotions WITHOUT dealing with them, *As It Pleases God*. Unfortunately, it will only cause a CORTISOL DUMP.

What is Cortisol? Cortisol is a hormone that is produced by the adrenal gland in response to stress. It is often referred to as the 'stress hormone' because it plays a vital role in the body's response to stressors or fear. Suppressing or blocking our emotions creates high levels of cortisol and can have adverse effects on the body, including weight gain, decreased immune function, and increased risk of chronic diseases, contributing to the *Funny Feeling*.

Meanwhile, according to the Heavenly of Heavens, you must become an expert at dealing with your emotions by managing your responses with self-control and identifying your triggers while using the Fruits of the Spirit as a developmental strategy. All of which preserves your sanity, allowing the psyche to reset itself from negative to positive to handle your *Spiritual Needs* accordingly.

What if we do not have Spiritual Needs? We are all Spiritual Beings having a human experience; therefore, we all have *Spiritual Needs*, even if we deny it or do not understand its role. So, let us go deeper.

Spiritual Needs

We need the Spirit of God, and the Spirit needs us in Earthen Vessels to carry out the Divine Fulfillment for this day and age. Yet, we must know what we need from the Realm of the Spirit while placing a DEMAND on it. How can we demand God? Is this not rude? Maybe or maybe not, but I did not say to demand God; I said to place a DEMAND on it. Here is what

The Power of Kindness

we must know: 1 Peter 2:9 says, *"But you are a chosen generation, a royal priesthood, a holy nation, His own special people, that you may proclaim the praises of Him who called you out of darkness into His marvelous light."*

In *Divine Etiquette*, when dealing with *Spiritual Needs* or when becoming a work-in-progress, *As It Pleases God*, a DEMAND is similar to placing a request, call, proclamation, or petition to what belongs to us. Amid all this, when working out our own salvation, the only issue is that if we place a Spiritual Demand on what DOES NOT belong to us, we will have a problem. For this reason, Philippians 2:12-13 advises: *"Therefore, my beloved, as you have always obeyed, not as in my presence only, but now much more in my absence, work out your own salvation with fear and trembling; for it is God who works in you both to will and to do for His good pleasure."*

With whom will we have a problem if we place a demand on what does not belong to us? We will have a problem with God Almighty, especially if He sees us as an enemy violating the free will of others who are not deemed as our children. Can this really happen? Of course, especially when disobedience and rebellion are involved. Do not take my word for it; let us take it to Scripture: *"But they rebelled and grieved His Holy Spirit; so He turned Himself against them as an enemy, and He fought against them."* Isaiah 63:10.

What should we do to avoid becoming an enemy of God Almighty? To avoid enmity of any kind when dealing with our *Spiritual Needs* or not, Ephesians 4:1 says this: *"I therefore, the prisoner of the Lord, beseech you to walk worthy of the calling with which you were called."*

What is considered walking worthy in the Eye of God? Here is a list of Divine Worthy Charactorial Traits, but not limited to such:

The Power of Kindness

☐ Obedient	☐ Generous	☐ Serving
☐ Loving	☐ Courageous	☐ Open-Minded
☐ Submissive	☐ Wise	
☐ Humble	☐ Just	☐ Joyful
☐ Respectful	☐ Peaceful	☐ Good-Hearted
☐ Polite	☐ Patient	
☐ Helpful	☐ Forgiving	☐ Resourceful
☐ Proactive	☐ Hopeful	☐ Purposeful
☐ Calm	☐ Faithful	☐ Willful
☐ Usable	☐ Disciplined	☐ Repentant
☐ Teachable	☐ Grateful	☐ Agreeable
☐ Shareable	☐ Resilient	☐ Aware

In my opinion, we are Blessed beyond what we could ever imagine. We have all the Spiritual Tools available at our fingertips that our Forefathers did not have. Proverbs 16:7 even says, *"When a man's ways please the Lord, He makes even his enemies to be at peace with him."*

Listen, we have the Holy Spirit as our Comforter and Guide, the Blood of Jesus as our Formal Sacrifice, the Fruits of the Spirit for self-correcting, Christlike Character to govern the heart, and the Word of God for Spiritual Alignment. But, most of all, we are privy to having a *Spirit to Spirit* Relationship with our Heavenly Father to connect and download information from the Heavenly of Heavens. And what do we do? We fail at using it to the full, *As It Pleases God*, only to find fault in the Divine System designed to liberate us from the inside out.

To take this a step further, place a check in the appropriate box of *Spiritual Needs* before moving to the next level.

- ☐ Do you need Spiritual Understanding?
- ☐ Do you need Spiritual Instructions?
- ☐ Do you need Spiritual Favor?
- ☐ Do you need Spiritual Insight or Foresight?
- ☐ Do you need Spiritual Inspiration?
- ☐ Do you need Spiritual Investments?

The Power of Kindness

- ☐ Do you need Spiritual Involvement?
- ☐ Do you need Spiritual Covenants?
- ☐ Do you need Spiritual Authority?
- ☐ Do you need Spiritual Proclivity?
- ☐ Do you need a Spiritual Commencement?
- ☐ Do you need Spiritual Wisdom?

Whatever you need, you can incorporate the need into your daily prayers. Feel free to use the checklist if you need all of them. All I ask is that you make sure you are ready. Why must we be ready? They will come with *Spiritual Testing* to make sure you are worthy of receiving what is Divine.

Spiritual Testing

Clearly, in *Divine Etiquette: As It Pleases God®*, I am not determining or judging someone's worthiness. All I am saying is that the Heavenly of Heavens will do its homework on us to ensure we are worthy of receiving Kingdom Secrets, Treasures, Wisdom, Notches, and Downloads.

The Kingdom of God is not a fly-by-night Divine Establishment, nor does it play around with those possessing this mentality. Painstakingly, it will put us through vigorous *Spiritual Testing* to determine what we are made of or our level of readiness.

What if we are not ready? Our lack of readiness does not necessarily mean we are bad people or unusable, even amid making mistakes. It only means that we must go back to the Spiritual Classroom for development, training, updates, and growth. Besides, no one is exempt from this process or classroom. In Earthen Vessels, we must all pass through this phase while remaining on a constant Spiritual Learning Curve, *As It Pleases God*.

The Power of Kindness

For the record, I was once in this stage, failing miserably with zero help outside of the Holy Trinity. When I say zero outside help, I really mean it. I had to wing it with the Holy Trinity (The Father, Son, and Holy Spirit), learning how to really trust and look toward the Heavens from which my strength cometh.

While in my Spiritual Classroom, one thing for sure is that I documented the information to provide a PATHWAY for the next in line, making it easier, understandable, useable, and accurate, *As It Pleased God*. When transcending human understanding, what Divinely Pleases God in one season of our lives may not be applicable to the next season. So, it is only wise in *Divine Etiquette* to become Spirit-Led.

In the Eye of God, we must allow ourselves to be guided by Spiritual Truths and Absolutes from the Heavenly of Heavens, rather than solely by earthly knowledge, understanding, or societal norms. This process helps us to avoid misalignments with our Spiritual Paths or Principles.

We are often taught to TEST the Spirit, but for some odd reason, we do not like being *Spiritually Tested*. What if we fail? Failing the *Spiritual Testing* processes without correction can lead to turmoil, dissatisfaction, confusion, and a sense of disconnection from our Divine Purpose or Predestined Blueprint. But it can also be the Spiritual Training Ground needed to thrust us forward. Here is the deal: Even if we fail, we have the Divine Authority to reverse-engineer it for the Greater Good. Here is how I see it:

- ☐ Failing a *Spiritual Test* can develop and refine our character traits, *As It Pleases God* to break our selfish bonds.

- ☐ Failing a *Spiritual Test* can develop a clearer understanding of our Divine Path.

The Power of Kindness

- ☐ Failing a *Spiritual Test* can equip us with the insights necessary on what to do and what not to do.

- ☐ Failing a *Spiritual Test* can prepare us for upcoming challenges.

- ☐ Failing a *Spiritual Test* can help us respond correctly and with wisdom.

- ☐ Failing a *Spiritual Test* can teach us how not to react out of fear, frustration, or anger.

- ☐ Failing a *Spiritual Test* can thrust us into a growth spurt.

- ☐ Failing a *Spiritual Test* can invoke our attention to a matter.

- ☐ Failing a *Spiritual Test* can offer hidden opportunities that we would not have received otherwise.

- ☐ Failing a *Spiritual Test* can strengthen our faith, hope, and love bonds.

- ☐ Failing a *Spiritual Test* can build our patience, humility, understanding, and trust in God's Divine Timing.

- ☐ Failing a *Spiritual Test* can lead to greater clarity regarding our Divine Purpose, Spiritual Gifts, Hidden Creativity, and Heavenly Calling.

- ☐ Failing a *Spiritual Test* can provide Divine Insight to guide our thoughts, decisions, words, and actions.

The Power of Kindness

- ☐ Failing a *Spiritual Test* allows us to move beyond surface-level thoughts, conversations, actions, and beliefs to Divine Engagement from the Heavenly of Heavens.

- ☐ Failing a *Spiritual Test* helps to prevent us from detrimental derailments.

- ☐ Failing a *Spiritual Test* builds faith, understanding, and discernment.

Sometimes, failing is not bad at all; actually, it could be a good thing hidden in the appearance of what we perceive as bad. With this buried component of learning through experience, I always advise everyone:

- ☐ To leave no stone unturned.
- ☐ To leave no one untouched by a positive impact or experience.

Even if we are rejected, the psyche knows the difference between kindheartedness and unkindness, even amid the lies. Above all, at the end of the day, my question is always, 'What did you learn?'

If we learned absolutely nothing or documented nothing, then rest assured, the *Spiritual Testing* is not over! Who am I to judge, right? No judgment is intended, but we cannot become an authentic Spiritual Teacher, *As It Pleases God*, without learning from the lessons presented. Unfortunately, it makes us stiff-necked and dull in the Eye of God. Plus, this is how we get the mean self-appointed instead of Divinely and Kindly Anointed, leading God's sheep.

The Power of Kindness

With all due respect and from experience, the meanest and cruelest people I have come in contact with are in the church, proclaiming to be led by the Holy Spirit. Actually, this is the reason why I was led to write this book, *Divine Etiquette: As It Pleases God®*. In my opinion, it does not make any sense for worldly individuals to exhibit more Spiritual Fruits and Poshness out of habit than those in the Kingdom of God.

Are we being *Spiritually Tested* on Kingdomly or *Divine Etiquette* right now? Absolutely! Treating God's sheep as if they were junkyard dogs in His Name is an abomination in His Divine Eye, severing our Divine Connections to the Heavenly of Heavens.

Clearly, this is not a matter of losing our Salvation...it is not lost at all because it is Spiritually Sealed with the Blood of the Lamb. Conversely, we lose our Spiritual Power and Authority within our Heaven on Earth Experiences while giving into mockery, trickery, confusion, and shamefulness.

What is the purpose of *Spiritual Testing* when we know and understand right from wrong as a Believer, and everything works out for our good anyway? At its core, *Spiritual Testing* challenges us to confront our beliefs, thoughts, habits, desires, and words to refine our character traits and align with Divine Principles. While simultaneously assessing and challenging our faith, tenacity, proactiveness, and commitment. In the Eye of God, the Spiritual Classroom needed to facilitate our *Spiritual Needs* is not designed to punish or humiliate us but rather to foster Spiritual Growth, self-awareness, and internal introspection, *As It Pleases Him*.

When you become Spirit-Led and Trained on Kingdom Laws, Protocols, and Principles, it helps you avoid Spiritual Strikes.

What is considered a Spiritual Strike? It will vary from person to person; however, it is the moment when we must become Spiritually Chastised. Yes, God is a God of second

The Power of Kindness

chances, third chances, and many more, full of GRACE and MERCY, but the correction will occur at some point. Here is the deal: We must FORGIVE and REPENT all of our known or unknown mishaps, making an honest attempt to change for the better, using the Fruits of the Spirit. If change does not occur, we ignore positive change, or we choose to become bitter, manipulative, conniving, evil, grudgeful, or hateful, we can reap generational curses upon ourselves, as well as into our Bloodlines.

More importantly, we must tread with caution when doing whatever with whomever, keeping it positive, fruitful, and Christlike. Why must we exhibit caution when doing our thing? When it is violating the will of another, causing unwarranted harm, or becoming a contributor to the spillage of innocent blood from a Mental, Emotional, Physical, or Spiritual Perspective, the Spiritual Strike has more of an impact. Is this fair? Absolutely!

If we allow ourselves to become Spiritually Blind, Deaf, or Mute, we will not know who is who. In this condition, if we target one of God's Anointed Ones, it is like we are contending with God Himself. How is this humanly possible? If the person is operating in their Divinely Blueprinted Purpose according to the Will of God, it comes with Supernatural Spiritual Protection. So, from my perspective, if we use the Fruits of the Spirit, exhibit Christlike Character, and keep the Holy Trinity at the forefront at all times, we have nothing to worry about.

On the other hand, if we are in the Will of God, doing what we should do in the Kingdom, and a Spiritual Strike or Correction is taking place, it is imperative to take a step back, doing a checkup from the neck up. If we are indeed in the Kingdom of God, and we feel as if we are a victim, everyone is doing us wrong, or we are always getting the short end of the deal, it should send up multiple RED FLAGS to tread with caution.

The Power of Kindness

Spiritually, this is designed to alert us, letting us know that we need to head over to the Spiritual Classroom because we are missing a vital lesson or have a kink in our system. At this point, if we choose not to query ourselves accordingly, déjà vu will reimpose the same lessons with different scenarios and characters until we finally get it. What do we need to get? We must get whatever our 'it' is or is not! Frankly, until we peel back the layers or get to the root or crux of the matter, we will miss the mark in or out of the Kingdom, regardless of how well we put on a show or play pretend.

How do we know if we are putting on a show or playing pretend? It is most often detected in the questions we secretly ask ourselves behind closed doors or when no one is looking. For example, but not limited to such:

- ☐ Are you asking, 'Why did You allow me to go through this?'
- ☐ Are you asking, 'Why me?'
- ☐ Are you asking, 'Why did You mess up my life?'
- ☐ Are you asking, 'How can I go through this when I am faithfully serving You?'
- ☐ Are you asking, 'Why is life so difficult?'
- ☐ Are you asking, 'How am I going to make it through?'
- ☐ Are you asking, 'Why did You cause this?'
- ☐ Are you asking, 'What kind of God are You to let this happen?'
- ☐ Are you asking, 'God, are You real?'
- ☐ Are you asking, 'Why should I serve You?'
- ☐ Are you asking, 'What is wrong with me?'
- ☐ Are you asking, 'How could You do this?'

Unbeknown to most, these types of questions indicate emotional issues that we are covering up, or we are downplaying our Divine Connection with the Heavenly of

Heavens. Yet, all is not lost; the Kingdom of God is on our side. We need to restructure our querying process by assuming responsibility first, even if it is by no means our fault.

Why must we pivot with a different mindset or perspective? Every challenge comes as a Lesson, Testing, Insight, Revelation, Red Flag, or Blessing. For this reason, we must seek out the hidden Elements of Wisdom in what we are going through or are going to. By doing so, we can reverse any form of negativity.

As It Pleases God, the minute we learn the benefits of the Spiritual REVERSAL process, we are better able to flip the script of our story. Our lives are a series of chapters, and if we miss the mark, we have to rewrite it, or it will recalculate itself until we get it right. For this reason, I do not particularly appreciate wasting time or redoing what I can get right the first time around. So, I learn how to ask the right questions to properly query myself to extract the Lesson, Testing, Insight, Revelation, Red Flag, or Blessing, creating a win-win, and then sharing it to activate the Law of Reciprocity.

More importantly, *As It Pleases God*, we cannot get caught up in too many negative distractions leading us away from our Divine Blueprint. If we do, we will find ourselves living our lives through the lenses or opinions of another, putting on a show of pretense, causing us to become easily sidetracked, brainwashed, or triggered in the areas where we are weak or traumatized.

Although we will not become an expert overnight, I promise that if we take one step at a time, they will add up, giving us a story worth remembering, especially if we become fully committed to the Kingdom of God, using the Fruits of the Spirit and Christlike Character as our Spiritual Weapons.

The Power of Kindness

Divine Illumination

As a part of the *Divine Illumination* from the Heavenly of Heavens, an essential part of this process is knowing when to move, hold, fold, prune, shut down, or walk away. This Spiritual Process helps us out of the dark areas into the LIGHT, yet we must know and understand the difference.

The pruning process of life is a way of strengthening our weak areas and making them stronger. Still, I have a few questions. 'How long has it been since you have pruned your life?' 'How long has it been since you eliminated the unproductive and the unfruitful things?' Or, better yet, 'What about the leeches or the people, places, and things sucking the life out of you?'

As we grow, the pruning process becomes a part of life; however, the leeches are chosen. Most often, we do not like admitting the truth about the leeches. Why do we avoid the truth about them? We may very well be a leech ourselves in some way, shape, or form. Therefore, we must analyze our leeches in 2 ways:

- ☐ Who are the leeches?
- ☐ Are we becoming a leech?

We must first start with the weak, sensitive, or most painful places in the pruning process. I know that the sting of the pruning process may hurt, but the long-term benefits may very well be more profitable than what we are experiencing right now.

In the *As It Pleases God Movement*, you must make it your business to limit the time spent with people who are complacent with a joker or dull mentality. To be clear, this is not a matter of judging others; it is choosing your environment carefully, protecting your sanity as well as your Temple.

In reality, it is not people, places, and things deceiving us; most often, we deceive ourselves based on our expectations and perceptions, or we outright ignore the apparent fruits presented. According to the Heavenly of Heavens, our ability to deceive ourselves causes more behavioral mishaps or problems than we care to admit.

In the *Divine Illumination* process, for example, we have a loving, giving, and affectionate person. Still, their perception of being constantly mistreated, short-changed, abused, left out, or rejected begins to group everyone in this category. So, guess what? This good person will begin to have personal conversations with themselves about the way they feel negatively. The more they talk to themselves in this manner, the more they think about it, proving Proverbs 23:7 correct. It says, *"For as he thinks in his heart, so is he. 'Eat and drink!' he says to you, but his heart is not with you."* Well enough, the more they create a melting pot in such a manner, they invoke a *Self-Fulfilling Prophecy* of their own making.

Self-Fulfilling Prophecy

As per the Spiritual Law of Seedtime and Harvest, the positive or negative SEEDS will feed and nourish the situations, circumstances, or events placed before us. In addition, the thoughts we constantly envision or play back to ourselves will manifest as a *Self-Fulfilling Prophecy*, proving us right in our own eyes.

Why would *Self-Fulfilling Prophecies* happen to a good person? Believe it or not, beyond mere psychological curiosities and myths, it happens to us all, positively or negatively. Proverbs 4:23 warns us about the profound connection between our beliefs, expectations, and reality,

The Power of Kindness

regardless of whether we think we are a good person or not. It says, *"Keep your heart with all diligence, for out of it spring the issues of life."* Now, in *Divine Etiquette, As It Pleases God*®, in order to get to the good issues of life, we must:

- ☐ Keep our hearts guarded and nurtured, *Spirit to Spirit*.
- ☐ Maintain a positive outlook and mindset.
- ☐ Break free from the chains of limiting beliefs.
- ☐ Manifest the best versions of ourselves.
- ☐ Uphold high moral standards.

We must understand how the bad issues enter our camps, Mentally, Physically, Emotionally, Spiritually, and Financially.

In my opinion, this is similar to the picturesque account found in Numbers 12:1-15 when Mariam, Moses' sister, spoke out against her brother negatively, questioning his authority, decisions, and Divine Mission. This event is a compelling example of how criticism can become a *Self-Fulfilling Prophecy* without having a clue about what we are doing.

The truth is that Mariam's elements of discord stemmed from her underlying enviousness, prolonged jealousy, embedded coveting, and secret competitiveness as she compared her role to that of her brother. How do I know? She said, *"Has the Lord indeed spoken only through Moses? Has He not spoken through us also?"* Above all, her negative expectations and oughts were contending with God Almighty to create communal strife.

And then, after the *Self-Fulfilling* outburst, swiftly and severely, God steps in, and Mariam is afflicted with leprosy and placed outside the camp. This *Self-Fulfilling Prophecy* is how she felt about the situation; as a result, she invited this affliction into her headspace.

The Power of Kindness

In addition, we must also understand how our afflicted headspace influences our actions, thoughts, beliefs, and self-talk in such a way that they ultimately come true. All of which lead to self-sabotage, constant failure, constant disappointments, or prolonged feelings of rejection.

The issues of life are based on the expectations we set for ourselves through the following items, but not limited to such:

- ☐ The issues of life are exacerbated with constant negative and uncorrected self-talk, rehashing the 'woe unto me' mentality. Here is what James 1:8 says about this type of person: *"He is a double-minded man, unstable in all his ways."*

- ☐ The issues of life are exacerbated when neglecting to counteract or overcome negativity with the Fruits of the Spirit. Here is how Matthew 12:34 feels about this matter: *"Brood of vipers! How can you, being evil, speak good things? For out of the abundance of the heart the mouth speaks."*

- ☐ The issues of life are exacerbated when overlooking the importance of casting down negativity and exhibiting Christlike Character in our thoughts, actions, spoken words, and reactions. Here is what 2 Corinthians 10:5 advises: *"Casting down arguments and every high thing that exalts itself against the knowledge of God, bringing every thought into captivity to the obedience of Christ."*

- ☐ The issues of life are exacerbated by not using positive affirmations as a form of hopeful and faithful interjections or counteractions. Here is what Proverbs 3:5-6 says to do: *"Trust in the Lord with all your heart, and*

The Power of Kindness

lean not on your own understanding; in all your ways acknowledge Him, and He shall direct your paths."

- ☐ The issues of life are exacerbated by not interjecting the Holy Trinity amid the negative chatter, especially when we have the opportunity to ask but instead choose not to do so. Here is the Spiritual Seal: James 1:5 says, *"If any of you lacks wisdom, let him ask of God, who gives to all liberally and without reproach, and it will be given to him."*

- ☐ The issues of life are exacerbated by not consciously REGRAFTING the root causes of whatever with whomever, while not giving thanks, or when becoming too anxious. Here is what Philippians 4:6-7 says: *"Be anxious for nothing, but in everything by prayer and supplication, with thanksgiving, let your requests be made known to God; and the peace of God, which surpasses all understanding, will guard your hearts and minds through Christ Jesus."*

- ☐ The issues of life are exacerbated when constantly interjecting justified or unjustified negativity of someone's life into ours, with or without their permission. Then again, it can come forth when we outright refuse to behave sober-mindedly. Here is what 1 Peter 1:13 has to say: *"Therefore gird up the loins of your mind, be sober, and rest your hope fully upon the grace that is to be brought to you at the revelation of Jesus Christ."*

- ☐ The issues of life are exacerbated by not creating a WIN-WIN while accepting or settling for the negative, leeching offers of life. Here is what Psalm 37:5 contributes: *"Commit your way to the Lord, trust also in Him, and He shall bring it to pass."*

The Power of Kindness

☐ The issues of life are exacerbated by not waiting on God or preparing, *As It Pleases Him*. Here is what Isaiah 40:31 shares with us: *"But those who wait on the Lord shall renew their strength; they shall mount up with wings like eagles, they shall run and not be weary, they shall walk and not faint."*

When dealing with *The Power of Kindness* with the issues of life, you must MASTER the *Elimination Process*, getting rid of the unnecessary stuff weighing you down.

The Elimination Process

What does kindness have to do with *The Elimination Process*? In a world often overshadowed by negativity and strife, *The Power of Kindness* emerges as our beacon of hope and resilience. It clears our Spiritual Vision, Hearing, and Language with the Heavenly of Heavens, eliminating the unneeded clutter, hindrances, and yokes that hinder our *Spirit to Spirit* Connection with our Heavenly Father.

From my perspective, King David was on to something with the Divine Elements of Kindness. Here is what Psalm 63:3 says, *"Because Your lovingkindness is better than life, my lips shall praise You."* *"For His merciful kindness is great toward us, and the truth of the Lord endures forever. Praise the Lord!"* Psalm 117:2. *"Let, I pray, Your merciful kindness be for my comfort, according to Your word to Your servant."* Psalm 119:76. Although it sounds so simple, but all so powerful in the Eye of God.

The Elimination Process, while sometimes necessary, according to *Divine Etiquette*, does not have to be brutal, unkind, mean, demeaning, or cold. When choosing *The Power of Kindness* as the Spiritual Principle, *As It Pleases God*, it can

The Power of Kindness

transform a difficult situation into a more manageable experience for all involved.

Engaging in *The Elimination Process* to foster growth and positivity may involve parting ways with a job, ending a relationship, severing a friendship, stopping engagements with the wrong crowd, breaking bad habits, shedding outdated beliefs, or removing toxic elements draining our energy or stifling our potential. At the core of holding on, whether it is through procrastination, unhealthy thinking, underlying trauma, or negative self-talk, the process of letting go of what we like may not always be an easy task. But still, it can also become a transformative act to create space for what truly matters in the Eye of God.

When approaching difficult situations, we must maintain a mindset that aligns with Spiritual Values, Standards, and Principles. Ultimately, the Spiritual Journey in *The Elimination Process* is not really about loss; it is more about gaining Divine Clarity, Supernatural Understanding, and Wise Focus on what genuinely enhances our lives, *As It Pleases God*, and makes room for our next. However, the Vicissitudes and Cycles of Life will inevitably present us with difficult situations, challenging our resilience and testing our character to determine what we are made of, but we still have choices.

According to the Heavenly of Heavens, in *Divine Etiquette*, when choosing correctly, the best way to grow is to let go, granting free-willed freedom without attempting to control the narrative. What can letting go of control do for Believers? Letting go of our personal agendas and giving God Almighty Divine Control helps our discerning faculties function as they should, enabling us to look for opportunities instead of problems. Confronting our hardships, successes, or failures, *As It Pleases God*, will create moments to look beyond the surface and understand the deeper lessons hidden. Once embraced in such a manner, we will become wiser, stronger, and more astute as setbacks become our point of redirection, a renewed sense of purpose, or a way of connecting to others for the Greater Good.

Embracing a selfless *As It Pleases God* Mindset and directing our thoughts and intentions toward what is true, noble, just, pure, lovely, and praiseworthy empowers us to thrive in the Spirit of Excellence. To become rooted in positivity and virtue, *As It Pleases Him*, here is the Spiritual Seal in *The Elimination Process* according to Philippians 4:8: *"Finally, brethren, whatever things are true, whatever things are noble, whatever things are just, whatever things are pure, whatever things are lovely, whatever things are of good report, if there is any virtue and if there is anything praiseworthy, meditate on these things."*

Operating in the Spirit of Excellence does not mean ignoring life's challenges or pretending everything is perfect, or that we are without fault. Rather, it is about choosing to highlight the beauty, wisdom, positivity, and goodness that exist alongside these challenges. This shift in focus can help us remain in a work-in-progress Spiritual Posture with the Holy Trinity at the forefront, even when people are trying to steal, interfere, or taint our Divine Destinies.

How can people steal our Spiritual Destinies? First, Spiritual Destinies are not merely about personal goals, desires, or ambitions. It is connected to our Divine Purpose, Spiritual Identity (our reason for being), and our Predestined Blueprint. Secondly, when we operate *As It Pleases God*, we are Divinely Protected from Spiritual Invaders or Pirates, shielding us from negative forces, inner turmoil, or influences that could derail us. Thirdly, if we operate selfishly to please ourselves, we can inadvertently uncover ourselves. Then again, we can put a kink in our Spiritual Armor, allowing a Spiritual Intrusion to harness, oppress, or zap our energy.

When *Divine Etiquette* is not used, *As It Pleases God*, or we act out of selfishness, we can get derailed, and our Divine Blueprint will be withheld to prevent unauthorized access.

Chapter Twelve

Divine Etiquette

We can tiptoe around the normal etiquette of being prim and proper, but when it comes to the Kingdom of God, we play by a different playbook that has been foolproofed from the Ancient of Days. The goal is to turn our external well-behaved manners into a State of Divineness from within, *As It Pleases God* with *The Crème de la Crème People Skills for Believers*.

By the time you get to this chapter, I firmly believe that you will be ready to become the *Crème de la Crème* in *Divine Etiquette*, shifting the Spiritual Dynamics, *As It Pleases God*.

In the pursuit of Authentic Godliness or our Divine Birthrights, we have Divine Dominion to cultivate our genuine State of Being, evolving into what is already within.

Divine Etiquette: As It Pleases God® challenges us to dig deeper within the psyche, examining our words, thoughts, motivations, beliefs, postures, and desires. In addition, we also unveil the 'How-To' aspects to properly align ourselves with the Divine Will of God, according to our Predestined Blueprinted Mission. Simply put, we do not leave anyone hanging without having access to Divine Instructions, Executable Roadmaps, Kingdom Understanding, or Supernatural Wisdom.

When we step beyond the constraints of conventional etiquette and embrace this transformative Spiritual Approach that aligns the Mind, Body, Soul, and Spirit with Divine Principles, *As It Pleases God*, we can indeed open up the Floodgates of Heaven on our behalf and that of another.

Having so-called 'good manners' in public is often commended in social settings, but in the Kingdom of God, we take this to another level using the Fruits of the Spirit. Why the change? Kingdom Protocol has never changed; unfortunately, we have changed! For this reason, God is not just dealing with our public personas; He is dealing with a few things, but not limited to such:

- ☐ He is dealing with what goes on behind closed doors.
- ☐ He is dealing with our idolatrous comfortabilities.
- ☐ He is dealing with what we are doing when no one is looking.
- ☐ He is dealing with how we treat those we do not like or need.
- ☐ He is dealing with our masks.
- ☐ He is dealing with how we are lying to ourselves.
- ☐ He is dealing with how we are faking the funk.
- ☐ He is dealing with how we are becoming comfortable in our folly.
- ☐ He is dealing with the conscience.
- ☐ He is dealing with our mindsets.
- ☐ He is dealing with heart and mind postures.
- ☐ He is dealing with how we know nothing about the Fruits of the Spirit.
- ☐ He is dealing with how we avoid behaving Christlike.
- ☐ He is dealing with a lack of love for Him, ourselves, and others.

Divine Etiquette

☐ He is dealing with our flawed people skills.

Divine Etiquette is about recognizing and utilizing the Divine Sacredness hidden in our relationships and our interactions with God, ourselves, and others with love, kindness, patience, and humility. These Divine Principles from the Heavenly of Heavens can enhance our impeccable people skills to uplift, build, and inspire rather than judge, destroy, or criticize.

God desires that His Shepherds and sheep not only practice good behavior but also develop the *Crème De La Crème* people skills rooted in Divine Love, Grace, Favor, and Authenticity. With this Divine Shift, *As It Pleases Him*, we can return the ball back to our courts with justice, dignity, and equality for all mankind.

In *Divine Etiquette: As It Pleases God*®, no one is better than the next man; we are all children of the Most High God. Thus, He wants us to be authentically real, relatable, and usable. In addition, He also wants us to engage in winning the hearts of His precious sheep with empathy and understanding. Conversely, He does not want us operating in morbid cruelty or underhanded antics, demeaning each other as if He made a mistake when He created us.

What is the big deal, especially when having free will to choose our own level of etiquette? Although we have free will, we also must understand that our interactions are opportunities to reflect the character of Christ in the world. If we opt out of doing so, we can also forfeit the Spiritual Benefits or Blessings associated. How does the forfeiture occur? Unfortunately, based on our free will choice, it occurs through Spiritual Blindness, Deafness, or Muteness. Here is what Matthew 15:14 shares: *"Let them alone. They are blind leaders of the blind. And if the blind leads the blind, both will fall into a ditch."*

Suppose we want to avoid the ditch mentality or probability. In this case, we must be willing to step into the

Divine Etiquette

Spiritual Classroom to become better, stronger, and wiser, *As It Pleases God* to showcase the Divine Astuteness of the Kingdom of Heaven in our everyday lives with our *Crème de la Crème* people skills.

Ultimately, for a time such as this, embracing humility, respect, love, and positive communication can guide us toward Divine Harmony with ourselves and others. Still, it may take a *Spiritual Classroom* to train us in the Divine Ways of God from a Heavenly Perspective on how to deal with His precious sheep.

So, if you are ready to learn *Divine Etiquette: As It Pleases God*®, take a seat, *Spirit to Spirit*, and allow the Spiritual Teacher to teach you...thus saith the Lord of Host.

Spiritual Classroom

In or out of the *Spiritual Classroom* or *Divine Etiquette*, and checking boxes, *As It Pleases God*, the Divine Essence of Christ in our interactions is on the Spiritual Table right now. Why? The Bridegroom is presently seating the table in preparation for His BRIDE (The Church). Yet, until now, we walk around behaving like beasts while proclaiming to walk in the Divine Anointing from the Heavenly of Heavens with false promises, deceptive claims, shattered hope, and rotten fruits.

To be clear, I am not calling anyone a beast here. I am only referring to the BEHAVIOR of beasts (The unspoken dark thoughts, desires, emotions, words, traumas, or behaviors). All of these are manifested through anger, hatefulness, lust, envy, jealousy, coveting, pride, greed, competitiveness, and, most of all, fear. Then again, they all can also incite betrayal against God, ourselves, and others, hindering our Spiritual Growth Process.

Even Revelation 13:18 gives us Divine Wisdom by saying, "*Here is wisdom. Let him who has understanding calculate the number of*

Divine Etiquette

the beast, for it is the number of a man: His number is 666." When Divine Wisdom says here is wisdom, we need to listen carefully. With Revelation 13:18, there is no way to possibly get this confused unless we make a willful choice to deny Divine Truths or miscalculate the enemy's wiles!

Although we often think 666 has some form of Spiritual Taboo to fear, once again, it is the number of a man. As we search high and low to figure out who he is, we do not realize that we should be afraid of ourselves and what we are capable of doing. The bottom line is that Spiritual Duality lives within each person, whether good, bad, or indifferent. If we do not get a grip, *As It Pleases God*, deception lies in wait to trick us with what we already know. Even 1 John 1:8-9 forewarns: *"If we say that we have no sin, we deceive ourselves, and the truth is not in us. If we confess our sins, He is faithful and just to forgive us our sins and to cleanse us from all unrighteousness."*

Everything for our Heaven on Earth Experience in Earthen Vessels is already recorded on the Tablet of our Hearts. Only if we wake up from our slumber, *Spirit to Spirit* with *Divine Etiquette: As It Pleases God®*, can we gain Divine Access to the Spiritual Scroll that is already.

Plus, there is no need to look for the Big Beast elsewhere; we must look from within, focusing on the seedling internal beastful minions first. Then, we can tackle this dilemma outwardly, establishing Divine Dominion, *As It Pleases God*. The moment we take our eyes off the prize (We, as God's Prize Possessions, having Divine Dominion), we will 'get got' by deceptive measures with identity crises to follow suit.

In this *Spiritual Classroom*, let me say this: The Spirit of Cain is not playing around with us. How do I know? Right now, we are indeed doing the most, especially to our brothers and sisters in Christ Jesus. For the record, wishing for the downfall or demise of our Brethren is an absolute

Divine Etiquette

abomination in the Eye of God. All for what? To feel superior over the next man for selfish reasons or gain!

Let us talk about Cain, the firstborn son of Adam and Eve. In Genesis 4, we read about Cain's offering to God, which was rejected in favor of his brother Abel's offering. Unfortunately, this rejectional factor ignited a fierce wave of anger, envy, jealousy, hatred, competitiveness, and resentment within Cain. As a result of his unbridled emotions, thoughts, words, and desires, he killed Abel, his brother, as if he were not his brother's keeper.

Cain's failure to embrace humility, lovingkindness, correction, accountability, and righteousness led him down a path of moral decay and corruption. This very same path is now plaguing mankind with his hidden behaviors, Mentally, Emotionally, and Spiritually, more so than Physically. In my opinion, this makes throwing the rock and hiding our hands much easier than the visible edifices of shedding or spilling blood outright, leaving definitive evidence behind.

From the Ancient of Days, moral failure, rebellion, and the consequences of sin resonate deeply within the human psyche of mankind, revealing the darker aspects of our human nature and its implications while appearing as LIGHT. In deceiving ourselves, we avoid the *Spiritual Classroom* at all costs, only to become openly or privately ensnared in the end, as if we did not see it coming. When engaging in real-life affairs, we often forget what Proverbs 17:15 says about how God feels about deception: "*Acquitting the guilty and condemning the innocent—the Lord detests them both.*"

In the Eye of God, 'To see and not want to see' contains the underlying charactorial traits of rebellion and selfishly blurring the lines, which He does not like at all. So, you see...the characteristics of the beast mirror those of Cain. What does this mean, especially for a Bloodwashed Believer? We, as humans, can feel when the beast is rising from within but choose to ignore it or lie about it. How do I know? The

Divine Etiquette

conscience is designed to warn us through our senses, and if it does not, it means we are heavily consumed in debauchery, warping our Spiritual Compass and Discernment Faculties. When this happens, it brings Isaiah 5:20 to the forefront of our lives, saying: *"Woe to those who call evil good, and good evil; who put darkness for light, and light for darkness; who put bitter for sweet, and sweet for bitter!"*

From the Book of Genesis to Revelation, we all have a beastful side within us, and we must face it instead of hiding or wrestling with it without Divine Assistance. Unfortunately, this is one of the reasons we have a lot of failed Spiritual Tests. Really? Yes, really!

In Genesis 32:22-32, Jacob even wrestled with an Angel, where he struggled with Divine Transformation, laying to rest all of his fears and anxieties. More importantly, with his *Spirit to Spirit* Encounter, he had to contend with his old and new natures. At some point in our lives, similar to Jacob, we must confront our past and seek the Divine Blessing and Promises from God Almighty.

When it comes to the rich tapestry of struggle, identity, purpose, and transformation, *As It Pleases God*, no one can do this for us; we must step into the ring with Him and duke it out, *Spirit to Spirit*. Listen, the struggle between good and evil is real; even if we walk away with a limp like Jacob did, we can still exit with faith, hope, dignity, and, ultimately, Divine Grace and Favor.

The moment we think we have arrived at a state of perfection outside of the Will of God, we will get called back into the *Spiritual Classroom*. For what? To deal with the hidden forms of idolatry and receive formal updates on *Divine Etiquette* to break free from the patterns of the Spirit of Cain and the beastful underlying charactorial traits. Even Romans 1:25 shares how we get sidetracked: *"They exchanged the truth of God for a lie and worshiped and served created things rather than the Creator—who is forever praised. Amen."*

What if we are NOT bad people? Listen, there is good and bad in everyone; it just depends on which one dominates and how well we self-correct. Plus, a bad person does not usually admit they are bad. Actually, they will proclaim goodness while exhibiting bad character traits, allowing their fruits to unveil the truth. Conversely, if one admits they are a devilish spawn, then BELIEVE them, peacefully love them with a long-handled spoon, and keep it moving in the Spirit of Excellence.

In the Eye of God, the DUALITY of our human nature can indeed be tamed, *As It Pleases Him*, especially when we exercise our authority over it. Jude 1:10 shares the fact that we, as 'Dreamers,' have a choice in opting out of behaving like bruting beasts and the way of Cain. It says, *"But these speak evil of whatever they do not know; and whatever they know naturally, like brute beasts, in these things they corrupt themselves. Woe to them! For they have gone in the way of Cain, have run greedily in the error of Balaam for profit, and perished in the rebellion of Korah."*

Where are we going wrong? Frankly, in this *Spiritual Classroom*, I am not here to point the finger because we all have issues, we all have something to work on, and we all have the option to become a work-in-progress. Still, when God, our Heavenly Father, is not in the equation, our lives will reflect on the serious consequences of unwise or unprincipled behaviors, thoughts, beliefs, habits, words, and desires. All of which undermine our Moral and Spiritual Integrity, leading us away from the Kingdom of God instead of toward it.

Nonetheless, here is what Jude 1:8 hints about a 'Dreamer's' point of erring and beastlike tendencies that compromise our overall well-being. It says, *"Likewise also these dreamers defile the flesh, reject authority, and speak evil of dignitaries."* Once this happens, the cascading effects lead to various forms of suffering, pain, or disdainment, making it so much easier to

Divine Etiquette

develop Mental, Physical, Emotional, and Spiritual Spots. In all simplicity, we will develop BLIND SPOTS, leading to all types of rashes, sores, and wounds, ushering us into a *Spiritual Classroom* for Divine Change or Correction.

Before going any further with the Spiritual Spots, please allow me to Divinely Align this matter Spiritually. *"These are spots in your love feasts, while they feast with you without fear, serving only themselves. They are clouds without water, carried about by the winds; late autumn trees without fruit, twice dead, pulled up by the roots; raging waves of the sea, foaming up their own shame; wandering stars for whom is reserved the blackness of darkness forever."* Jude 1:12-13.

As Dr. Y. Bur, the WHY Doctor, I understand this may be hard to swallow regarding the beastlike sides that thrust us into a spotted or checkered state, leading to some form of blindness, but we need to know this. So, let us dig a little deeper into this matter, especially since we are in a *Spiritual Classroom* anyway. For example, but not limited to such:

- ☐ **Mental Blind Spots**: In this State of Being, anxiety, depression, confusion, and a lack of focus can arise, especially when disobedience, arrogance, dullness, and rebellion are present. Unfortunately, this is what causes us to continuously reject authority, disrespect the Laws of the Land, and engage in harmful behaviors while appearing right in our own eyes. Jude 1:16 says, *"These are grumblers, complainers, walking according to their own lusts; and they mouth great swelling words, flattering people to gain advantage."*

- ☐ **Physical Blind Spots**: In this State of Being, our bodies can reflect our internal turmoil, resulting in illness or fatigue when we neglect our health and well-being. While at the same time knowing nothing about the chemical imbalances we trigger or the hormones we do not release to counterbalance.

- ☐ **Emotional Blind Spots**: When our heart and mind postures are distorted, we may find ourselves thinking everyone else has a problem, not realizing we may be the cause or culprit. More importantly, the lack of positive relationships and constant negativity can create emotional scars, wounds, and traumas, leading to feelings of loneliness, rejection, depression, deflection, or projection. Jude 1:17-19 shares this: *"But you, beloved, remember the words which were spoken before by the apostles of our Lord Jesus Christ: how they told you that there would be mockers in the last time who would walk according to their own ungodly lusts. These are sensual persons, who cause divisions, not having the Spirit."*

- ☐ **Spiritual Blind Spots**: When we are out of the Will of God, doing our own thing with no regard to our Predestined Blueprint, we will experience a longing from within. As a result, it prevents us from seeing what we should have, overlooking what we should not have, or remaining where we do not belong, creating distance from God and diminishing our Spiritual Vitality.

In this *Spiritual Classroom*, here is how to reverse engineer spots, blemishes, sores, or wounds *As It Pleases God*, according to Jude 1:20-23: *"But you, beloved, building yourselves up on your most holy faith, praying in the Holy Spirit, keep yourselves in the love of God, looking for the mercy of our Lord Jesus Christ unto eternal life. And on some have compassion, making a distinction; but others save with fear, pulling them out of the fire, hating even the garment defiled by the flesh."*

Divine Etiquette

Are Spiritual Spots of Blindness real for us as Believers? No one is exempt from Spiritual Blindness, Deafness, or Muteness. The moment we allow the beast (human nature) from within to arise and take over negatively for the lesser good, it inhibits our Spiritual Clarity, Attunedness, and Voice. Therefore, it should be tamed at all times, including when there is an uprising within the psyche. Do we have the power to do so? Absolutely!

The destructive behavior, if left unchecked when triggered by stress, trauma, chaos, or societal pressures, can result in a downfall from the inside out. Through Spiritual Guidance, Self-Control, Moral Clarity, Self-Reflection, and Self-Awareness, we have the power to overcome, subdue, or eradicate with an ongoing commitment to our Heavenly Father, ourselves, and others to become a work-in-progress, *As It Pleases Him.*

The secret to bringing forth our Divine Blueprinted Purpose *As It Pleases God* is to 'RISE' to the occasion! Why must we rise from the comfort of where we are? In the Kingdom, if we think we can sit back and expect the Kingdom to serve us without us getting up out of whatever and with whomever, we are sadly mistaken. We cannot be zapped into a righteous state of being without wanting to be in one. Why not? It violates Spiritual Laws and the Divine Elements of Choice. We are not robots; therefore, we must willingly make the free will effort to positively change for the better.

What if the *Spiritual Classroom* does not work? Frankly, it means that we are in the WRONG CLASSROOM! Whenever we are in a *Spiritual Classroom* for *Spirit to Spirit* Training, there is no need to worry about not having what we need. As long as we are WILLING to obey the Will and Word of God while aligning with our Divine Blueprint with the Holy Trinity at the forefront, we will come out adequately equipped with the Spiritual Tools necessary with the Whole Armor of God.

Divine Etiquette

So, once in the *Spiritual Classroom*, it behooves us to get an understanding, *As It Pleases God*, to ensure we are not playing ourselves short with the lessons we need to learn, the necessities encapsulated in the lesson, or what it will take to break or reverse a yoke of bondage.

By pinpointing the ROOT of our wavering faith, we can take ownership of it while bringing about some resolve or regrafting quickly. If we GIVE UP on or do not REGRAFT ourselves amid the waver, then it may be an automatic forfeiture. What is more, I do not want anyone to lose their Birthright due to the lack of understanding from a Spiritual Perspective.

When it comes down to Divine Change, the moment we think we are NOT ready for our Divine Purpose or the odds are against us, our change or transformation will take place. On the other hand, there are times when we think we are ready, but in God's Divine Eye, we are not! As a result, He sends us back to the drawing board of reality, which may feel like failure, rejection, loss, or a setback.

Why does God send us back to the *Spiritual Classroom*? The reasons may vary from person to person because we all have some form of Spiritual need, trauma, or deprivation. The *Back to the Spiritual Classroom* Chart unveils most reasons, but is not limited to such.

- ☐ You are failing the People Test.
- ☐ You have atrocious communication skills.
- ☐ You have secrets or unrepentant sins.
- ☐ You are corrupting God's credibility or your integrity.
- ☐ You are not using the Fruits of the Spirit.
- ☐ You are unforgiving or hateful.
- ☐ You are engaging in the things that God hates.
- ☐ You are on the wrong track.
- ☐ You are too emotional or reckless.
- ☐ You are exhibiting too much doubt or unworthiness.

Divine Etiquette

- ☐ You are too negative or doubtful.
- ☐ You need a checkup from the neck up.
- ☐ You are engaging in too much folly.
- ☐ God is regrafting your character.
- ☐ You are under a generational curse.
- ☐ You have hidden your Gift, Talent, or Calling.
- ☐ You are clueless about WHO you are and WHY.
- ☐ You allow your psyche to take the wheel instead of the Holy Spirit.
- ☐ You are Spiritually Asleep, Lukewarm, or Dull.
- ☐ You are outright disobedient or a stiff-necked person.
- ☐ You are operating under a Pharisee's or Jezebel Spirit.
- ☐ You are consumed by an ungoverned tongue.
- ☐ You are bound by envy, jealousy, pride, greed, coveting, or competitiveness.
- ☐ You lack SELF-CONTROL.

Why do we need these lists in *Divine Etiquette*? It jogs the memory of the psyche. The moment we try to read others, most often, we are reading the echoes of ourselves, especially if we are not Spiritually Trained to read through the Heavenly Lens of Divine Discernment. Unfortunately, this is why there is a lot of backwardness and hurt among those who truly love God.

For me, I am the first to admit that I am not perfect and that I am still a work-in-progress. Plus, the more Divine Wisdom and Spiritual Principles I share regarding what I have learned, the more God TRUSTS me with the Divine Overflow of Wisdom, Knowledge, and Understanding. Above all, you are no different...if you follow instructions, you too can SUPERSEDE me if the *Divine Etiquette: As It Pleases God*® Spiritual Principles are placed at the forefront of your life. Really? Yes, really!

Divine Etiquette

Here is the deal: From a Spiritual Perspective, most people attempt to read the physical eyes of man, which is proven to be inaccurate at times. According to the Heavenly of Heavens, it is not the physical eyes we should be reading; it is the Spiritual Eye. How is this possible? It is possible based on this one question, *"Can the blind lead the blind? Will they not both fall into the ditch?"* Luke 6:39.

We must develop the ability to SEE *Eye to Eye* Spiritually or *Spirit to Spirit* Relationally, to develop preciseness and accuracy to see correctly, *As It Pleases God*. If not, our perceptions and biases can cloud our ability to read the true contents of the soul based on man's system of operation. Now, in *Divine Etiquette: As It Pleases God*, all we need is to establish a *Selfless Commitment* to the Will of God and our reason for being in Earthen Vessels.

Selfless Commitment

The Commitment to God is short and sweet, saying, *"Now to Him who is able to keep you from stumbling, And to present you faultless Before the presence of His glory with exceeding joy, To God our Savior, Who alone is wise, Be glory and majesty, Dominion and power, Both now and forever. Amen."* Jude 1:24-25.

A commitment to personal excellence, *As It Pleases God*, is derived from the DESIRE to become better, until our better becomes our best, and our best becomes our Greatest. Here is a piece of Divine Wisdom from Proverbs 28:26, which says: *"He who trusts in his own heart is a fool, but whoever walks wisely will be delivered."*

Without a doubt, we are all driven by some form of achievement, recognition, responsibility, or growth; still, we must add God into the equation. Why should we add Him, especially when we are our own person? Our level of

Divine Etiquette

commitment determines our level of performance, and it sparks the amount of excellence we can experience at any given moment.

So, if we add God into our lives, *As It Pleases Him*, with the mindset of, "*I can do all things through Christ who strengthens me,*" according to Philippians 4:13, we inadvertently allow the Divine Multiplying Factors into the *Selfless Commitment* with Spiritual Growth working on our behalf. On the other hand, if we do not add Him into the equation and engage in selfish commitments, we are on our own with our self-induced or self-led whatever! Is this not a little insensitive? Maybe or maybe not, but Proverbs 12:1 specifically says, "*Whoever loves instruction loves knowledge, but he who hates correction is unwise.*"

What is the purpose of *Selfless Committing*? First, we must understand that selfishness is a repellent, pushing people, places, and things away from us and corrupting good character. In addition, selfishness spoils good fruits and the whole bunch, even with good-willed intentions.

Secondly, we must know that selflessness is alluring, drawing people, places, and things toward us while influencing our level of sustainable attraction and social connections. Once released, *As It Pleases God*, it branches off into a few types of allurants, whether it is romantic, platonic, or work-related:

- ☐ Physical Allurants: Appealing physical features.
- ☐ Behavioral Allurants: Great attitude and demeanor.
- ☐ Emotional Allurants: Pristine emotional intelligence.
- ☐ Situational Allurants: Excellent people skills.

By understanding these various forms of allurants included in *Divine Etiquette: As It Pleases God*® according to our DNA, we can better selflessly navigate our interactions with others. Be it physical, behavioral, emotional, or situational, they foster genuine connections of authenticity and understanding when used correctly.

Thirdly, we must also realize that we operate in both selfishness and selflessness simultaneously, according to the Spiritual Law of Duality. However, we must position ourselves to allow our selflessness to become the most important component of our physical traits, behavioral characteristics, or even situational contexts. Doing so in Earthen Vessels brings forth the magnetic gravitational pull between individuals and our Divine Destiny.

Plus, let me say this before moving on: If someone says to me, 'I do not have a selfish bone in my body.' All types of red flags go up, and I would not trust them at all. Why not? The Spiritual Law of Duality is real, relevant, and accurate. More importantly, selfishness has a positive and negative trigger, especially when it relates to our survival or well-being. Simply put, our bodies will naturally go into a selfish survival mode, releasing cortisol into our system by default. Therefore, if they can lie about having a selfish bone, I already know the Spirit of Deception is at work.

In my opinion, picturesquely, this is similar to a married man who would naturally become selfish if another man attempted to steal his wife. If this does not occur, and he willfully allows another man to bogart his home, taking what should belong to him, it means his heart is with another! Selfishness and selflessness must become balanced according to the situation at hand, so we should always approach all things with God in our equational efforts.

Now, getting back to *Selfless Commitments*, when we are committed to something or someone, there is little or no hesitation in giving up so easily. Actually, we will put in the work or do what it takes to make sure everything is copacetic on our behalf.

Divine Etiquette

Conversely, without a commitment on any level, we will inadvertently suffer from hesitation, doubt, or resistance based on our selfish needs, wants, or desires without having the willingness to bring forth a mutual agreement. In my opinion, this is more like the 'Whatever happens, happens' mentality.

In the realm of Divine Growth and Spiritual Development, *As It Pleases God*, when operating in outright uncertainty, we become problematic in the Eye of God. How so? In the pursuit of excellence, clarity, and purpose, He views uncertainty and the lack of commitment as double-mindedness. Here is what James 1:8 says about a person operating in uncertainty: *"He is a double-minded man, unstable in all his ways."* For sure, we cannot get to a Divine Status in the Kingdom until we master our Heaven on Earth Experiences, weeding out inner conflict or indecision.

Why must we master the certainty process as Believers? In the Kingdom of God, when dealing with the Divine Secrets, Wisdom, Treasures, or His precious sheep, we must be able to think on our feet. We do not have time to deal with an internal tug-of-war, frustration, anxiety, and a lack of direction. We must be ready, equipped, and proactively prepared for what is next. Then again, we may have to put our issues aside to become laser-focused, waiting for our Spiritual Cues.

When we are Divinely Representing the Kingdom of God, for real, for real, we will be tried, tested, provoked, rejected, and tempted. If we trip over ourselves, our thoughts, our emotions, or our traumas, it means we go back to the Spiritual Classroom for updates. Fortunately, this is conducted for our safety and to protect our known or unknown vulnerabilities.

Why must we remain safe? The enemy will have us for lunch if we tackle Spiritual Things without an understanding of them, especially when we are weak Mentally, Physically, Emotionally, or Spiritually while thinking we are okay. Not knowing who we are in Christ Jesus reminds me of the sons of Sceva, seeing the power of Paul's ministry, who had not received the Holy Spirit and attempted to invoke the name of Jesus to expel an evil spirit.

Here is the story: *"Then some of the itinerant Jewish exorcists took it upon themselves to call the name of the Lord Jesus over those who had evil spirits, saying, 'We exorcise you by the Jesus whom Paul preaches.' Also there were seven sons of Sceva, a Jewish chief priest, who did so. And the evil spirit answered and said, "Jesus I know, and Paul I know; but who are you?" Then the man in whom the evil spirit was leaped on them, overpowered them, and prevailed against them, so that they fled out of that house naked and wounded."* Acts 19:13-16.

Now, if we think we are any different when it comes to the wiles of the enemy, we are sadly mistaken. As a result of God's Divine Love and Mercy for us, He blocks us from certain Elements of Spirituality until we develop a genuine *Spirit to Spirit* Relationship with Him while building ourselves up in the FAITH.

The embodiment of Divine Authority and Power is for Believers to use, not to abuse. Nevertheless, if we are out of the Will of God or operating in the Spirit of Selfishness, Disobedience, or Rebellion, we can picturesquely stub our big toe.

Get Off The Sideline

Listen, we can talk Bible all we like, but if we cannot apply it, *As It Pleases God*, cover ourselves with the Blood of Jesus as Spiritual Atonement, or become Spirit-Led by the Holy Spirit, we can get hurt dealing with Spiritual Matters. When on Spiritual Milk or when profusely crying over spilled milk, we are vulnerable, becoming easy bait, an easy target, or fresh meat.

Divine Etiquette

What is more, according to the Heavenly of Heavens, when operating with all types of rotten fruits and uncorrected character traits that are unpleasing to God, we will get SIDELINED while thinking we are in the game. How do we know if we are sidelined? The psyche knows automatically, but it is in denial. So, it (meaning the psyche) goes on a negative rambling stage with our thoughts, words, desires, and habits, with a feeding frenzy until we get fed up, awakening from our slumber.

According to the Heavenly of Heavens, to keep the psyche of mankind in check, *As It Pleases God*, we must assess our lives, ensuring we have or create balance in all areas, including business. More importantly, with *Divine Etiquette* and to avoid half-stepping, we must use the Fruits of the Spirit and behave Christlike at all times to maintain Divine Leverage on our behalf. Colossians 3:2 advises us on the ideal mindset to practice, *As It Pleases Him* to help us self-correct at the drop of a dime. It says, "*Set your mind on things above, not on things on the earth.*" Is this realistic? Absolutely!

In a world inundated with noise, lies, fakeness, and distractions, my ability to write, speak, and articulate thoughts clearly is a Heavenly Gift ordained for a time such as this. For me, this Spiritual Ability is not just a skill; it is deeply intertwined with my Authentic Identity and Predestined Blueprinted Purpose. By Spiritually Aligning everything *As It Pleases God*, it gives me Divine Leverage to do, *Spirit to Spirit*, what most cannot at this present moment.

Here is the deal on how I got off the sideline: I articulate and DOCUMENT my thoughts, words, ideas, or revelations as a Spiritual Testimony for the Kingdom of God. Why for the Kingdom of God? Because everything I share with others is born and bred from experience, deep reflections, unanswered questions, and a commitment to authenticity.

Divine Etiquette

So, there is no possible way to exclude Him, especially when I am truly living because of Him and His Divine Interventions.

Being that I had to make a conscious choice to depend on the Breath of Life to *Get Off The Sideline*, when I write, I draw from those life experiences, hard lessons, and Divine Downloads from the Heavenly of Heavens. All of which shaped who I am, going deeper into God, *Spirit to Spirit*, to extract Divine Wisdom with zero shame attached. In the Eye of God, this Heavenly Authenticity resonates with readers and listeners, making my words relatable, pliable, understandable, impactful, and relevant.

By opening up about my struggles and triumphs, the goal is to get us back in the game, bridge gaps, heal wounds, set captives free, and spark good conversations, *As It Pleases God*. Once again, if one follows the instructions in this book, *Divine Etiquette: As It Pleases God*®, they can supersede what I do. How so? In the Kingdom of God, the students must become better than the Spiritual Teacher with multiplying factors. If not, there is a Spiritual Glitch in the Divine System.

Through God's Divine Grace and Mercy, I have put in the work, doing what I am Spiritually Called to do, and now it is time for you to do your part in sharpening your iron. What does iron have to do with anything? *"As iron sharpens iron, so a man sharpens the countenance of his friend."* Proverbs 27:17.

With a commitment to improve and to *Get Off The Sideline*, you must know firsthand what is important to you. Below is a list of things you must know, but not limited to such:

- ☐ You must recognize your NEED for God while understanding who you are in Christ Jesus. *"What is man that You are mindful of him, and the son of man that You visit him? For You have made him a little lower than the angels, and You have crowned him with glory and honor."* Psalms 8:4-5.

Divine Etiquette

- ☐ You must KNOW that you were created in the Image of God. Genesis 1:26-27 says, "*Then God said, 'Let Us make man in Our image, according to Our likeness; let them have dominion over the fish of the sea, over the birds of the air, and over the cattle, and over all the earth and over every creeping thing that creeps on the earth.' So God created man in His own image; in the image of God He created him; male and female He created them.*"

- ☐ You cannot become ATTACHED to materialistic things. It invokes selfishness, pride, greed, envy, jealousy, coveting, and competitiveness. Here is what 1 Timothy 6:9-10 shares with us: "*But those who desire to be rich fall into temptation and a snare, and into many foolish and harmful lusts which drown men in destruction and perdition. For the love of money is a root of all kinds of evil, for which some have strayed from the faith in their greediness, and pierced themselves through with many sorrows.*"

- ☐ You must be willing to CANCEL your negative thoughts by replacing them with positive ones. Here is what Romans 12:2 wants us to know: "*And do not be conformed to this world, but be transformed by the renewing of your mind, that you may prove what is that good and acceptable and perfect will of God.*"

- ☐ You must become TRANSPARENT with your weaknesses and inconsistencies to God. In *Divine Etiquette: As It Pleases God®*, repeat this daily: "*Search me, O God, and know my heart; try me, and know my anxieties; and see if there is any wicked way in me, and lead me in the way everlasting.*" Psalm 139:23-24.

Divine Etiquette

- ☐ You must be WILLING to do everything in the Spirit of Excellence with outright integrity. Here is a Wisdom Nugget from Proverbs 22:29: *"Do you see a man who excels in his work? He will stand before kings; He will not stand before unknown men."*

- ☐ You must have COMPASSION and MERCY with yourself and others, focusing on interdependency. If you cannot become a team player in your home, it is hard to become a loyal team player elsewhere without having your ego overshadow your true Greatness. Here is what Ecclesiastes 4:9-10 shares with us: *"Two are better than one, because they have a good reward for their labor. For if they fall, one will lift up his companion. But woe to him who is alone when he falls, for he has no one to help him up."*

- ☐ You must DETACH yourself from worldly power, super-inflated egos, and manipulation. 2 Corinthians 10:5 says, *"Casting down arguments and every high thing that exalts itself against the knowledge of God, bringing every thought into captivity to the obedience of Christ."*

- ☐ You must become GRATEFUL for everything, the good or bad, right or wrong, just or unjust, etc., while *"Casting all your care upon Him, for He cares for you."* 1 Peter 5:7.

- ☐ You must EXTRACT the positive and discard the negative in any given situation, getting rid of worry. Matthew 6:34 tells us what to do: *"Therefore do not worry about tomorrow, for tomorrow will worry about its own things. Sufficient for the day is its own trouble."*

Divine Etiquette

- ☐ You must be FORGIVING and KIND-HEARTED. James 5:16 specifically says, *"Confess your trespasses to one another, and pray for one another, that you may be healed. The effective, fervent prayer of a righteous man avails much."*

- ☐ You must be willing to CAST DOWN the Spirit of Envy or Jealousy immediately. Here is a Spiritual Insight from James 3:16. It says, *"For where envy and self-seeking exist, confusion and every evil thing are there."*

- ☐ You must be willing to WALK AWAY from anything and anyone taking you in a destructive direction. Know this: *"For I know the thoughts that I think toward you, says the Lord, thoughts of peace and not of evil, to give you a future and a hope."* Jeremiah 29:11.

- ☐ You must have a desire to become INTERNALLY JOYFUL through your relationship with God, yourself, and others, in this order. Romans 15:13 says, *"Now may the God of hope fill you with all joy and peace in believing, that you may abound in hope by the power of the Holy Spirit."*

- ☐ You must FIGHT THE TEMPTATION to control or bully others, especially the faint of heart. Repeat this over and over: *"I can do all things through Christ who strengthens me."* Philippians 4:13.

- ☐ You must GET RID of the hidden negative motives of deception. It is best to make people aware of your intentions up front to ensure you are not violating their free will. *"As obedient children, not conforming yourselves to the former lusts, as in your ignorance; but as He who called you is holy, you also be holy in all your conduct."* 1 Peter 1:14-15.

Divine Etiquette

- ☐ You must CONTROL your negative responses regarding your Gifts, Calling, Talents, Creativity, or Divine Blueprint. Matthew 25:21 gives us the ideal response we want: "*His lord said to him, 'Well done, good and faithful servant; you were faithful over a few things, I will make you ruler over many things. Enter into the joy of your lord.'*"

- ☐ You must REPENT of your wrongdoings or mistakes. Here is what Proverbs 28:13 wants us to know: "*He who covers his sins will not prosper, but whoever confesses and forsakes them will have mercy.*"

- ☐ You must become COMFORTING while sympathizing with others. Hebrews 4:15-16 shares: "*For we do not have a High Priest who cannot sympathize with our weaknesses, but was in all points tempted as we are, yet without sin. Let us therefore come boldly to the throne of grace, that we may obtain mercy and find grace to help in time of need.*"

- ☐ You must put a LIMIT on your worry by taking it to God in prayer and leaving it there. Isaiah 26:3 wants us to trust and know this: "*You will keep him in perfect peace, whose mind is stayed on You, because he trusts in You.*"

- ☐ You must allow yourself time to REFLECT creatively or figuratively. Philippians 4:8 shares: "*Finally, brethren, whatever things are true, whatever things are noble, whatever things are just, whatever things are pure, whatever things are lovely, whatever things are of good report, if there is any virtue and if there is anything praiseworthy—meditate on these things.*"

- ☐ You must ASSUME RESPONSIBILITY for your role in everything. No more tit-for-tat blaming games.

Divine Etiquette

Timothy 2:15 says, *"Be diligent to present yourself approved to God, a worker who does not need to be ashamed, rightly dividing the word of truth."*

- ☐ You must become a PEACEMAKER while finding an exit with the fire starters. 1 Thessalonians 5:11 says, *"Therefore comfort each other and edify one another, just as you also are doing."*

- ☐ You must EXTRACT the lesson from your obstacles, setbacks, and atrocities. And then, *"Commit your works to the Lord, and your thoughts will be established."* Proverbs 16:3.

- ☐ You MUST listen, learn, grow, sow, till, and execute. *"And that you put on the new man which was created according to God, in true righteousness and holiness."* Ephesians 4:24.

According to the Heavenly of Heavens, the Spiritual Platform of Commitment to the Kingdom has Spiritual Conditions, Prerequisites, and Principles associated. Better yet, know this: Anything having Spiritual POWER is conditional.

Why does God place conditions on power? In the Eye of God, it is for protective measures for us and the Kingdom. According to our human nature, with ungoverned control or dominance, we would become reckless or impulsive with Heavenly Commodities, especially without being properly vetted and tested, *As It Pleases Him*. Then again, power is not freely bestowed upon everyone because they cannot handle it properly.

As we all know by now, in our interactions, power has always been a highly sought-after commodity, not only from a human perspective but also in the Realm of the Spirit. If we

Divine Etiquette

do not understand the foundational principles of *Divine Etiquette: As It Pleases God®*, we can become self-serving, self-reliant, and self-defeating rather than community-minded, people-oriented, and authentically relatable.

When we are granted authority or power without appropriate guidance or readiness, it can lead to destruction, abuse, and suffering if left ungoverned. In the Eye of God, the sacred trust of real power is designed to unselfishly build, uplift, regraft, and transform for the Greater Good.

To *Get Off The Sideline*, we do not need to be perfect; still, growth and maturity are needed to grow GREAT, *As It Pleases God*. If we are watching from the sideline, how do we go about getting off of it as Believers? We must have a willing desire and workable ethics to become a positive work-in-progress in the Spiritual Regrafting phase. While at the same time, developing the Fruits of the Spirit and Christlike Character according to the Principles of the Kingdom.

Additionally, this may include overcoming trials, engaging in character-building experiences, accelerating in the Spiritual Growth Process, and cultivating virtues such as humility, empathy, and wisdom. Doing so gives us the Spiritual Edge needed to bring UNITY from within, spreading outwardly while understanding what we need from the Realm of the Spirit.

We are sadly mistaken if we think we DO NOT need anything from the Realm of the Spirit. Why? We are Spirit first, and human second. The moment we put our humanness before our Spirit, we create an imbalance by default. How is this possible when we are sold out for the Kingdom of God? Sold out or not, according to our Divine Blueprint, when we are Spiritually Asleep, we cannot become used to our full capacity in Earthen Vessels. Then again, if we think we have all the right answers, behave unrepentantly, or think we have an unblemished record, needing nothing from God or anyone

Divine Etiquette

else for this matter, we tend to make the biggest mistakes while becoming Spiritually Grounded.

In so many words, by omitting the real reason we came to Earth in the first place, we become limited. Why are we limited in the Kingdom of God, especially when faithfully serving Him? Our Heavenly Father desires a *Spirit to Spirit* Relationship with us. Also, He wants us to COVER ourselves with the Blood of Jesus and become Spirit-Led by the Holy Spirit...if we cannot do any of the above, then we will become Spiritually Limited to our Divinely Blueprinted Mission.

Now, if we want God to come to our level doing what we want Him to do, while secretly pimping and prostituting Him for selfish gain, we will invoke our own limits, Mentally, Physically, Emotionally, and Spiritually. What does this mean in layman's terms? The human psyche controls what we are doing and why, while sometimes using God as a cover-up instead of a COME-UP!

What is the cover-up all about for Believers? Usually, it becomes a massive covering for our deep-seated emotions of fear, anger, and unforgiveness. All of these create a barrier that separates us from our authentic selves and hinders our *Spirit to Spirit* Relationship with God. Nevertheless, in *Divine Etiquette*, to deal with them all, *As It Pleases God*, we must get to the root of the matter, which is *Dealing With Anger*.

Why not deal with the other two, fear and unforgiveness? They both have an underlying root or a big WHY. Most often, it is the Root of Anger or Bitterness that hides the resentful turmoil from within, giving us a false sense of peace, love, and prosperity. As a result of this underlying deficiency from within the psyche, it invokes a build-up of fears, paranoia, and a nest to harbor unforgiveness. Unfortunately, this can make us toxic with distorted perceptions, clouding our sense of good judgment.

Divine Etiquette

Dealing With Anger

When our emotions imprison us, we can limit our Freedom Experience and Restorative Power in Christ Jesus. For this reason, it behooves us to engage in *Dealing With Anger* from a Divine Perspective. By dismantling the negative wall and barriers surrounding our anger, we can hopefully eradicate the one-sided feelings or issues surrounding our selfish behaviors, thoughts, beliefs, desires, words, neediness, and readiness.

What does readiness or neediness have to do with *Dealing With Anger*? Most often, we lack readiness due to unresolved anger that causes pitch-fork wounds in dealing with betrayal, creating rifts that complicate our relational interactions and erode trust. In contrast, our ungoverned neediness will cause us to look for and tolerate people, places, and things to satiate our underlying insecurities. The two critical factors of readiness and neediness play crucial roles in our emotional responses when faced with feelings of betrayal or unresolved issues, which exempt no one in human form. Above all, they also determine our REACTIVENESS or PROACTIVENESS in or out of the Kingdom.

In a microwave world with instant everything at the click of a button and where appearances often outweigh authenticity, we often overlook whether we are being reactive or proactive. All of this can be due to our upbringing, environmental conditioning, societal pressures, unresolved traumas, and personal experiences, which can also cause us to deal with, redirect, and project, positively or negatively.

The concept of *Divine Etiquette* serves as a reminder of the profound truths hidden on the surface and beneath the surface in plain sight. How do we make this make sense? Although everyone is a little different, here is an example of our basic triggers having NOTHING to do with Demonic Possession. However, if this is the case, one would need a

Divine Etiquette

Spiritual Psychologist to assist. Ordinarily, with a positive and negative do-it-yourself Approach, *As It Pleases God*, we deal with Surface, Emotional, Cognitive (Mental), and Rooting Triggers:

- ☐ The Surface Triggers are:

    - ☐ Hunger.
    - ☐ Fatigue.
    - ☐ Bodily pain.
    - ☐ Daily stress.
    - ☐ Daily frustrations.
    - ☐ Poor communication.
    - ☐ Reaction to unkind people skills.
    - ☐ Poor customer service.
    - ☐ Being cut off in traffic.
    - ☐ Receiving an unexpected bill.
    - ☐ When someone interrupts you while speaking.
    - ☐ Losing your keys or phone.
    - ☐ Missing a deadline.
    - ☐ Loud or disruptive neighbors.
    - ☐ A wrong order at a restaurant.
    - ☐ Misplacing important documents.
    - ☐ A canceled event or meeting.

- ☐ The Emotional Triggers are:

    - ☐ Feeling a profound emotional connection.
    - ☐ Feeling disrespected or respected.
    - ☐ Being ignored or included.
    - ☐ Feeling insulted or respected.
    - ☐ Dishonesty or honesty in a conversation.
    - ☐ A feeling of jealousy or envy.
    - ☐ Coveting or contentment.
    - ☐ Competitiveness or togetherness.

Divine Etiquette

- ☐ Experiencing acceptance or rejection.
- ☐ Met or unmet needs or expectations.
- ☐ Lack of recognition or validation.
- ☐ Experiencing the absence or loss of a loved one.
- ☐ Feeling guilt for actions or decisions made.
- ☐ Experiencing embarrassment or humiliation.
- ☐ Feeling connected or disconnected.
- ☐ Experiencing happiness from positive events.
- ☐ Feeling frustration or rage in response to a situation.

☐ **The Cognitive Triggers Are:**

- ☐ The desire to learn or discover something new.
- ☐ Feeling a sense of release after overcoming a challenge.
- ☐ Feelings of justice or injustice.
- ☐ Fear of losing control.
- ☐ Positive or negative self-talk.
- ☐ Ungoverned mental chatter.
- ☐ Inferiority complex.
- ☐ Hopefulness or powerlessness.
- ☐ Positive or negative statements to self.
- ☐ Visualization of positive or negative outcomes.
- ☐ Setting and striving for achievable goals.
- ☐ Failing at our goals.
- ☐ Acts of kindness or rudeness.
- ☐ Being in nature or avoiding it.
- ☐ Perfectionism or a destroying mentality.

☐ **The Rooting Triggers Are:**

- ☐ Past or present traumas.
- ☐ Unresolved emotional pain.
- ☐ Learned behaviors and mindsets.

Divine Etiquette

- ☐ Suppressed emotions and desires.
- ☐ Internal battles with shame, abuse, and neglect.
- ☐ Bruised ego.
- ☐ Power hungry.
- ☐ Desperate to be seen.
- ☐ Lacking love.
- ☐ Feeling unsafe.
- ☐ Lack of worthiness.
- ☐ Abandonment issues.
- ☐ Experiences of bullying.
- ☐ Conflict between personal and cultural identity.
- ☐ Guilt from past actions.
- ☐ Parental expectations or pressure.
- ☐ Relationship betrayals or infidelity.
- ☐ Witnessing or experiencing violence.
- ☐ Financial instability in childhood.
- ☐ Chronic illness or health issues.
- ☐ Neglect or emotional unavailability.
- ☐ Long-standing family conflicts.

In the Eye of God, when dealing with a Divine Perspective, *As It Pleases Him*, the ones who pretend to be so strong and have it all together are usually the most insecure and sensitive. Really? Yes, really!

How is it possible for someone to seem so composed and poised while grappling with intense inner turmoil from within? They must constantly lie to themselves to display confidence and control. Unfortunately, with this façade of strength, those who are close to them can see through their lies, causing them to develop all types of masks.

Masks that are camouflaged with anger often lead them into a web of disillusionment, becoming secretly or openly abusive or controlling, Mentally, Physically, Emotionally,

Spiritually, or Financially. Then again, they can become outright defensive about everything, especially in the areas where they fall short.

On the other hand, the ones who are the most humble, understanding they are a work-in-progress, are usually the strongest. How do we equate humility with strength? According to the Heavenly of Heavens, it is due to their honesty, transparency, and willingness to make the necessary adjustments while self-correcting to become better, stronger, and wiser continually.

To better understand this dynamic, let us delve into how anger influences our ability to establish and respect boundaries, whether it is from a friend, family member, colleague, partner, or foe. Without the ability to process, manage, and express our anger constructively, we risk perpetuating a cycle of conflict, misunderstanding, confusion, revenge, and resentment, eroding our communication or people skills. In addition, it puts a damper on our ability to self-correct, self-reflect, and exhibit self-control, *As It Pleases God*.

For instance, we have someone who sets foolproof boundaries to keep people out of their relationship. But one person (the one who initiated the boundaries) violates the established borders due to the unsurety of their own making without advising the other party of the changes, violations, or struggles.

As a result, the person with unwavering trust and faithfulness, who adhered to the boundaries without a hitch, is put to shame, looking like boo-boo the fool and feeling blindsided. So, not only is one person dealing with unresolved anger, but we now have two angry people dealing with secret measures of unforgiveness due to silent grievances, betrayals, or unmet expectations. And now, we have two hurt people struggling to get back on track with

Divine Etiquette

their Divine Connection while questioning their Authentic Divinity.

According to *Divine Etiquette*, to move forward in the Spirit of Excellence, *As It Pleases God*, both individuals must be willing to address the unresolved anger, repent of misunderstandings, forgive each other, and formally reestablish trustworthy boundaries with a triple-braided cord mindset. What caused the rift in the first place? When we bring people's opinions into the equation without adding God wholeheartedly, we can unravel the top or bottom part of the triple-braided cord. How so? The ends were not Spiritually Sealed with the Word of God and the Blood of Jesus to make it a Divinely Anointed Triple-Braided Cord. Unfortunately, this is how Power Couples lose their power or fizzle out.

Here is the deal: Unforgiveness is a state of mind in which a person holds onto negative emotions, refusing to forgive someone who has wronged, traumatized, abandoned, shamed, outed, or hurt them. It is a common experience we will all go through at some point in our lives. Still, unforgiveness can have severe consequences for our mental and emotional well-being, as well as our relationships. In all simplicity, the relationship we have with God, ourselves, others, and our health will suffer as a result of unforgiveness.

Unforgiveness is derived from unresolved anger, bitterness, conditioning, biases, frustrations, fears, or traumas. In Earthen Vessels, our quality of life is paramount; therefore, we should not subject ourselves to the Spirit of Anger when we have the power to cast it down.

To be clear, we will definitely be presented with something or someone designed to provoke us, but we cannot allow anger to fester negatively. We must forgive, regardless of the trespasses. Even if we do not like the situation or what is happening around us, we must counteract it with GRATEFULNESS while interjecting the Fruits of the Spirit

Divine Etiquette

and Christlike Character. Honestly, there are times when it becomes challenging to do, especially when someone is casting doom and gloom over us. Still, it is doable in the Eye of God.

In the Kingdom, when using *Divine Etiquette: As It Pleases God*, anger is two-fold. It can work for us as a means of motivation, or it can be used as a tool to destroy us and others. The signs of anger problems from others can also give us a warning about things to come. When people show us who they are, we must believe them to safeguard our sanity. Yes, we are to forgive, but it does not mean subjecting ourselves to becoming a victim or casualty, especially when dealing with a few items, but not limited to such:

- ☐ Verbal Outbursts.
- ☐ Physical Aggression.
- ☐ Mood Swings.
- ☐ Blame Shifting.
- ☐ Chronic Lying and Deceitfulness.
- ☐ Passive-Aggressive Behaviors.
- ☐ Massive Destroyer (engaging in breaking things).

According to Proverbs 22:24, it says, "*Do not associate with a man given to anger, or go with a hot-tempered man.*" Now, if we were this person, we would have work to do. Why is work required of us? If we put up a smokescreen regarding anger, it will cause us to become Mentally, Emotionally, Physically, and Spiritually tapped out, causing temper tantrums when we least expect them.

According to our DNA, it takes a lot of energy to become and remain angry, harbor unforgiveness, or hold a grudge. More importantly, we can only hide anger for a certain amount of time before the mask comes off, exposing our true colors, including the areas in which we are blowing smoke.

Divine Etiquette

Aggression, violence, and disrespectfulness are the result of undealt with anger and fear. In today's time, some people think it is cool or funny to pop off, but in all actuality, anger can create a great disservice, especially in the Eye of God. For example, in the Bible, Moses could not enter the Promised Land due to his uncontrollable anger, which led to his act of disobedience.

As we know, the Root of Obedience is a required trait when dealing with the Fruits of the Spirit and Christlike Character. We cannot allow our anger to frighten, disobey, or hurt innocent people. On this note, James 1:19-20 gives us wise counsel on this matter: *"So then, my beloved brethren, let every man be swift to hear, slow to speak, slow to wrath; for the wrath of man does not produce the righteousness of God."*

If we are frustrated, we can take a walk, pray, dance, or exercise to release bottled-up energy. Never become accusatory or point the finger. Why should we NOT point the finger, primarily when we are justified in doing so? It depletes our POWER. Plus, Colossians 3:8 says this: *"But now you yourselves are to put off all these: anger, wrath, malice, blasphemy, filthy language out of your mouth."*

When expressing how we feel with *Divine Etiquette*, speak in the 'I' form, not the 'You' form (you did this, you did that). The you, you, you, is out! Here is what I would say, but not limited to such:

- ☐ 'I allowed myself to get upset because of _____.'
- ☐ 'I got a little frustrated because _____.'
- ☐ 'I apologize for getting upset because I felt that _____.'
- ☐ I feel frustrated when our conversations do not lead to understanding; what can I do better?
- ☐ I recognize that we have different perspectives, and I want to understand yours.

Divine Etiquette

- ☐ I want to take a moment to cool down before discussing this further.
- ☐ I am committed to finding a solution that works for both of us.
- ☐ I feel hurt when my opinions are not considered, and I would very much appreciate a listening ear, please.
- ☐ I want to listen actively to your concerns so that we can find common ground.
- ☐ I realize that I might not have all the answers, but I am open to suggestions.
- ☐ I need to ask for a little space right now to collect my thoughts.
- ☐ I feel overwhelmed, and I would appreciate a little more patience as we work through this together.
- ☐ I want to avoid pointing fingers and focus on how we can move forward together on _____.
- ☐ I believe that our relationship is important, and I want to nurture it by resolving this conflict.
- ☐ I am willing to compromise if it means reaching a solution we can both agree on.
- ☐ I need us to set aside some time to really dive into this issue together.
- ☐ I understand that I may have contributed to the conflict, and I am ready to take responsibility regarding _____.
- ☐ I appreciate the willingness to discuss _____ together.
- ☐ I hope we can both express our feelings about _____ together without judgment or defensiveness.
- ☐ I feel relieved when we can talk things through instead of avoiding the issue.
- ☐ I am optimistic that we can resolve _____ and strengthen our connection together.

Divine Etiquette

When we own how we feel, we can take action and shift the atmosphere or energy. However, if we deny it, then there is nothing to resolve. I would say go ahead, own it, and get over it quickly. Amid all things, here is what Ephesians 4:26-27 advises: *"Be angry, and do not sin: do not let the sun go down on your wrath, nor give place to the devil."*

Dealing With Injustices

Who said forgiving would be easy? Well, it is not. Our lives are full of choices day in and day out. Some choices we want to make, and some we do not. The decisions we do not want to make often serve as an injustice, forcing us to make a decision.

Injustices are a part of life, coming with Spiritual Lessons, Blessings, Opportunities, and Tests to prevent a lifestyle of déjà vu. As life would have it, an injustice (being wronged) comes into your life for two reasons:

- ☐ To let you know that it is NOT YOUR BLESSING.
- ☐ To cause you to DOUBT your Blessing.

If you can find your way through wrongness, there is rightness on the other side; however, you must find out what your injustices are trying to convey to you. Once you find out, you must repent, forgive, and prevent yourself from being consumed by negative emotions that will cause history to repeat itself.

How do we make injustices make sense as Believers displaying self-control? The enemy is going to shoot his shots, doing what he does best. If it lands without a positive, effective, and righteous counteraction on our behalf or if we do not put on the Whole Armor of God, *As It Pleases Him*, we will 'get got' even if we are Believers. In Earthen Vessels, it is for this very reason that Ephesians 6:13-16 tells us: *"Therefore take up the whole armor of God, that you may be able to withstand in the evil day, and having done all, to stand. Stand therefore, having girded your waist with truth, having put on the breastplate of righteousness, and having shod your feet with the preparation of the gospel of peace; above all, taking the shield of faith with which you will be able to quench all the fiery darts of the wicked one."*

In *Divine Etiquette*, the Word of God is both a GUIDE and a WEAPON. In Spiritual Warfare, if we use the Fruits of the Spirit, *As It Pleases Him*, and behave Christlike, we do not have to put our hands on anyone. Nor do we have to lie down to become trampled over by the injustices placed before us or become violent. Here is how this works according to Isaiah 49:2, *"And he made my mouth like a sharpened sword, in the shadow of his hand he hid me; he made me into a polished arrow and concealed me in his quiver."*

When we are in Purpose on purpose according to our Predestined Blueprint and *As It Pleases God*, there is a level of Divine Protection associated with our READINESS and PRECISION that will put the enemy to boot. On the other hand, if we are out of purpose, doing our own thing without God anywhere in the equation, we become limited in the amount of protection needed. Is this fair? Absolutely. If we are not ready and we are constantly missing the mark with God nowhere in sight, then what needs protecting? If we think He is going to protect our mess, then we are sadly mistaken.

From my perspective, when dealing with injustices, we must begin making our mess into a Testimony that is usable and palatable for the Kingdom. What can this do for us? As an instrument of change, it helps us to begin turning our Divine Purpose into a Spiritual Arrow that the Heavenly of Heavens polishes up. Additionally, it assists in bringing us closer into the Arms of God, our Heavenly Father, for Divine Protection. Ultimately, this makes Psalm 91:1-2 even more powerful: *"He who dwells in the secret place of the Most High shall abide under the shadow of the Almighty. I will say of the Lord, 'He is my refuge and my fortress, my God, in Him I will trust.'"*

Does Psalm 91:1-2 really work? Of course! First, it is the Word of God. Secondly, if we are in Purpose on purpose, *As It Pleases Him*, the Secret Place must be Divinely Protected. Thirdly, if we think we are big and bold enough to touch someone in a Secret Place protected by the Holy of Holies, touch them and see what happens. I promise you that you will know that God is real, and He does not play around when it comes to those who are Divinely Aligned with the Heavenly of Heavens.

What is the Secret Place? The Secret Place is IN HIM! John 15:5 gives a picturesque view of how this works: *"I am the vine, you are the branches. He who abides in Me, and I in him, bears much fruit; for without Me you can do nothing."* And then, Acts 17:28 concurs, saying: *"For in Him we live and move and have our being, as also some of your own poets have said, 'For we are also His offspring.'"*

When in a Secret Place, *As It Pleases God*, everyone's experience will be different because our Predestined Blueprints were all created differently, similar to our fingerprints, eye-prints, footprints, and mind-prints. Plus, their LEVEL of Spiritual Training or Commission will determine the expansiveness of their Secret Place. Furthermore, it will also determine the Divine Protection required to keep them safe to do what they were called to do.

What is so special about those who are truly in a Secret Place? Most often, no one knows who they are unless the Spirit of God unveils it. Let me say this: They are so humble, kind, and pleasant, faithfully using the Fruits of the Spirit and behaving Christlike to the point we would think they are weak. But they are all so POWERFUL in the Eye of God.

Divine Etiquette

In times of uncertainty, let me remind you: You have the key to open the door to your Spiritual Lessons, Tests, Opportunities, and Blessings, enhancing your life beyond what you could ever imagine. However, to get to this point, you do not want to exhibit any form of disrespectfulness or unforgiveness toward what the Spirit of the Lord is pointing out or unveiling.

Now, before moving on to *Dealing with Unforgiveness*, know this: *"For we are His workmanship, created in Christ Jesus for good works, which God prepared beforehand that we should walk in them."* Ephesians 2:10. All this means is that you have what it takes, period! Regardless of where you are or what you are going through, there is hope for you, IN HIM. As Paul says in Colossians 2:10, *"You are complete in Him, who is the head of all principality and power."*

Dealing With Unforgiveness

According to the Heavenly of Heavens, you need to understand a few Spiritual Principles about forgiveness. Forgiving is the channel through which you can release your deepest hurts and fears. Yes, it would be best if you forgave all who have trespassed against you. As a Believer, this does not mean that you have to hang around them, be with them, or even associate with them, but you must forgive, even if it is with a long-handled spoon.

Unbeknown to most, harboring unforgiveness could render you incapable of functioning normally. Why would we become overwhelmed or function abnormally as Believers? Due to the constant overwhelming thoughts of getting even or secret plotting when hurt, wounded, betrayed, rejected, or traumatized. Unforgiveness is like a ton of bricks weighing you down, draining all of your mental energy with a secret

Divine Etiquette

guise of denial or uprightness, as your mental chatter tells the real story of what is hidden within the psyche.

Unforgiveness is nothing more than holding a grudge, eventually leaving you angry, bitter, and frustrated from the inside out. Of course, no one knows what that person may have done to you or how that person's actions may have affected you. However, you must think about what unforgiveness is doing to you right now. You must show mercy and forgiveness, regardless of the wrong done to you. Here is how to do so, but not limited to such:

- ☐ You must ACKNOWLEDGE that you are holding onto negative emotions.
- ☐ You must RECOGNIZE and AGREE that the negative emotions associated are not serving you.
- ☐ You must IDENTIFY the source of your unforgiveness.
- ☐ You must EXAMINE the situation or trigger that caused the feeling.
- ☐ You must UNDERSTAND the reasons behind whatever or whomever.
- ☐ You must MIRROR the situation, circumstance, or event from a different point of view.
- ☐ You must REPENT of your associations with whatever or whomever.
- ☐ You must FORGIVE and let go of the negative emotions.
- ☐ You must REPLACE negative emotions with positive ones.
- ☐ You must PINPOINT the win-win or lesson.
- ☐ You must DOCUMENT your findings with a Testament or Testimony for the GREATER GOOD.
- ☐ You must RECONCILE with whom you have exhibited unforgiveness.

Divine Etiquette

Will this list really help us? Absolutely! Thus, we must use the list, *As It Pleases God*. Operating *As It Pleases Him* profoundly impacts our lives, allowing us to tap into Heaven's Reservoir of Divine Wisdom, shaking loose the inner trauma that has the potential to sabotage, contaminate, distract, or derail us or our Bloodline.

Why do we get derailed? No one is perfect, and we all have something to work on or work at. Here is what the Word of God shares with us: *"For many times, also, your own heart has known That even you have cursed others. All this I have proved by wisdom. I said, 'I will be wise'; But it was far from me. As for that which is far off and exceedingly deep, Who can find it out? I applied my heart to know, To search and seek out wisdom and the reason of things, To know the wickedness of folly, Even of foolishness and madness. And I find more bitter than death The woman whose heart is snares and nets, Whose hands are fetters. He who pleases God shall escape from her, But the sinner shall be trapped by her."* Ecclesiastes 7:22-26.

Who Are We Pleasing?

In a world filled with innumerable opinions, countless biases, insurmountable perspectives, and shifting morals, in *Divine Etiquette: As It Pleases God*®, it is imperative to know the ins and outs of WHOM we are Pleasing and WHY we are doing so. As a beacon of Divine Guidance from the Most High God, although we do not like ordinary standards, principles, and protocols, there are many Spiritual Ones that are required of us in Earthen Vessels.

Clearly, we are not under the LAW because the Blood of Jesus fulfilled it for our sake; still, we must heed the Spiritual Principles set forth from the Ancient of Days. What can Spiritual Principles and Protocols do for us, especially if we already have it going on? Respectfully speaking, having it

Divine Etiquette

going on in a worldly realm to please ourselves and others CANNOT equate to having it going on in the Spiritual Realm, *As It Pleases God*. In all simplicity, seemingly earthly power, notoriety, and influence can never equate to Divine Power, Influence, and Wisdom. Therefore, we have a decision to make.

Once we come into AGREEMENT with our Heavenly Father, *Spirit to Spirit*, to become a work-in-progress, *As It Pleases Him*, He will begin shaping our thoughts, actions, words, and desires in a manner that resonates with His Divine Intentions and our Predestined Blueprint (our reason for being).

What is the purpose of being reshaped, *As It Pleases God*? The best answer to this question is found in 1 Samuel 16:7, which states: *"But the Lord said to Samuel, 'Do not look at his appearance or at his physical stature, because I have refused him. For the Lord does not see as man sees; for man looks at the outward appearance, but the Lord looks at the heart.'"*

For our Heaven on Earth Experiences to pan out as they should to develop our heart and mind postures, *As It Pleases God*, we must Spiritually Align the Mind, Body, Soul, and Spirit to Divinely Download from the Heavenly of Heavens. What does this mean for Believers? First, we need a willful commitment to understanding how God created us. Secondly, we need to possess *Divine Etiquette* through the use of the Fruits of the Spirit to capture the true essence of His Divine Presence, *Spirit to Spirit*. Thirdly, we must allow the Blood of Jesus to cover us as Spiritual Atonement. Lastly, we need the Divine Presence of the Holy Spirit to guide us in all things Spiritual to ensure we remain Divinely Pure, Holy, and Righteous, *As It Pleases Him*, with a work-in-progress mindset and heart posture.

To truly embody *Divine Etiquette*, we must first explore the Divine Nature of God through His Divine Attributes,

Divine Etiquette

Perspectives, Character Traits, and Expectations. In addition, we must also know what is required of us to go from sheep to Shepherd status, *As It Pleases Him*.

Why do we need to know information about sheep and Shepherds when dealing with our Kingdom Status? In the Eye of God, due to the Blood of Jesus for our Salvation, we all have a sheep status by default. Conversely, just because we claim the status of being a Shepherd does not mean that we are one in the Eye of God. Nor does it mean that the Heavenly of Heavens is endorsing our status, even if we are self-proclaimed or man-endorsed. Please allow me to Spiritually Align this matter: *"The prophets prophesy falsely, and the priests rule by their own power; and My people love to have it so. But what will you do in the end?"* Jeremiah 5:31.

How do we know the difference between a Divinely Ordained, man-appointed, or self-proclaimed Shepherd? Once again, *"Therefore by their fruits you will know them."* Matthew 7:20. In addition, they are also known by whether or not they are leading God's sheep toward or away from the Kingdom. Here is how 2 Timothy 4:3-4 sums it up: *"For the time will come when they will not endure sound doctrine, but according to their own desires, because they have itching ears, they will heap up for themselves teachers; and they will turn their ears away from the truth, and be turned aside to fables."*

In *Divine Etiquette: As It Pleases God*®, here are a few questions to ask yourself according to Galatians 5:22-23 to avoid having itching ears:

- ☐ Are they operating in LOVE?
- ☐ Are they operating in JOY?
- ☐ Are they operating in PEACE?
- ☐ Are they operating in PATIENCE?
- ☐ Are they operating in KINDNESS?
- ☐ Are they operating in GOODNESS?

Divine Etiquette

- ☐ Are they operating in FAITHFULNESS?
- ☐ Are they operating in GENTLENESS?
- ☐ Are they operating in SELF-CONTROL?

Is this not judging people? Absolutely not! There is no law against querying fruits for the sake of our well-being. Actually, it is openly insulting or disrespecting others that gets us in hot water with God. Thus, we must govern our tongues accordingly without pointing the finger while operating in the Spirit of Lovingkindness and Excellence.

Now, getting down to the nitty-gritty, we are required to inspect our own fruits and those of another to determine if we are equally or unequally yoked. Then again, when conducting a fruit analysis on ourselves with a work-in-progress mindset, according to Matthew 12:33, it gives us an option: *"Either make the tree good and its fruit good, or else make the tree bad and its fruit bad. For a tree is known by its fruit."* If we opt out of doing either of the two, determining the type of yoke or engaging in the self-correcting process, we can 'get got' by the enemy's wiles.

The use of the Fruits of the Spirit is for our edification and development, first and foremost. How so? It is impossible to recognize something accurately if we do not possess or understand it. For this reason, once we begin to use the Fruits of the Spirit, *As It Pleases God*, it develops our discerning faculties. Secondly, if we do not use them, *As It Pleases Him*, we will find ourselves engaging in Spiritual Woes of getting people, places, and things all wrong while appearing right in our own eyes. Here is the Scripture: *"Woe to those who call evil good, and good evil; who put darkness for light, and light for darkness; who put bitter for sweet, and sweet for bitter!"* Isaiah 5:20.

Granted, we are all subjected to error, but there are certain things we should not get wrong when being Divinely Led by the Holy Spirit. How do we make this make sense?

Divine Etiquette

According to our Divine Design, we all have a conscience and senses, whether distorted or on high alert. More importantly, we all know the difference between right and wrong, even if we ignore it or do not understand it! Who am I to judge, right? No judgment intended...but if our bodies release the appropriate hormones for the occasion, it means the psyche knows it and can feel it.

In cultivating the proper heart of righteous intentions with a usable and serviceable Spirit, *As It Pleases God*, in *Divine Etiquette*, the Mind, Body, Soul, and Spirit Connections are vital. In navigating the complexities of life, we definitely need an understanding of the Divine Prewiring designed to SAVE us from ourselves. What if we have it all together? Then, I would say, 'Congratulations!' However, what I do know is that we are all a work-in-progress. Therefore, we must remain on a continuous Spiritual Tilling and Growth Cycle to avoid lying to ourselves about our current status in or out of the Kingdom of God.

For the record, as long as the SEASONS change on the face of this Earth, we are required to do likewise. In Earthen Vessels, we are interconnected with the Vicissitudes, Cycles, and Seasons of Life, and if we do not do our part in becoming better, stronger, and wiser, it will view us as a Canker Sore, making its best attempts to purge us from this Earth. Really? Yes, really!

Unfortunately, when we stop learning or growing, our lives are thrust into a cycle of déjà vu or a wandering process like the Children of Israel until we learn what needs to be learned. We often think the wandering in the desert in the Book of Exodus for the Children of Israel was just a story to share with other Believers. Still, in the Eye of God, this story holds valuable Spiritual Principles and Etiquette, taking us from where we are to the Divine Promise that is already within each of us.

Divine Etiquette

What if we opt out of learning? Then, we will transfer the MANTLE to the next in line prematurely, causing them to learn what we refused to learn. When, in all actuality, we should have become the TEACHER with Divine Meat but opted to remain a student sipping milk in a remedial state of being. Can this really happen? It is happening, for real, for real!

According to the Heavenly of Heavens, the way of escape is hidden in WHO we are PLEASING. What does this mean? We have a few options for who or what we are pleasing:

- ☐ We Please God (With Selflessness and Serving).
- ☐ We Please Ourselves (With Selfishness and Lack of Self-Control).
- ☐ We Please Others (With People Pleasing, Coveting, and Competitiveness).

If God is indeed our first choice, it encapsulates a level of WISDOM beyond human understanding.

What if we are not that smart? When it comes down to the Kingdom of God, we do not need to be intelligent, articulate, or whatever, nor do we have to worry about what people think about us. We need to become Kingdomly Usable for Divine Wisdom to rest according to our Predestined Blueprint and Spiritual Giftings.

What will Divine Wisdom do for us? Divine Wisdom will lead you where ordinary knowledge will not. Then again, knowledge changes and can fail us, but Divine Wisdom is absolute, unchanging, and unfailing, granting us the courage that will put our enemies to boot. Here is what we need to know: *"Who is like a wise man? And who knows the interpretation of a thing? A man's wisdom makes his face shine, And the sternness of his face is changed."* Ecclesiastes 8:1.

Secrets of Discipline

With the *Secrets of Discipline*, the one thing that makes forgiveness such a Source of Gratitude is the person who can love despite another's weakness. We all make mistakes, but God demands wholehearted forgiveness without reservation. Choosing to forgive does not always mean you will forget, but it does mean you will let go of the issue, circumstance, or situation and never bring it up again.

What is the big deal about forgiveness? Unbeknown to most, forgiveness helps us with an invaluable commodity we need the most, called DISCIPLINE. What does discipline have to do with forgiveness? It is like the secret bonding agent to all the other charactorial fruits in or out of the Kingdom.

According to Kingdom Standards, the Crown or the Cloak of Favor is really determined by our charactorial discipline, our ability to give thanks, and the maximization of the Fruits of the Spirit. Simple enough, right? Here is how they work together for our good:

- ☐ It takes a lot of prayer and discipline to exhibit compassion when people hate on you. In *Divine Etiquette*, know this: Matthew 5:44 says, "*But I say to you, love your enemies, bless those who curse you, do good to those who hate you, and pray for those who spitefully use you and persecute you.*"

- ☐ It takes a lot of discipline to exhibit joy from within when you are faced with devastation. In *Divine Etiquette*, know this: Colossians 4:2 says, "*Continue earnestly in prayer, being vigilant in it with thanksgiving.*"

- ☐ It takes a lot of discipline to exhibit peace when there is war all around you. In *Divine Etiquette*, know this:

Divine Etiquette

Philippians 4:6-7 says, *"Be anxious for nothing, but in everything by prayer and supplication, with thanksgiving, let your requests be made known to God; and the peace of God, which surpasses all understanding, will guard your hearts and minds through Christ Jesus."*

- ☐ It takes a lot of discipline to exhibit patience when you feel that you are in dire need. In *Divine Etiquette*, know this: Galatians 6:9 says, *"And let us not grow weary while doing good, for in due season we shall reap if we do not lose heart."*

- ☐ It takes a lot of discipline to exhibit kindness when people are rude, vindictive, and abusive to you. In *Divine Etiquette*, know this: Ephesians 4:32 says, *"And be kind to one another, tenderhearted, forgiving one another, even as God in Christ forgave you."*

- ☐ It takes a lot of discipline to exhibit goodness when you are being treated like a junkyard dog. In *Divine Etiquette*, know this: James 1:19-20 says, *"So then, my beloved brethren, let every man be swift to hear, slow to speak, slow to wrath; for the wrath of man does not produce the righteousness of God."*

- ☐ It takes a lot of discipline to exhibit faithfulness when that is all you have left. In *Divine Etiquette*, know this: James 1:12 says, *"Blessed is the man who endures temptation; for when he has been approved, he will receive the crown of life which the Lord has promised to those who love Him."*

- ☐ It takes a lot of discipline to exhibit gentleness when you are faced with the cruelty of life. In *Divine Etiquette*, know this: Proverbs 15:1 says, "*A soft answer turns away wrath, but a harsh word stirs up anger.*"

- ☐ It takes a lot of discipline to exhibit self-control when temptation is all around you. In *Divine Etiquette*, know this: Proverbs 25:28 says, "*Whoever has no rule over his own spirit is like a city broken down, without walls.*"

- ☐ It takes a lot of discipline to love those who do not love you while spitefully using you. In *Divine Etiquette*, know this: Matthew 5:44 says, "*But I say to you, love your enemies, bless those who curse you, do good to those who hate you, and pray for those who spitefully use you and persecute you.*"

- ☐ It takes a lot of discipline to help those who walk all over your kindness. In *Divine Etiquette*, know this: Romans 12:20-21 says, "*Therefore 'If your enemy is hungry, feed him; If he is thirsty, give him a drink; for in so doing you will heap coals of fire on his head.' Do not be overcome by evil, but overcome evil with good.*"

- ☐ It takes a lot of discipline to give and expect nothing in return. In *Divine Etiquette*, know this: 1 Peter 3:9 says, "*Not returning evil for evil or reviling for reviling, but on the contrary blessing, knowing that you were called to this, that you may inherit a blessing.*"

As a Word to the Wise, no one is exempt from these feelings, but the ability to exhibit faith and favor makes them doable!

Life is a complex journey woven with experiences, lessons, emotions, and relationships, and none of us is immune to making mistakes. Nonetheless, according to *Divine Etiquette*:

Divine Etiquette

As It Pleases God®, how we respond to those mishaps, missteps, or folly is what truly defines our character and shapes our growth, positively or negatively.

Even when I make mistakes or experience these same feelings, I am quick to REPENT, FORGIVE, and SELF-CORRECT the behavior by applying the Fruits of the Spirit on a moment-by-moment basis. Plus, with this trifecta, I will engage in pinpointing the CAUSE or my WHY to align my actions, thoughts, beliefs, and words with my Spiritual Values, Principles, and Protocols for Kingdom Development, *As It Pleases God*.

According to the Heavenly of Heavens, the Divine Journey of repentance, forgiveness, and self-correction is an ongoing process. All of this is designed to keep us Spiritually Connected to God, our Heavenly Father, *Spirit to Spirit*, for our Heaven on Earth Experiences and to evolve into what we were created to do from the onset. By committing to this path, we must begin to view our mistakes, traumas, or wounds as opportunities for learning, growth, and preparation to become the best version of ourselves for the Greater Good.

Although it may not be easy at first, so here is a Wound Release Contract that will help you come into AGREEMENT with the Spirit of Discipline with *Divine Etiquette* working in your favor:

In becoming Disciplined, As It Pleases God, I, _____, release the pain of my Emotional Wounds into the Hands of God, this __ Day of _____, _____. I lay this Emotional Wound list on the Altar in the Name of the Father, Son, and Holy Spirit, and I will leave them there at Your Doorpost. As Your Word becomes a Lamp unto my feet and a Light unto my path, I REPENT of all of my known and unknown sins of unrighteousness. By the Blood of the Lamb of my God in Heaven, I claim

Divine Etiquette

my Divine Healing today, putting on the Whole Armor of God in the Name of Jesus. Thank you. Amen.

_____
Signature

In conclusion, the foundation of *Divine Etiquette: As It Pleases God* is wrapped in Spiritual Discipline. As a matter of fact, Spiritual Discipline serves as the BEDROCK upon which the Kingdom Principles of *Divine Etiquette* were built to ANCHOR your faith in Christ Jesus, allowing the Holy Spirit to do what He does best.

Without Spiritual Discipline, *As It Pleases God*, you can become unraveled without realizing it. But know this: Everything in this book has strategically prepared you for what is NEXT, providing the Spiritual Tools necessary to face future challenges, setbacks, and opportunities.

This Divine Guide of Practicalities, *As It Pleases God*, was written with you in mind to shape your character and influence your interactions with others. Henceforth, with the use of your dynamic people skills with a heart and mind posture of submissiveness and receptiveness, the Divine Whispers of the Holy Spirit can go to work on your behalf to bring forth what is already.

As Dr. Y. Bur, the WHY Doctor, in addition to your prayers, here is what I need you to do:

- ☐ TRUST the process, *As It Pleases God*, and use the Fruits of the Spirit faithfully.

- ☐ COVER yourself with the Blood of Jesus as Spiritual Atonement.

Divine Etiquette

- ☐ MASTER Spiritual Duality with the Holy Spirit guiding you on how to reverse negatives into positives, wrongs to rights, bad to good, unjust to just, and so on.

- ☐ REPENT and FORGIVE wholeheartedly while remaining humble consistently.

With the *Secrets of Discipline*, once you can automatically turn a lose-lose into a win-win with a positive mindset, you will become a Confident and Powerful Force to be reckoned with, GUARANTEED.

From me to you, in Growing Great as the *Crème de la Crème of Kingdom Poshness*, please remember that my Divine Voice as an intercessor will SPEAK to you, *Spirit to Spirit*, as we become ONE with Christ Jesus on this Spiritual Journey, *As It Pleases God*. As you move forward with a commitment to continuous improvement in the Spirit of Excellence, carry this message: I BELIEVE in you. Embrace every moment, and let your Spirit ROAR and SOAR to the Highest Heights. Many Blessings!

Dr. Y. Bur

www.ingramcontent.com/pod-product-compliance
Lightning Source LLC
Chambersburg PA
CBHW071704160426
43195CB00012B/1574